THE BLACK POWER MOVEMENT
AND AMERICAN SOCIAL WORK

The Black Power Movement and American Social Work

Joyce M. Bell

COLUMBIA UNIVERSITY PRESS   NEW YORK

COLUMBIA UNIVERSITY PRESS
Publishers Since 1893
New York   Chichester, West Sussex

cup.columbia.edu

Copyright © 2014 Columbia University Press
All rights reserved

Library of Congress Cataloging-in-Publication Data
Bell, Joyce Marie.
   The Black power movement and American social work / Joyce M. Bell.
       pages cm
   Includes bibliographical references and index.
   ISBN 978-0-231-16260-9 (cloth : alk. paper) — ISBN 978-0-231-53801-5
(e-book)
   1. African American social workers—History—20th century.   2. Black
power—United States.   3. Social workers—United States—History—20th
century.   4. Social service—United States—History—20th century.   I. Title.
   HV40.8.U6B45 2014
   361.3089'96073—dc23

                                                                2013045297

Columbia University Press books are printed on permanent and durable acid-free paper.
This book is printed on paper with recycled content.
Printed in the United States of America

c 10 9 8 7 6 5 4 3 2 1

COVER DESIGN: Chang Jae Lee

References to websites (URLs) were accurate at the time of writing.
Neither the author nor Columbia University Press is responsible for URLs
that may have expired or changed since the manuscript was prepared.

CONTENTS

TODAY IT IS NOT REMARKABLE that Kenya Robinson,[1] an engineering major, is active in the National Society of Black Engineers, minored in African American studies, socialized at the Black Cultural Center on campus, and graduated with a kente cloth stole from a major flagship university. Nor is it odd that she jumped the broom when she married Jamal, a journalist who tutors teen writers through the National Association of Black Journalists. Though their lives have been indelibly shaped by Black Power, they are remarkably mainstream as African Americans go.

In 1966, however, civil rights leaders like NAACP executive director Roy Wilkins called Black Power a "reverse Hitler and a reverse Ku Klux Klan." Not to be limited to comparisons to mass murders and terrorists, the leader of the oldest civil rights organization also referred to Black Power as the "mother of hate and the father of violence." The objectives of the Black Power movement were wrong-headed and pernicious, he and other civil rights leaders argued. They insisted that black studies programs would leave students ill prepared for the workforce and that black student unions were promoting dangerous "re-segregation" on college campuses. The various black professional organizations that sprouted like wildfire in the late 1960s "reversed the progress" of the civil rights movement, they reasoned. Yet Black Power, as an ideological phenomenon, was so significant that its effects pervade not just black America but the country itself. It has even shaped other communities of color in important ways. Among African Americans in particular, its legacies are so ubiquitous that they are often overlooked and ignored—even by the very scholars who explore the black freedom movement.[2]

Scholars have been examining the scope and impact of the black freedom movement in the United States in ever more sophisticated ways over the past decade. Prior to the mid-2000s, the grand narrative among historians of the civil rights movement positioned Black Power as a fundamentally disruptive force to a beloved community created by a multiracial group of activists who sacrificed their lives to dismantle codified forms of white supremacy. Despite revisions to this narrative, the conventional history remains unchanged up to a point. Civil rights activists, the narrative goes, strategized and boldly challenged the hatred and violence of an intractable system of racism and oppression. Hospitals, schools, and public accommodations such as pools and parks were exclusively white throughout communities in the South. White supremacists in local, state, and federal legislatures urgently attempted to defend these discriminatory institutions, as local authorities also beat, maimed, and jailed activists who sought to secure voting rights. Southern states banned and repressed civil rights groups in innovative, intimidating ways. Not to be deterred, grassroots activists met in churches, schools, and basements and forged a new vision of America. National civil rights groups—including the National Association for the Advancement of Colored People (NAACP), the National Urban League (NUL), the Southern Christian Leadership Conference (SCLC), the Student Nonviolence Coordinating Committee (SNCC), and the Congress on Racial Equality (CORE), also known as the Big Five—represented a strong, sober, hopeful, and disciplined struggle towards integration. They were a striking contrast to the brutish, violent, and ugly agents of some of the most explicit forms of white supremacy represented by terrorist groups like the Ku Klux Klan. The above remains an essential part of the new narratives on the black freedom movement, as well. But complications and nuances to this narrative arise when scholars address the role of black nationalism and Black Power in the black freedom movement. Moreover, one of the most fundamental elements to pivot on this conversation was the efficacy of integration itself as an essential goal of black uplift.

No figure represents this "heroic era" of the black freedom movement more than the Reverend Dr. Martin L. King Jr., co-founder of the SCLC. His commitment to integration and nonviolence is iconic. King and others presented to the world powerful images of well-dressed men, women, and children being beaten and attacked by white law enforcement officers or white civilians. This positioned civil rights activists on the moral high ground in the court of public opinion. Nevertheless, as the modern civil rights movement unfolded in the late 1950s and early 1960s, another foil emerged in the landscape of racial politics in the United States—the Nation of Islam. Called the "Black Muslims" by the white and black press alike, the Nation was the largest black nationalist organization in the country and had a national spokesman with incredible appeal as a new construction of black defiance. Malcolm X was tall, good-looking, and forceful yet also charming, with impeccable oratory skills and a conspicuous cadre of stern, upright black men as security. The Nation of Islam proved anathema to the civil rights movement in many ways. It rejected the legitimacy of racial reconciliation, integration, and even American citizenship for black people. It also forcefully and vituperatively denounced the efficacy of nonviolence and integration with whites. It celebrated self-defense, self-determination, and black pride in ways that no civil rights organization had ever. It celebrated the beauty, history, and abilities of black people. The organization simultaneously offered a cathartic space for anger to be expressed at white supremacy without any particular deference to any "good whites" who were as committed to see blacks free, as they were to see themselves free. The Nation was sui generis.

Though historians have downplayed the significance of the Nation of Islam, by the early 1960s, Malcolm X had become the country's most interviewed black person. By the late 1960s, the Nation of Islam had become the richest black organization in the United States and published *Muhammad Speaks*, the most widely read black newspaper in America. One member, Muhammad Ali, was heavyweight champion of the world and one of the most famous black people alive. In fact, Ali's own colorful style and defiant politics made an indelible imprint on an entire generation of African Americans. The Nation was the first major organization to insist that "black" exclusively replace "Negro," helping to retire the word "Negro" in the Anglophone world. More importantly, the Nation was a chief benefactor to a new style of political expression and social activism that became known as the Black Power movement.

While the Black Power movement had many sources of influence, the Nation was essential in developing a framework for resistive politics that (1) privileged black self-determination, and (2) did not see integration as the panacea for exigencies faced by black people. The Nation, however, was no activist group, and most black people were not willing to believe in universal white devilry or sacrifice their right to expect and demand civil rights. Black Power also inherited important elements from the civil rights movement, including a belief in activism as a means to affect change within white-controlled institutions. This point of activism was a distinct difference between black nationalists who typically rejected activist politics and insisted on creating black institutions—social, religious, cultural, economic, etc. From the Universal Negro Improvement Association through the Nation of Islam, territorial separatism—the creation of a black nation state—had been the cornerstone of black nationalism. And while they sought a black nation state either in North America or Africa, nationalists created a veritable black nation through networks of black institutions designed to meet the basic needs of black people. From schools, to supermarkets, restaurants, factories, and farms, "nation building" was a pervasive dictum in nationalist circles. U.S. citizenship was not the ultimate ambition, nor was the realization of civil rights. Black Power, however, assumed and asserted civil rights, even as it insisted and organized around black self-determination within a context of being both black and American. It was a merging of two seemingly irreconcilable beliefs—black nationalism and racial integration—that forged a new politics which permeated black America. Moreover, despite what historians and others have argued, it was Black Power, not the dream of a racially integrated America, that ultimately became a dominant expression among African Americans.

.   .   .

It is from this departure that Joyce Bell adds considerable depth, dimension and sophisticated analysis to the scholarship on the development of black professional associations during the age of Black Power. By focusing on the National Association of Black Social Workers (NASBW), she contextualizes the emergence of these groups during an era of unprecedented black access to white professional groups. What becomes abundantly clear in this study is that groups like the NABSW, though undoubtedly affected by the victories and thrust of the civil rights movement, owe their existence to the ideological force of Black Power. It was the call for a conspicuous celebration of blackness, racial pride, and black self-determination that spawned scores of black professional groups. Though civil rights leaders saw integration as the Promised Land in the early 1960s, by 1970 many African Americans came to a significant shift in the way in which they envisaged the racial landscape of a new America. In fact, many who were reared in black schools and churches, attended black colleges, and belonged to black fraternities, sororities, and social clubs could not come to see black organizations and spaces as inherently inferior to white ones. From fashion and hairstyles to music, to literature, sports, religion, academia, and even to the naming of children—no facet of black life went unaffected by Black Power. While the afro, James Brown's "Say it Loud (I'm Black and I'm Proud)," Kwanzaa, black studies, and the Black Panther Party are obvious outgrowths of Black Power, many have only recently begun to explore the degree to which black professional associations, from the Afro-American Patrolmen's League to the National Association of Black Journalists (NABJ), were as well.

As Joyce Bell so eloquently demonstrates, the manner in which Black Power emerges in institutional spaces "is the most understudied outcome of the movement and social scientists' dismissal of it has led to an underestimation of the transformatory power of the movement." As a social scientist, she contributes to the scholarship on both the civil rights and Black Power movements by framing much of her discussion around social movement theory. She explores the process of civil institutionalization, defined as "the implementation of movement goals, ideas, and practices in the institutions of the civil sphere—those that exist between the level of the household and the exercise of state power." Using the NABSW as a primary subject, this study gives important nuance and depth to an organization that represents professionals with considerable visibility in the black community. Examining leadership models and the role that intra-organizational dynamics have played in shaping the NABSW, this study offers a new point of analysis for understanding social movements and the development of black professionals who—like students, prisoners, athletes, musicians, academics, and even publicly elected officials—were touched by a new framework of thinking about race and power.

Jeffrey O. G. Ogbar

ACKNOWLEDGMENTS

I AM DEEPLY GRATEFUL to all of the people who supported and tolerated me through the writing of this book. While all of its shortcomings are mine, this book was a community effort in more ways than one and for that I am forever grateful.

This project started as my doctoral dissertation at the University of Minnesota. For their constant support I would like to thank Rose Brewer, Doug Hartmann, and Keith Mayes. I am also grateful to Liz Boyle and Ann Hironaka for their mentorship in my early years of graduate school and to Robin Stryker and Chris Uggen, who have always looked out for me. I am especially indebted to my dissertation advisor Ron Aminzade. It was when I sat in his seminar on social movements that I knew I made the right decision to go to graduate school. He has always encouraged me and held me up. I am thankful that I've had him on my side and honored to represent his mentorship in my academic endeavors.

This research wouldn't have been possible without the support, guidance, and assistance of the people at the Social Welfare History Archives. I want to thank archivists David Klaasen and Linnae Anderson, as well as the numerous student workers that assisted me in the development and execution of this project. I also want to thank the social workers who graciously gave their time, resources, and wisdom in support of this project.

I also benefited from institutional support in the sociology and African American studies departments at the University of Georgia and the sociology department and the Center on Race and Social Problems at the University of Pittsburgh. Both of these intellectual homes have nurtured the ideas here. I am especially grateful for Derrick Alridge, Kathy Blee, Cheryl

Dozier, Aisha Durham, and Kecia Thomas who have pushed me intellectually and spent time both writing and thinking with me. I am particularly thankful for my colleague and writing partner Waverly Duck, whose friendship and support were essential to the end stages of this project. In addition, I owe an intellectual debt to several academic giants who laid the groundwork for this project: Eduardo Bonilla-Silva, Kimberlé Crenshaw, Joe Feagin, Elizabeth Higginbotham, Peniel Joseph, Robin D. G. Kelley, Joyce Ladner, Manning Marable, Aldon Morris, Jeffrey O. G. Ogbar, Robert C. Smith, Kwame Ture, and Cheryl Townsend-Gilkes.

Jennifer Perillo, Stephen Wesley, and Kathryn Jorge at Columbia University Press and several anonymous reviewers provided insightful feedback important to the development of this project. I am also thankful for the wide range of colleagues who have provided comments, guidance, and critiques of the book that have shaped it.

It is also important to me to thank the University of Minnesota's Upward Bound and McNair Scholars programs and staff, particularly Aloida Zaragoza and Bruce and Sharyn Schelske. The journey to this book began with them. They were each instrumental in helping me look beyond my situation when I was a kid who didn't even see a diploma. I truly treasure the guidance, understanding, and unconditional friendship that I have had in my life since I was thirteen because of them. I would be a different person had my life not been touched by their influence.

There are a number of women in my life who, because of the love and support they have given me, should really be listed as co-authors of this book. DeAnna Cummings, Tiffany Davis, Lisette Haro, Wendy Leo Moore, Carrie Williams, and Keegan Xavi—you are my counsel, my mirror, and my sanity. Thank you for being my unconditional friends. I would also like to thank Ryan Schleif and Amanda Hill Harris who opened their homes to me when I needed space to just sit and write. Your generosity was crucial to this project.

My mother Jean Annan, my brothers Eugene and Maurice Dunn, my in-laws Brenda Bell-Caffee and Jessie Caffee, and my spiritual mother Amoke Kubat have provided an unshakable foundation for my life and this project. I can't thank them enough for all they give to my family. Without them, this project wouldn't have happened.

My partner in life, Tyehimba Bell, is my solid ground. He has been the cool to my hot and the steady to my shaky. He has been my support, my distraction, and my peace through this whole process. He has believed in me like no one else and constantly reminds me that I have everything I need inside myself. Our son, Tyehimba Ralasi, is an amazing young man who started this journey as a much younger (and shorter) child. He has heard, "Mama's too tired," or "I have to work now," more times than I want to admit. But he has somehow understood that I love him more than anything else—ever. If my work on this book can teach him any lessons, it is already a great success.

I have the great fortune of having many good friends, a family who loves me, and several people around me and across the world who have touched my life and have supported this project, in ways big and small. There's no way I can name them all, but I thank you—my friends (both old and new), my family and extended family, and people whose ideas inspire me, whose music has made writing easier, and whose courage gives me strength. I truly am rich in loved ones.

*THE BLACK POWER MOVEMENT
AND AMERICAN SOCIAL WORK*

1

Introduction

ON WEDNESDAY, MAY 29, 1968, a group of black[1] social workers took over the 9:00 A.M. general assembly meeting of the 95th Annual National Conference on Social Welfare (NCSW).[2] There were 8,200 registrants— the largest NCSW conference to date (Vasey 1968). The theme of the conference was "An Action Platform for Human Welfare," a timely title for a conference being held in the wake of the assassination of Martin Luther King Jr. and the ongoing urban riots that followed. The group, made up of black social workers from around the country, had arrived early, cordoned off the center section, and asked all black social workers to sit together there.[3] Several men were given the job of blocking the doorways once the meeting was under way, and both men and women were assigned to float through the audience to encourage other black social workers to sit in the middle section.[4] Vic Brabson, Lenore Delaney, Larry Gary, and Will Scott joined T. George Silcott on stage while they waited for the crowd to file into the meeting room of the San Francisco Civic Center (Johnson 1975).

Once people had settled into their seats, Silcott took over the microphone and presented the group's position statement (Jaggers 2003; Vasey 1968). The ten-point statement of the newly constituted National Association of Black Social Workers (NABSW) began by calling attention to the contradiction between the action theme of the forum and the very constitution of the conference, which precluded social action by claiming that "it does not take an official position on controversial issues and adopts no resolutions except occasional resolutions of courtesy."[5] The NABSW recommended that the preamble of the constitution be changed to reflect the current action theme of the conference. The statement went on to claim that the NCSW was a white institution whose board and planning committee did not reflect the "ethnic composition commensurate with its expressed concern."[6] They also called for NABSW representatives to be appointed to powerful committees of the NCSW. Furthermore, they demanded that "people who speak, write, research, and evaluate the Black community be Black people who are experts in this area," while white social workers "involve themselves with solving the problem of white racism," which they cited as "America's number one mental health problem."[7] Silcott concluded the delivery of the statement by asserting, "We are committed to the reconstruction of systems to make them relevant to the needs of the Black community and are therefore pledged to do all that we can to bring these things about by *any means necessary*" (Jaggers 2003).

As planned, after Silcott finished reading the statement, the five men on the stage walked down the center aisle. Nearly all of the black social workers present got up and followed them from the meeting room, out of the civic center and across the street to the Glide Memorial Church[8] to hold their own meeting.[9] The scene was powerful, and the general assembly was taken by surprise. In retrospect, Dr. Shirley Better, a founder of the Los Angeles chapter of the NABSW and central to the organizing efforts in San Francisco, spoke about the shock registered by everyone's white colleagues that they had walked out.[10] She recalled, "This was so unusual, you know? We were supposed to be working *with* liberal whites, so this division was very startling to the whites."[11]

This walk-out of black social workers, which was the result of national organizing and led to the founding of the National Association of Black Social Workers, is but one example of how the Black Power movement was articulated in organizational spaces all across the United States. From the growth of black studies programs on college campuses and campaigns for community control of neighborhood services to fights for black representation on boards of directors of non-profits and the rise of black professional associations, Black Power was informing struggles for change in all sorts of organizational contexts. As the dominant tenor of black politics shifted from the civil rights movement's search for integration to the Black Power challenge to white racism, African Americans embedded in various organizations sought to create change in their work, school, and social lives. Yet this process of bringing Black Power into institutional spaces is the most understudied outcome of the movement and social scientists' dismissal of it has led to an underestimation of the transformatory power of the movement.

In the popular imaginary, the Black Power movement is all afros, dashikis, berets, and guns. As a new student of the movement, I was also fascinated with the image of the "new negro" emerging unafraid from the disappointments of the civil rights movement with a new attitude, a new swagger, ready to take on white racism by any means necessary. There is certainly an affinity between my generation, the hip-hop generation, and the black power generation that drove my initial interest. Much of hip-hop culture in the late 1980s and early 1990s reflects an admiration of those black power figures that were willing to risk everything to say "enough is enough" and reframe the movement for black liberation so that white racism became the primary target of action. This fascination, however, has limited both the way we remember the movement and the importance we place upon it when assessing black power's impact on U.S. society.

Indeed, much of what social scientists have had to say about the Black Power movement treats it as: (1) merely an aside to the mainstream civil rights movement, which did little beyond assisting the implementation of the more moderate demands of that movement, and (2) never having been institutionalized to any extent because it was "radical." But in order to understand the long-term impacts of the Black Power movement, it is necessary to look beyond those elements of our popular imagination and extant social science literature to examine if and how the ideas, values, norms, strategies, and tactics—the essential stuff—of the movement were carried into the institutions that make up our society.

I do this by examining the Black Power influence on the professions. I look specifically at the rise of black professional associations and use the specific case of American social work to illustrate the role of the movement in shaping the professions. Black social workers' effort to translate the aims and gains of the Black Power movement into their line of work serves as a prime example of how African Americans imported black power into U.S. institutions in the latter half of the modern movement for black liberation. Placing the activism of black social workers during the late 1960s and early 1970s in the context of the institutionalization of the rights revolution and the expansion of Black Power politics, I argue that the rise of black professional associations in general—and within social work in particular—is a primary example of the institutionalization of the Black Power movement in U.S. society.

Studies of the black liberation movement have generally followed predictable storylines: the early years are depicted as the emergence of the movement, the peak is the height of direct action, and the downswing is marked by radicalization, riots, and a decline into irrelevance. Despite some slight variations in this story, very little research examines any activity beyond formal movement organizations, movement events, and urban rebellions. But there is something more than this, something that reveals a pervasive and far-reaching movement impact beyond state policy reforms that traditional accounts fail to acknowledge. During the Black Power movement, black professionals found themselves engaged in a battle to implement change in institutions from within. Moving beyond calls for increased access and representation within professional fields, and more than calls for improvement of the delivery of professional services to the broader community, the grievances motivating the collective actions of black professionals included demands for respect, the enforcement of new racial language, and the development of a new black professional ethic. These demands indicate that while black professionals may have been empowered by the civil rights movement, they were inspired and emboldened by the Black Power movement.

Relying on extensive archival research and oral history interviews, I examine the movements of two groups of black social workers within their national professional associations. Through a comparison of the process of black dissent within the National Federation of Settlements (NFS) and the National Conference on Social Welfare (NCSW), this book traces the Black Power influence on the development of black professional associational life in the United States in the late 1960s and early 1970s. My findings reveal that the movement within the NFS was eventually forgotten as black social workers were granted some concessions within the national organization. On the other hand, the workers who mobilized within the NCSW used a separatist strategy and became the National Association of Black Social Workers (NABSW), which exploded into the national spotlight in the 1970s with their controversial stand on transracial adoption. This book seeks to understand the divergent paths of these movements and to understand their relationship to the larger structure of the Black Power movement.

In addition, by making use of primary sources previously unexplored by sociologists, I examine the process by which movement gains became institutionalized within formal organizations. I also explore the conflicts over new racial norms that were ushered in by the Black Power movement within professional organizations. Not all Americans were willing, enthusiastic participants in the rights revolution and were certainly not interested in anything called "Black Power." Black people who were embedded in social institutions had to continue to push the contexts of their lives to catch up to the new racial norms that were being forged in the Black Power revolution.

The development of black professional associations in the late 1960s and early 1970s reflects a larger process by which black professionals brought the ideas, values, norms, strategies and tactics of the Black Power movement into their professional lives. The rise of black professional associations was a form of black activism specifically rooted in the Black Power tradition. Moreover, I see this specific case as providing a lens through which to view a larger moment of movement institutionalization, in which elements of the Black Power movement were imported not only into the professions but also into education (black studies, black colleges, and Afrocentric education) and culture (black museums, black holidays, etc.). By focusing in depth on the institutionalization of Black Power politics into the professions, particularly social work, I hope to draw attention to the broad reaching impact of the Black Power movement on U.S. society.

RACE, RESISTANCE, AND CIVIL SOCIETY

There is no doubt that the movements of the civil rights era changed the institutions that structure our lives for the better. While institutional racism is still a part of the post-civil rights landscape, civil rights legislation certainly changed the racial atmosphere of formal organizations. Indeed, most of us take much for granted about the racial practices of the institutions we encounter as a part of the post-civil rights generation. Moving from signs that say "Negroes Need Not Apply" to having laws against discrimination in employment is a monumental gain of the civil rights movement. However, passing laws is not a wave of a magic wand. As Crenshaw (1988) puts it, "Racial hierarchy cannot be cured by the move to facial race-neutrality in the laws that structure the economic, political, and social lives of Black people" (1378). Recall that the 1954 Supreme Court decision in *Brown v. Board of Education* to desegregate public schools was met with such virulent resistance that court orders are still needed to enforce school desegregation more than fifty years later. And even then, as a result of white flight from inner cities or into private schooling, public schools in the United States remain as segregated today as they were prior to the *Brown* decision (Orfield 2001). Clearly, changes to the law cannot tell the whole story of how institutions are transformed. The families, educators, and administrators—both black and white—who participated in the fight to end segregation in schooling engaged in a complex series of struggles and negotiations that went far beyond the law.

Sociologists have recently pushed to develop frameworks for understanding the persistence of racial inequality and the new dynamics of American race relations in the post-civil rights era (cf. Bonilla-Silva 2001, 2003; Carr 1997; Crenshaw 1997; Doane and Bonilla-Silva 2003; Gallagher 2003). Recognizing the monumental shift in racial practice in the United States ushered in by the civil rights movement, these scholars have attempted to explain that, since the civil rights era, racism has taken on a new form: colorblind racism. This racism is subtler, more behind-the-scenes, and deceptive than the in-your-face—indeed, legal—segregation of pre-civil rights America, and characterizes much of contemporary racial discourse and practice. However, there is insufficient research into the actual transition process. How did this change come about? What are the processes by which changes in racial norms and practices dispersed throughout society? Did the movements of the era make it into non-state sites? How so? Which movements had an effect outside of the state apparatus? In short, how did these shifts in how we do race spread?

Shifts in race relations happened within the vast arrangement of organizations that make up the landscapes of our lives. These institutions (and the people in them) that organize our social life—the schools and colleges, health-care facilities, professions, academic disciplines, community based associations and so forth—were not automatic converts to new ways of "doing race" in the United States. On the contrary, these changes were only possible through a complex set of negotiations, with actors within these spaces participating in a complicated and slow reworking of racial boundaries to remake the rules of racial interaction. These struggles to change everyday practices and procedures shaped the face of each institution.

Race and Radical Marches

Generally, the focus on action against the state and public policy in the social movements literature has meant that, with few notable exceptions (cf. Lounsbury, Ventresca, and Hirsch 2003; Katzenstein 1998; Raeburn 2004; Skrentny 2002), studies of social movements have failed to recognize how movements affect other types of institutions. Moreover, the lack of focus on the time period at the end of and directly following the black liberation movement (1966–1976) means that, in many ways, social scientists have missed out on where the "real action" happens. As students of social movements, we have little understanding of what happens in the rest of society "when the marching stops" (Walton 1988). Yet, if we begin with the understanding that power relations are embedded throughout society, we must ask questions about how movements foster (or fail to foster) change in institutions outside of the state. In this way, contemporary sociological race theory has a crucial contribution to make in shaping studies of race-based movements. Indeed, knowing that the civil rights era marks a transition period in the racial structure of the United States (Bonilla-Silva 2001; Omi and Winant 1994; Wacquant 2001) necessitates a fuller analysis of the ways in which the incipient cultural transformation was at times coaxed and at others coerced by the black community.

Dominant racial ideologies and practices are not simply produced and regulated by the state, nor are they merely manifestations of individual choices and preferences. On the contrary, racial ideas and practices that reflect the interests of the dominant group permeate all social institutions, small group formations, and individual actions in society (Bonilla-Silva 2003; Feagin 2001). Analysts must thus examine contentious racial politics in institutional settings outside of the state. Yet, in both popular thinking and academic accounts, the routine practices of social organizations tend to be "ignored or minimized" as processes that perpetuate racial inequality (Brown et al. 2003:19). In this view, racism is seen as a problem of a few bad apples, or a couple bigots acting contrary to the rules of supposedly egalitarian institutions, such that access to institutions that once excluded people of color is seen as the primary goal when it comes to dealing with racial injustice (Brown et al. 2003; Feagin 2001). The problem with this is that the form, ideas, and practices of these organizations were developed out of racial exclusion. As Joe Feagin (2001) argues, "from the beginning,

European American institutions were racially hierarchical, white suprema-cist, and undemocratic" (5). People of color were integrated into institu-tions with little thought given to how to transform these organizations to actually incorporate previously excluded groups (Brown et al. 2003). Because of this, "any analysis of racial inequality that routinely neglects organizations and practices that intentionally or unintentionally generate or maintain racial inequalities over long periods of time is incomplete and misleading" (Brown et al. 2003:19).

The real issue at hand is how to conceive of the nature of power relations in society. The exercise of power is not only conducted by or through the state. Rather, power relations and struggles over unequal power relations are embedded throughout society. As Michel Foucault (1980) instructs, in order to understand power relations in modern society, the study of power "should not concern itself with the regulated and legitimate forms of power in their central locations . . . on the contrary it should be concerned with power at its extremities, in its ultimate destinations, with those points where it becomes capillary, that is, in its more regional and local forms and institutions" (96). The notion that the state is aided in exercising domina-tion over society by the civil sphere is also central to Antonio Gramsci's for-mulations of hegemony. At the most basic level, Gramsci theorizes that the ruling class is able to dominate society as a whole not only through the law and the exercise of force, but also through "private forces" or "civil society." Taking this perspective on power requires a focus on the disperse nature of power in societies where hegemony is exercised in the institutions of civil society (Hall 1996). Recognizing the society-structuring properties of these other realms of social life—the churches, voluntary associations, cultural organizations, and so forth of the civil sphere—means that it is important to point our attention to "wars of position" (or movements to change dom-inant practices and ideas in society) in arenas beyond the state.

This conception of power relations is central to much of the body of race-based critical theory in the sociological tradition (see Hartmann and Bell 2011). For example, Gramsci's sense of social formation and hegemony is integral to the formulation of Omi and Winant's (1994) classic theory of racial formation, wherein they conclude that race is a "fundamental axis of social organization in the U.S." (13). Since the United States is a "racial-ized social structure," they argue that this structure in turn "shapes racial experience and conditions meaning." On the other hand, "our ongoing interpretation of our experience in racial terms (also) shapes our relations to the institutions and organizations through which we are imbedded in social structure" (60). A primary claim for Omi and Winant is that race is socially constructed, meaning that at the most basic level our understanding about race and racial groups changes over time and is different in different places. These "rearticulations" of race—shifts in what race means ideologically and materially in a given society—occur through various "racial projects," which do the ideological work of changing conceptions of race at several levels. To support this argument, Omi and Winant (2004) detail how the black liberation movement in the United States marked a "great transformation" in race relations. In fact, they argue that the greatest triumph of the black liberation movement in the U.S. was its ability to redefine the meaning of racial identity and consequently of race itself (99). These redefinitions take place through complex interactions in all arenas of social life, from individual interactions to large-scale political and economic processes.

The bottom line here is not only that race is foundational to U.S. society—functioning as a primary axis of social differentiation—but also that conflict, protest, and contestation of racial meanings, racial identities, and racial inequality are inherent in societies structured by race. To explain this Feagin (2001) develops the concept of systemic racism. For Feagin, "systemic racism includes the complex array of anti-black practices, the unjustly gained political-economic power of whites, the continuing economic and other resource inequalities along racial lines, and the white racist ideologies created to maintain and rationalize white privilege and power" (6).

The term "systemic," for Feagin (2001), means that, "the core racist realities are manifested in each of society's major parts. . . . Each major part of U.S. society—the economy, politics, education, religion, the family—reflects the fundamental reality of systemic racism." Despite the tendency of many Americans to view racism as an individual problem, Feagin argues that, "systemic racism is perpetuated by a broad social reproduction process that generates not only recurring patterns of discrimination within institutions and by individuals, but also an alienating racist relationship—on the one hand, the racially oppressed, and on the other, the racial oppressors. The former seeks to overthrow the system while the latter seeks to maintain it." Social oppression, and the resulting persistent inequality, "leads to subtle or overt resistance by black Americans and other Americans of color" (6).

This idea is also central to Eduardo Bonilla-Silva's (2001) concept of racialized social systems. In opposition to mainstream social scientific frameworks on racism, Bonilla-Silva proposes an alternative theory in order to capture the "society-wide, organized, and institutional character of racism" (37). A racialized social system is a society "in which economic, political, social and ideological levels are partially structured by the placement of actors in racial categories or races" (37). Bonilla Silva summarizes his approach in five points: "First, racialized social systems are societies that allocate differential economic, political, social and even psychological rewards to groups along racial lines, lines that are socially constructed." This process leads to "a set of social relations and practices based on racial distinctions . . . at all levels." The whole of this is what Bonilla-Silva calls the "racial structure of a society." Secondly, he argues that, "races are historically constituted according the process of racialization." In other words, "races" are the outcome of oppositional relationships between racialized groups. Third, a racial ideology develops based on this structure. This isn't simply a reflection of the racialized system but actually works as an "organizational map that guides the actions of racial actors in society." Fourth, he states that "most struggles in a racialized social system contain a racial component," but sometimes these struggles "exhibit a distinct racial character." This "racial contestation" or struggle over racial meanings (political, social, and economic) is a "logical outcome of a society with a racial hierarchy." Finally, racial contestation allows us to see the "different objective interests of the races in a racialized social system" (Bonilla-Silva 2001:44).

Taken together, the concepts of racial formation (Omi and Winant 1994), systemic racism (Feagin 2001), and racialized social system (Bonilla-Silva 2001) all point to the centrality of race and racism in American society. Further, they all point out that racism operates within and through social institutions. In other words, all of these theorists argue that racial meanings and racism are not only outcomes of state initiated processes, nor are they simply ideas that individuals can either subscribe to or not. Rather, race and racism are developed and expressed in and through the organizations and institutions in which we are all embedded. Finally all of these frameworks highlight the idea that resistance to racism is an expected outcome of societies characterized by persistent racial inequality and a dominant racist ideology. In this way, the perspective outlined here is an essential starting point for studies of race-based social movements. By incorporating the work of these scholars of race into studies of social movements—especially those movements that deal explicitly with racial issues—the study of contentious politics will be enhanced. Starting from here, it becomes clear that the work of changing racialized norms and practices, while necessarily a dispersed and somewhat amorphous process, was partially carried out in the institutions of civil society.

Social Movement Institutionalization

Given what sociologists know about the historical difficulty of implementing movement gains in legislation and policy, it makes sense to assume that some of the greatest movement gains occur in the non-state sites of civil society.[12] Starting from the understanding that power relations—whether those related to class, race, gender or otherwise—are embedded throughout society, it is my contention that movements that create change at the state level, or in law, must still be acted out in the institutional contexts of civil society in order to see widespread social change. To this end, I call attention to the process of civil institutionalization, or the implementation of movement goals, ideas, and practices in the institutions of the civil sphere—those that exist between the level of the household and the exercise of state power.[13]

Social movements scholars have examined the institutionalization of social movements primarily as three distinct, but overlapping processes:

1. Political institutionalization: shifting relationships between social movements and the state,
2. Cultural institutionalization: the embedding of social movement ideas in culture, and
3. Organizational institutionalization: the isomorphic tendencies of social movements.

(Walker 2005)

Political institutionalization "refers to the changing location of social movement actors from a position largely external to the state to one in which movement actors are either recognized members of the state, work in a close relationship to the state and assist the state in policy-making, or are directly funded by the state" (Walker 2005:12). Moreover, political institutionalization has been theorized temporally as marking the end of a movement (Karstedte-Henke 1980; Koopmans 1993; Tarrow 1983). The argument is that at the end of a movement cycle, moderates and their demands are generally incorporated or institutionalized while radicals remain outside of the polity, generally to become victims of extreme state repression (Karstedte-Henke 1980). In other words, social movement institutionalization is associated with the loss of the outsider status that made them a movement in the first place. Cultural institutionalization refers to "the institutional incorporation or acceptance of movement ideas (ideologies, cultural framings, and issue positions) or practices (tactical repertoires, strategies of action, and discursive and rhetorical styles), both within and beyond the movement" (Walker 2005:16). We see the cultural institutionalization of movements when the "stuff" of movements becomes normalized in society. Finally, organizational institutionalization refers to a kind of "iron law" institutionalization by which social movement organizations come to look more like "professional organizations" or advocacy groups because of environmental or funding constraints.

By themselves, these three ways of understanding movement institutionalization largely neglect the processes by which movements get brought into non-state social institutions, largely because of social movement scholars' near singular focus on movements aimed at the state (McAdam and Scott 2002, 2005). Thus, little research has focused on collective action targeted towards or outcomes based in central institutional sites in U.S. society.[14] Because of this, sociologists have made many studies of race-based movements that don't pay attention to race. In other words, studying the movements of black people, without paying attention to racial practice or how race actually works in society, has left a void in the study of the black liberation movement. Sociologists in particular have mostly conceived of movement outcomes as those changes that occur at the level of the state and government policy. The central outcome of the civil rights movement then is the passage of civil rights legislation. This means that there is little understanding of racial contestation as it occurred in the organizations and institutions that connect us to society.

Institutionalization as Social Movement

Examining the collective actions of black social workers reveals that the civil institutionalization of larger state-level social movements often takes place through the mobilization of social movement ideologies and strategies within organizations, a process I am calling "intra-organizational social movements" (IOSMs).[15] McAdam (1999) argues that social movements often emerge when an exogenous shock created by some broad social change destabilizes social and political relations, creating an atmosphere of uncertainty within various fields of social life. This uncertainty leads to sense-making activities by embedded social actors, which can lead to perceived threats or opportunities requiring action. Activists can then either appropriate existing structures or create new mobilizing structures for the purpose of carrying out innovative collective action. In other words, a widespread social movement that results in vast social changes can set in motion phases of emergent mobilization in smaller, non-state institutional settings to bring about changes related to the larger movement. These intra-organizational social movements, while following similar emergence patterns with society-level social movements, are both enabled and constrained by the organizations in which they take place.[16] In the case of black professionals, I argue that the legal gains of the civil rights movement, followed by the Black Power movement's push towards new black identity, advocacy of new norms for racial interaction, and call for the development of black institutional capacity, served as the impetus for black mobilization in the professions.

I examine not only the dynamics of the activists and movement organizations involved, but also the nature of the professional associations that were targeted. I pay particular attention to the ways in which activists within the profession exploited the organizational identity and culture of their target—in this case national social work professional associations (cf. Albert and Whetten 1985; Schurman 2004). Similarly, I focus on the interaction between the target organization's sense of legitimacy (Suchman 1995), or its sense that it is acting appropriately based on a set of relevant norms, and the way that these national professional associations responded to black mobilization. Operating in the atmosphere of uncertainty of the 1960s, the professional associations under attack were often unclear about what responses were appropriate. The negotiation of these decisions played a crucial role in the trajectory of these IOSMs.

Finally, it is important to note that examining movements within organizations requires a different way of thinking about movement tactics. Formal organizations typically have prescribed tactics for dealing with intra-organizational conflict, generally spelled out in its constitution or by-laws (Zald and Berger 1978). I questioned whether social movements within organizations worked within or outside of these normal channels, and my research reveals that IOSMs do use prescribed tactics for seeking change within organizations. However, their relationship to legitimate channels and the existing structures of the organization is important to note. For instance, while the act of interrupting a committee meeting with a set of demands is disruptive and represents an illegitimate way to express grievances in organizations, it most certainly relies on and exists in relationship to those tactics that are legitimate. In other words, meeting interruptions, conference disruptions, and unsanctioned mailings represent the hijacking of proper channels rather than their circumvention. To be sure, black social workers did not make a habit of picketing the offices of their professional associations. Rather, they took full advantage of their position as "outsiders within" and sought to redirect conversations, create spectacles, and change minds within the organizational structure in which they were embedded (Hill-Collins 1986). Therefore, while scholars generally treat social movement tactics as deriving from an overarching strategy (i.e., sit-ins as a tactic of the nonviolent civil rights movement), it is important to consider how activists interpret the possibility of particular tactics based on an interaction between strategy and organizational context. It is also important to account for how professional and organizational norms shaped the "repertoires of contention" (Tilly 1978) that developed during this period of organizing within the professions.

Civil Institutionalization

Within organizations like professional associations there is generally a lack of the kind of leadership that characterized the civil rights or Black Power movements. As a result, people who are invested in the goals of the broader movement create IOSMs. Based on my examination of the ways in which Black Power politics were brought into the social work profession, I propose a model for understanding movement institutionalization that places the actors responsible for demanding such change at the center. I suggest that these movements will necessarily perform three critical tasks in ushering in movement implementation. First, they are responsible for framing interests in a way that is relevant to the institution; that is, they do the work of translating the movement into their organizations. For example, black social workers translated a general tenet of the Black Power movement—the development of ideological and real connections to Africa for African Americans—into demands around Afro-centric education in social work. Secondly, they develop tactical repertoires that are both constrained and enabled by the institutional norms and practices of the target as well as the tactics of the movement. In the case of black social workers, the professional convention intersected with the Black Power movement in such a way that activities such as taking over conferences became a central tactic. Finally, these IOSMs do the day-to-day work of raising issues for discussion, getting movement goals onto institutional agendas, writing for publications, and generally facilitating the fusion of movement-related issues with the goals of the organization. Much of black social workers' movement activity was acted out in conversation and negotiation between themselves and white coworkers in a way that kept the issues they felt were important on the table.

This interactional process is also an explicitly emotional process on two levels: First, the emotional labor that challengers must engage in to either conform to or challenge the norms for emotional displays within their organizational context constitutes an important part of the work that IOSMs do. Secondly, challengers must also manage the emotional reactions that power holders within the organization have toward the movement. Emotional reactions to the prospect of power sharing and/or other forms of institutional change may affect relationships and interactions between challengers and power holders in such a way that movement-makers within organizations have to—whether explicitly or implicitly or both— engage with them. Black social workers, for example, often had to deal with and craft responses to their white colleagues' feelings of rejection at being told that their liberalism was not enough.

CASES

Social Work

In recalling his upbringing, historian Robin D. G. Kelley (2003) writes, "the cops, drug dealers, *social workers*, the rusty tap water, roaches, and rodents were constant reminders that our world began and ended in a battered Harlem/Washington Heights tenement apartment on 157th and

Amsterdam" (emphasis mine) (1). Kelley's memoir reflects a reality that poor people and people of color know all too well: social workers are a part of the constellation of actors and institutions that shape life in the ghetto. A part of that reality is that too often their collective influence works to constrain rather than enable and simply supervise rather than uplift. So while the period under examination witnessed black professional struggles in several fields, I focus on social work because of its centrality to the black experience. Social workers have played a central role in the lives of the black urban poor, yet while their role as social control agents of the poor and women has been well documented (cf. Gordon 1994), their role in the maintenance or disruption of the racial order has not been fully examined.

African Americans, however, have not only been on the receiving side of social work services. Indeed, African Americans have a long history in the profession and have not been immune to the class conflicts inherent within it. During the Progressive Era (1898–1918), while mainstream social work was developing a reform ethic in response to the dominant casework model, African American social workers were focused on racial uplift through self-help and mutual aid (Carlton-LaNey 1999). Proponents of the racial uplift ideology held that middle- and upper-class African Americans have a social responsibility to work for the betterment of lower-class African Americans (Gaines 1996). In discussing racial uplift among black women, Carlton-LaNey (1999) points out that while their leadership in the black community was service-oriented, class-consciousness and elitism were "constant hallmark(s)" of their achievement (314). The idea was summed up by W. E. B. Du Bois, a primary proponent of the ideology in his 1908 "The College-Bred Negro," arguing that, "the best of us should give of our means, our time, and ourselves to leaven the whole" (as quoted in Carlton-LaNey 1999:313). This "race work" that African American social workers were engaged in was chronicled by Du Bois in his works *Some Efforts of American Negroes for their Own Social Betterment* (1898) and *Efforts for Social Betterment Among Negro Americans* (1909) (as cited in Carlton-LaNey 1999).

This phenomenon has been well documented in the work of black women in social welfare. Race work among black women has often taken the form of social work. Citing the pioneering work of Ida Bell Wells-Barnett, Lugenia Burns Hope, Elizabeth Ross Haynes, and Janie Porter

Barrett, Carlton-LaNey and Alexander (2001) stress that black women's race work during the Progressive Era developed a strong foundation of black social work. The work that these women did embraced a broad definition of social work that saw meeting educational, health, and economic needs as essential to broader social welfare. As Higginbotham (1993) notes, much of black women's race work during this period can be characterized as racial uplift work, steeped in the politics of respectability. Their work also solidified an activist culture of black social work that focused on building institutions for this purpose. From Ida B. Wells-Barnett's settlement house to Mary McLeod Bethune's college and Charlotte Hawkins Brown's Palmer Memorial Institute, black women's early social work contributed to the development of black institutions.

Black social workers were also central to the development of black organizational life during this era, including: the National Association of Colored Women (NACW), organized in 1896; the National Association for the Advancement of Colored People (NAACP) in 1910; and the National Urban League on Urban Conditions Among Negroes (later renamed the National Urban League [NUL]) in 1920. These organizations were the "most significant social welfare and social reform organizations for African Americans in the Progressive Era" (Carlton-LaNey 1999:314). But they also performed an important second function: they laid the organizational groundwork for African Americans to thrive in the field of social work as the profession grew and changed.

In fact, the National Urban League organized the first social work course of study for African Americans at Fisk University in 1911 (Carlton-LaNey 1999). At the time when the NUL established the school, many were practicing social work without any training. But Eugene K. Jones, the second executive director of NUL, argued that professional social work was important. "Effective social work among Negroes," he contended, "will tend to raise the level of intelligence, of physical vigor & industrial status" (as quoted in Carlton-LaNey 1999:315). This sentiment became more important as education for social workers became more popular. Moving into the 1920s, two more social work schools were established for African Americans: the Atlanta School of Social Work and Tuttle School in Raleigh, North Carolina (Carlton-LaNey 1999).

During the 1960s unprecedented black access to higher education and jobs coincided with the rise of Great Society antipoverty programs (many of which required maximum feasible community participation) in such a way that many new African American professionals became concentrated in jobs serving the black poor. This had the effect of both placing African American professionals in a position to understand the experiences of their less well-off counterparts and reinforcing black class cleavages by disposing a class of black "helping professionals" as the new guardians and social control agents of the black poor. Because of this, examining how black social workers articulated and acted upon their grievances within the profession is critically important to understanding black professional mobilization during the Black Power era and to moving beyond functionalist accounts that fail to acknowledge the contributions of black professionals in challenging (while at times reinforcing) the racial order that was often maintained in the practice of their profession. Their mobilization reflected a frustration with the way their profession was progressing and a desire to hold all social workers accountable for the gains of the rights revolution and ideals of the Black Power movement.

Many black social workers who entered the profession during this period saw their careers as a way to create social change. However, they encountered a professional environment that was struggling with the tension between professionalization and social action. This conflict between a helping model and an action model of social welfare had long existed within the profession. Still, many black social workers, who were often times the direct products of the civil rights movement and rooted in the Black Power tradition, came into the profession with social change at the forefront of their professional goals. Furthermore, the profession of social work had a long tradition of white professionals (mostly women) working in social service positions serving people of color. From public welfare offices to community service centers, many African Americans who came into contact with social workers were receiving services from white workers and the white women who had long held leadership positions in the profession. As black social work professionals entered the profession in larger numbers, bringing with them new expectations for interracial interaction in the workplace and new ideas about how social work should approach work with black communities, white social workers often felt pushed aside and offended that their ways were being questioned. This dynamic made for a very tumultuous period in the history of the profession of social work.

Organizations

In his classic work on strategies for dealing with dissatisfaction in firms, Hirschman (1970) contends that unhappy firm members have two basic options: exit or voice—if you don't like it, you can leave or you can speak up. The model provides a simple but powerful way of thinking about strategic choices for the dissatisfied in many contexts. Clearly, social movements are also relational, and movement scholars have long been attuned to the fact that the environment in which social movements operate impacts their form and outcome. Along these lines, Turner and Killian (1971) argue that there are three conditions that affect whether a movement within an organization will be incorporated or separate from it:

1. The extent of integration of the dissenting group into the parent body,
2. The power of the parent body to enforce its legitimate actions and suppress dissent, and
3. The ability of the parent body to absorb dissent, either through changing in response to growing pressures or by encompassing internal variability."

(331)

In an extension of this theory, Harrison and Maniha (1978) argue that there are actually three potential relationships that can develop between challengers and target organizations: social movements can be suppressed and either "disintegrate or go underground," they can separate from the parent organization, or a "relationship of cooperation" could develop (219).

Black social workers' movements utilized both exit and voice strategies within the profession, reflecting the larger conflicts and complexities in black politics at the time. Further, they encountered different organizational structures as they challenged the profession. While my research does not examine individual social workers who exited the profession altogether, I find that some social workers fought for representation within white-dominated professional associations while others chose to form separate organizations. What accounts for these differences? I explore this question through a comparison of the process of black dissent within the National Conference on Social Welfare (NCSW) and the National Federation of Settlements (NFS). I chose these two particular cases because, while their similarities would suggest similar outcomes, they take different overall paths, as one formed a separate organization early in its trajectory and the other remained committed to gaining greater voice within the organization it was challenging.

The National Association of Black Social Workers (NABSW) was organized by black social workers in 1967 as a movement that was fought within the National Conference on Social Welfare (NCSW) to make changes to the profession of social work between 1968 and 1969. The NCSW was originally formed in 1874 as a forum for the exchange of information between social welfare workers before a real, structured network of social welfare professionals existed (Tropman and Stotzer 2005). It quickly became the central vehicle for bringing social workers together in the United States, and remained the primary professional organization for social workers until it disbanded in 1984, as the National Association of Social Workers (NASW, formed in 1955) emerged as the more dominant membership organization for social workers (Tropman and Stotzer 2005).

In 1969 the NABSW separated from the NCSW and formed an independent organization to work for change as a separate entity. NABSW activists focused on seeking changes to the profession on three levels. First, they wanted to expose and address the racism that affected them as workers in the profession. Secondly, they focused on the institutional racism within the field by seeking to change the way that the profession educated, hired, and trained social workers in order to eliminate the inherent biases in the professionalization process. Finally, they dealt with the racism they felt the profession projected onto black communities through social welfare practices that were racist in intent and/or outcome.

The other group of dissident black social workers in this study challenged the National Federation of Settlements (NFS). The National Federation of Settlements was formed in 1911 as a way to coordinate the service and reform efforts of settlements across the nation. The NFS was and continues to be the national coordinating body and membership organization for neighborhood-based agencies in the United States. These black social workers, who first called themselves the Black Caucus of Settlement Workers, organized in 1967. They rallied together around two major issues. First, they insisted on increased representation of black social workers in leadership and decision-making positions within the organization. Secondly, they focused on demanding that the NFS do more in the way of social action on behalf of black communities. The

Black Caucus of Settlement Workers eventually became known as the Techni-Culture Movement (TCM) in 1969, as they decided to become more multicultural in their orientation and focused on producing a Techni-Culture Conference, which would bring together settlement practitioners of color.

Both movements started as quests for greater voice and representation and were both embedded in the Black Power tradition. However, black social workers in NFS ultimately used a voice strategy. They fought to win control of key positions within the Federation and appropriated existing committees within the organization. In contrast, their counterparts in the NCSW used an exit strategy, their mobilization resulting in the separate National Association of Black Social Workers. Through an examination of the historical documents from the profession, each organization, and individual social workers, combined with oral histories with key informants in the movements, I find that differences in the organizational cultures of NFS and NCSW and strategic decisions made by the leaders of these groups of black social workers are important in explaining the divergent strategies. However, the larger context of black politics and the network of relationships between black social workers across the two organizations are also essential pieces of the puzzle. Exploring these two different paths sheds light on the wide range of factors that either promote or inhibit the incorporation of movement ideas into organizations.

OVERVIEW

This book has three overarching goals. It simultaneously offers a critique of state-centered studies of social movement outcomes, provides a step towards filling the empirical gap in the literature concerning the institutionalization of the black liberation movement, and represents an expansion of how we think about the long-term impacts of the Black Power movement. I argue, first of all, that bringing movements into organizations is a very movement-like process. I also find that Black Power was the central motivation and political lens for the creation of new racial practice within organizations in the late 1960s and early 1970s. Finally, I argue that the development of black professional associational life is a central outcome of the Black Power movement that has had long-lasting and broad implications in the professions.

Chapter 2 provides the historical context of the black liberation movement in the United States. After a brief history of the civil rights movement I introduce the social science literature and existing historiography of Black Power. I make the case that Black Power was not only the sort of political formation that is called to mind when we envision groups like the Black Panther Party. Rather, Black Power also morphed into a political form that is captured in the movement's call for "black faces in higher places." Motivated by a desire to create new institutional forms and/or carve out institutional space for African Americans, this black political strategy simultaneously ushered in new racialized norms within institutions and reinforced class cleavages within the black community. This facet of Black Power shaped the development of black mayoral and congressional politics and black convention politics, and spawned a sort of black radical march through the institutions, including the rise of black studies departments and black professional associations.

Chapter 3 explores this process by examining the development of black professional associational life during the Black Power era. Black professional associations were born out of a combination of two primary factors—unprecedented black access to both higher education and white-collar employment and the Black Power movement ideology of "closing ranks" by building independent black organizations. In addition, the concurrent rise of Great Society antipoverty programs (many of which were mandated to have "maximum feasible participation" from the communities they served) led to a concentration of newly minted black professionals in both government and non-profit programs serving the black poor. This makes social work an ideal case for examining the process of IOSMs. I also explicate the relationship between the action and organization of black social workers (among others) and the framing of the Black Power movement. I contend that the long-term impacts of the Black Power movement have been vastly underestimated, in part because of a failure to understand its impact on the development of the institutional capacity of the black community.

With the context of black professionals in social work delineated, chapter 4 goes on to examine the history of the service/activism tension in the profession of social work. I explore the debates that arose within social work organizations as the civil rights movement emerged and the effect that race riots and the emerging Black Power movement had on the debates and discourse about activism in the profession. During a social movement wave, activism often becomes defined by the practices of said movements. Groups like social workers, who straddle the fence between activism and some other role (like direct service or advocacy), are forced to rethink their roles in movements. For example, the leadership of the National Federation of Settlements had a major debate about whether or not to participate in the 1964 March on Washington. The conflict centered on the organization's identity, asking themselves: are we the kind of group that participates in civil rights marches? Moreover, this atmosphere of uncertainty created openings for dissenting social workers to seek change within the profession.

Then, in chapter 5, I trace the process of the mobilization of black social workers within the National Federation of Settlements (NFS). This process resulted in the emergence of the Black Caucus of Settlement Workers and its attempted transition from a black caucus to a multicultural campaign for representation in NFS known as the Techni-Culture Movement (TCM). I analyze the grievances, demands, strategies, tactics, and outcomes of their activism. Like the emergence of the NABSW, the growth of the Techni-Culture Movement takes place in the context of the expansion of Black Power politics. In this case, though, these social workers used a voice strategy and maintained a commitment to gaining representation throughout their mobilization, which ended in what has been called a "black takeover" (Trolander 1987). Because the social workers involved in the Black Caucus and the TCM made the choice to work within the organization to create change, these social workers encountered different forms of resistance, hence this chapter also deals with the emotional dynamics at work in the conflict within the organization.

Not all black social worker activism followed the same path, however. In chapter 6, I look at how black social workers capitalized on this atmosphere of uncertainty by telling the story of black social workers' challenge to the National Conference on Social Welfare. The social workers who participated eventually created an autonomous organization, the National Association of Black Social Workers (NABSW). I detail the historical context of the organization's emergence, analyzing their grievances, their demands, their strategies and tactics, and the outcomes of the mobilization. I also place the emergence of the NABSW in 1967–1968 in the larger context of shifting racial ideologies and the expansion of Black Power politics. Through an analysis of the content of their movement activities and the culture of the organization, I contend that their struggle, while it started as a demand for greater voice within the profession, ultimately employed an exit strategy, which led to their separation from the NCSW to pursue their goals independent of the perceived constraints of the larger professional organization.

With a clear understanding of the different strategies and tactics employed by these two organizations, chapter 7 moves on to compare the outcomes of black social workers' activism in these two relatively similar social work organizations. While the NABSW and the Techni-Culture Movement had similar goals, used similar tactics, and even had a cross-membership of activists, they pursued different strategies and had very disparate outcomes. I argue that leadership and organizational culture help to explain the different paths of these two IOSMs. Differences in the NFS's and NCSW's racial discourse and practices, in addition to organizational identities and legacies surrounding social action, shaped their organizational cultures such that black activists encountered very different targets. Further, the leaders of the NABSW and TCM made decisions that created key turning points in the trajectories of their mobilization campaigns that also help to explain their different outcomes. Here, I develop a model for understanding the role of intra-organizational social movements in civil institutionalization. Additionally, this chapter pays close attention to the role of emotional labor in these struggles.

Lastly, chapter 8 revisits popular conceptions of the Black Power movement in light of its role in the development of black professional associational life. This chapter also explores the idea of treating the Black Power era as a transition period in race relations. I also briefly address the state of contemporary black professional associations.

2

Re-envisioning Black Power

THE TREATMENT OF THE Black Power movement in academic research has been insufficient, and the result is an underestimation of its impact on U.S. society. Many scholars have concluded that while the movement did not have much of an effect on the state itself, it had profound psychological and cultural ramifications for African Americans (Van Deburg 1992). That the Black Power movement inspired and educated black people about Africa, democratic pluralism, and the liberatory function of art, as well as creating space to celebrate a uniquely black aesthetic, is central to what scholars have had to say about its influence. This, however, is an incomplete picture.

Black Power not only contributed to the development of race consciousness and solidarity but also "stimulated the formation of separatist black interest organizations, and sped up the process of black incorporation and cooptation into systemic institutions and processes" (Smith 1992:101). The Black Power influence on the emergent black organizations of the era cannot be overestimated. In fact, the creation of a network of separate black professional, educational, cultural, and political caucuses and organizations is a central outcome of the Black Power movement, one that led to greater incorporation of (at least) the black middle class (Ogbar 2004; Smith 1981).

An interdisciplinary body of literature, which has been referred to as "Black Power Studies," has emerged in the last fifteen years or so that attempts to rectify this mistreatment of the movement (Joseph 2008). In addition to several excellent histories of the movement as a whole (cf.

Jeffries 2006; Joseph 2007; and Ogbar 2004), scholars of the Black Power movement have significantly expanded our knowledge of the outcomes of the movement. Martha Biondi (2012), Stefan Bradley (2009), Ibram Rogers (2012), and Fabio Rojas (2007) have produced excellent studies that treat the rise of black studies departments across the United States as an outcome of the movement. Keith Mayes's (2009) book on Kwanzaa argues that the holiday was a result of the movement's focus on carving out space for blacks, even on the calendar. Andrea A. Burns's (2013) book on black museums brings attention to the Black Power influence on these institutions. Alondra Nelson's (2011) *Body and Soul* provides an account of the health related social programs of the Black Panther Party as a corrective to the popular one-sided academic treatments of the Party. These texts—and the subfield they represent—started the task that I take on in this book: revising the historical and social science account of the movement to include its impact on existing institutions and influence on the development of independent black institutions.[1]

Despite this growth in the historiography of the movement, sociologists have been particularly dismissive of Black Power, having mostly focused on the Black Power movement inasmuch as it affected the moderate civil rights movement upon its advent. What little has been written has primarily—whether explicitly or implicitly—centered on radical flank effect arguments. The radical flank effect refers to how radical factions of social movements affect their moderate counterparts. Haines (1997) defines both negative and positive flank effects and how they work. A negative flank effect occurs when the activities of radicals work to threaten the success of moderates because the latter become associated with the undesirable tactics and ideas of the former. On the other hand, a positive flank effect can occur "when the bargaining position of moderates is strengthened by the presence of more radical groups" (440). Haines's analysis of the Black Power movement bears out that it had a positive flank effect, with the threat of radical action by Black Power advocates making the organized, nonviolent civil rights movement look like a preferable alternative. This resulted in increased funding for organizations that remained moderate.

All in all, the sociological literature on social movements has been guilty of ignoring the enduring impacts of Black Power or, worse, lumping together Black Power activists as a ragtag group of illiterate, uneducated, and unorganized thugs. Doug McAdam (1982), for example, cites

Peter Goldman (1970) with no qualification when he calls the Black Power movement a "ghetto-bred generation with reputations no larger than a single city or neighborhood or even a particular block" (Goldman 1970, as cited in McAdam 1982:185). This characterization of Black Power activists and their impact on society is simply untrue.

It is important to note here that there are significant disagreements among sociologists and historians alike about whether the civil rights and Black Power movements constitute one shifting black liberation movement or two separate movements entirely. In my estimation, it is a bit of both. Clear temporal transitions occur among civil rights activists and organizations that mark a shift in the earlier movement towards a Black Power frame—take, for example, the transformation of the Student Nonviolence Coordinating Committee (SNCC) from the nonviolent inventors of the sit-in movement to foremost Black Power advocates. However, the moderate, integrationist thrust of the civil rights movement that dismantled legal segregation, while retreating from dominance in the face of Black Power, did not disappear; nor did black radicalism start with the Black Power movement of the late 1960s and early 1970s. Given this, I conceptualize the black liberation movement as encompassing both the civil rights and Black Power movements and use the term to refer to this larger constellation of black political movements.

Along these lines, a lack of clarity about the boundaries of these movements is one reason sociologists in particular have failed to recognize the impact of the Black Power movement. This is evident in the way scholars have handled its periodization. In the usual periodization of the movement the cycle of the black liberation movement has three important phases. Figure 2.1 illustrates the standard argument about the movement's cycle. The years 1955–1960 are considered the emergence; the years 1961–1965 are the heyday, marked by the height of direct action; and finally, 1966–1970 is the period of decline. It's important to note that the time period widely considered as the decline of the black liberation movement overlaps with the rise of Black Power politics. This is because the increasing radicalization of the movement is considered part of the reason that the movement ended.

In this narrative, the Black Power movement comes along and ruins everything for the moderate movement. Their brand of protest is unpalatable for elites so they become the subject of extreme repression and die off. It is certainly true that the Black Power movement was subjected to

TOTAL MOVEMENT INITIATED EVENTS

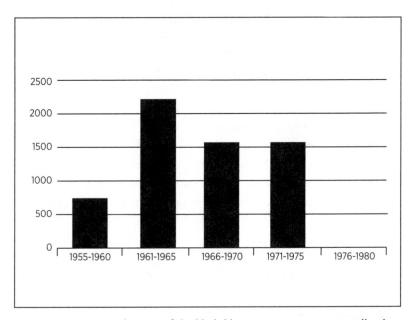

FIGURE 2.1 The periodization of the black liberation movement, as usually identified by scholars. Note how it follows an arc from emergence to climax and then decline.
Adapted from Doug McAdam's *Political Process and the Development of Black Insurgency,
1930–1970* (Chicago: University of Chicago, 1999).

repression. From government-sponsored infiltration by informants, to
unlawful surveillance, violent police repression, and the use of incarcera-
tion to quell movement activity, Black Power organizations experienced
severe state suppression. However, the notion that the radical movement
simply died ignores the ways in which the Black Power movement was
incorporated into the organizations of civil society.

If we accept these indicators—and this cycle—we miss out on where the
real action happens: the movement to implement the movement. Figure 2.2
shows the number of national level black professional associations founded
between 1955 and 1980. The division is based on the standard periodization seen previously in Figure 2.1, where the first time period represents the
emergence, the second time period the heyday, and third the decline. It is

NUMBER OF NATIONAL BLACK PROFESSIONAL
ASSOCIATIONS FOUNDED

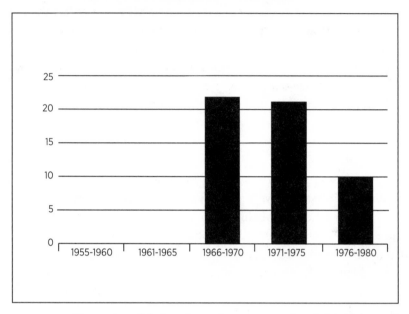

FIGURE 2.2   The number of black professional organizations founded, held against the standard periodization of the black liberation movement. The number of organizations actually reached its peak during the period scholars identify as the movement's decline. Adapted from Kristy A. Swartout, ed., *Encyclopedia of Associations*, 44th edition (Farmington Hills, Mich.: Gale Group, 2006).

during the period widely accepted as the decline of the movement that the founding of black professional associations actually peaked. By focusing only on traditional movement organizations, standard protest events, and the like, we miss the opportunity to understand another whole phase of the movement, which I am contending is at least partially captured by the rise in black professional associations, and is the same type of phenomenon as the black studies movement—a sort of black radical march through the institutions (Dutschke 1969).

Drawing on Gramsci's (1971) ideas, Rudi Dutschke (1969), the militant representative of the German student movement, proposed the notion of the long march through the institutions as a form of radical revolution. In arguing that universities cannot be the only site for the movement, he claims that revolutionaries "must regard the 'long march through the institutions' as a practical critical action in all social spheres" (249). Dutschke also went further, maintaining that the long march was necessary to bring the ideas of the movement into the organizations that structure our lives. This process of civil institutionalization is critical to understanding the ways in which the movement was institutionalized in U.S. society, and works to complicate our understanding of what happens at the so-called end of a movement cycle.

MOVEMENT HISTORY

Black professional associations are a direct outcome of the Black Power movement. In many ways, their patterns of emergence, structures, and general form reflected the shift from civil rights to Black Power politics and fit right into the larger history of black liberation movements in the United States.

Since the arrival of the first Africans to the United States, the long struggle for black liberation has taken on varying forms, but all of its permutations can largely be sorted into two parallel streams. As political scientist Cedric Robinson (1997) suggests, "by the second half of the nineteenth century, two alternative political cultures had arisen." The first, rooted in a black desire to claim "privileged political and social identities jealously reserved for non-Blacks," led to an "assimilationist Black political culture that appropriated the values and objectives of the dominant American Creed." The second, grounded in the desire of slaves to "form a historical identity that presumed a higher moral standard than that which seemed to bind their masters" led to an alternative political culture that promoted the rejection of white institutions, norms, and values and that espoused separatism at some level (96). As the civil rights movement gave way to Black Power in the mid-1960s, this second, more radical black political culture came into dominance. But these two cultures have always been complicatedly connected.

What I find is that it was the concerns of the of the Black Power movement, not those of the civil rights movement, that dominated the demands of black social workers as well as other black professionals in this era. Indeed, black social workers were very much products of their time in that they saw themselves as a part of the constellation of black political and cultural formations that were eschewing the integrationist goals of the civil rights movement. While a full discussion of the differences between and histories of the civil rights and Black Power movements is beyond the scope of this current project, it is important to understand the relationship of black social worker movements to the larger black political environment through a brief discussion of the history of the black liberation movement.

Civil Rights: The Heroic Period

The civil rights movement, normally placed between 1954 and 1964, is generally seen as encompassing the struggle for desegregation, voting rights, and against discrimination in general. The beginning of the "heroic period" (Joseph 2007) of the black liberation struggle is often marked as beginning in 1954 with the Supreme Court's *Brown v. Board of Education* decision because it signals the emergence of a surge of direct action. The roots of the *Brown* decision, however, date back to the 1896 *Plessy v. Ferguson* decision, when the Supreme Court held that segregation was constitutional so long as the separate accommodations were equal. Through law, the United States had become "two societies, one white, one black, separate and unequal" (United States National Advisory Commission on Civil Disorders 1968). The National Association for the Advancement of Colored People (NAACP) took up a monumental legal fight against the "separate but equal" clause of the *Plessy* decision, using education as the site of struggle.

The culmination of a twenty-year long legal battle, the Supreme Court's decision in the *Brown v. Board of Education* case outlawed segregation in public education, a critical outcome of the NAACP's legal strategy toward desegregation in public schooling. Following this civil rights victory, however, African Americans witnessed massive resistance to school integration across the country.[2] Southern whites resisted integration with school closures, refusal to integrate, and outright violence. In many ways, the direct action phase of the movement that we associate with the civil rights movement grew out of black reactions to white resistance to integration.

As Lewis Killian (1981) points out, the civil rights movement in its early years "was fundamentally and unrelentingly assimilationist" (43). The movement was preoccupied with ending legal segregation and gaining access to institutions previously reserved for whites only. Focused on equalizing access to public accommodations and services, movement campaigns not only targeted the state through actions aimed at integrating education and government programs, but also sought to integrate public transportation, eating establishments, and other public facilities. Overall, the movement was less about a restructuring of U.S. society or challenging the basic institutions of U.S. life than about reforming the country in such a way that African Americans would have equal access to existing U.S. political and social formations. The dominant rights frame employed by the movement claimed that each person in the United States should have the same rights as anyone else. In this way, the movement relied on an individual notion of freedom, appealing to American individualism by asserting that no person should be denied the basic rights of citizenship. Movement actors also attempted to appeal to Americans' moral conscience through tactical choices such as marches, sit-ins, boycotts, and other non-violent demonstrations.

There are several key marking points in the timeline of the movement. An early important moment was the Montgomery bus boycott. This campaign followed the now legendary arrest of Rosa Parks, who sat in the white section of a segregated bus on December 1, 1955. Parks's demonstration and subsequent arrest resulted in a mobilization that lasted a whole year and ended with a Supreme Court decision that desegregated Alabama's bus system in 1956. Despite the fact that it was actually the movement's second mass bus boycott, it was its first major success and the campaign catapulted Martin Luther King Jr. into the movement's spotlight.

The movement's integrationist values were largely shaped by King and the black church's adherence to the ideal of the beloved community. The dominance of King's Gandhian-Christian values was reflected in the central ideological and practical role the black church played in the movement (Morris 1984). Not only did the church provide organizing centers for the movement, but Christian values and ideals also shaped movement strategies and tactics in essential ways. King explicitly used Christian themes and language in describing the goal of the movement, which is clear in a speech he delivered reflecting on the successful Montgomery bus boycott: the goal was "to awaken a sense of shame within the oppressor and challenge his false sense of superiority. . . . The end is reconciliation; the end is redemption; the end is the creation of the beloved community. It is this type of spirit and this type of love that can transform opposers into friends" (King 1956, as quoted in Garrow 1986:81). The notion that "the end" should be reconciliation and redemption relies on a distinctly Christian notion of agape love—one that forgives, sacrifices, and is unconditional enough to move beyond the horrors of white racism into a meaningful beloved community. This sentiment distinctly shaped the movement's integrationist thrust.

Another centerpiece of the nonviolent civil rights movement was the sit-in strategy. This tactic was used to challenge the discrimination existing in the South's predominantly segregated public accommodations. Black students took the lead with the sit-in movement, often challenging lunch counter segregation at eating establishments across the region. The Student Nonviolent Coordinating Committee (SNCC), which would go on to become one of the most important organizing forces of the civil rights movement, was formed out of the sit-in movement's momentum.

Founded in 1960 at a student conference called by Ella Baker (then executive director of the Southern Christian Leadership Conference), the SNCC was conceived of as a student-centric wing of the nonviolent civil rights movement, and would coordinate sit-ins and other student actions. The organization was also an effort to come together as a student community within the larger civil rights movement. They initially adopted the dominant frames of the movement, such as the Gandhian-Christian principles of nonviolence and integrationism. However, unlike many of the other civil rights organizations at the time, they were not willing to impose those ideas on local leaders in a way that constrained the idea of radical militancy. The SNCC became a vital part of the wave of direct action that resulted in the passing of significant civil rights legislation such as: the Civil Rights Act of 1964, which outlawed segregation in public accommodations; the Voting Rights Act of 1965, which banned discrimination in voter registration; the Twenty-fourth Amendment to the Constitution, which outlawed poll taxes; Executive Order 1124, which required "affirmative action" in hiring; and the Civil Rights Act of 1968, which prohibited discrimination in housing.

As the organization's early focus shifted from desegregation to political rights, the SNCC's commitment to nonviolent direct action shifted to a form of radicalism shaped by their experiences in black communities. During this shift, which largely occurred in the aftermath of their Mississippi voting campaign that brought hundreds of college students to the state, the organization went into a period of reflection. This turn inward was particularly focused around whether they would remain committed to ideas of interracialism and nonviolence and whether the best path forward was to continue confronting existing institutions or to build independent institutions (Carson 1995). As SNCC members worked to define their path forward in the mid-1960s and to resolve internal conflicts, the organization moved towards a form of radicalism that would eventually be given the name "Black Power." As a result, the organization excluded white activists and created conflict with other civil rights groups over issues of radicalism and separatism. This development helped dissolve the coalition between civil rights organizations that had successfully resulted in civil rights legislation and racial integration in public life.

Between 1954 and 1965, while the nation's attention was riveted on the modern civil rights movement, there was a parallel movement for self-determination that was the precursor to Black Power. After all, the enormously influential Malcolm X was organizing with the Nation of Islam during this period and was only assassinated in 1965, well after the passing of key civil rights legislation. It is only after 1965 that this parallel movement came to the forefront of politics, and was given the name "Black Power."

The Transition to Black Power

In June 1966, James Meredith began a solo march across the South to protest the severe racism against African Americans in the region. Shortly after starting his trek, he was shot by a sniper and sent to the hospital for treatment. Upon hearing about James Meredith's lonely march and subsequent shooting, several civil rights activists decided to pick up where he left off and continue the march in his name. It was when the march reached Greenwood, Mississippi, that Stokely Carmichael delivered his now famous Black Power speech, sparking off what would become a new, controversial slogan for black organizing in the United States. Carmichael—by all accounts an oratorical genius—told the audience, "this is the twenty-seventh time that I've been arrested. I ain't going to jail no more. The only way we gonna stop them white men from whuppin' us is to take over. What we gonna start saying now is Black Power!" The crowd responded with unified shouts of "Black Power!" with the SNCC's equally passionate Willie Ricks leading the crowd in a call-and-response:

"What do you want?"
"BLACK POWER!"
"What do you want?"
"BLACK POWER!"

(Joseph 2006; Woodard 1999)

Black Power quickly moved from an extemporaneous rallying cry to a prominent, identifiable political and ideological force in American life. Following on the heels of the Watts Rebellion of 1965, Black Power gave voice to a generation of black young people who wanted more—more than the civil rights movement was asking for and certainly more than the "establishment" was giving. Indeed, Black Power provided a framework for many in the black community to express a wide range of reactions to the dismal situation in poor black communities. The Black Power movement soon developed as a loosely organized network of organizations and individuals committed to radical social change and independence in black economic, political, social, and aesthetic life. The movement challenged the wholesale acceptance of integration as the appropriate strategy for black people in the U.S., advocating instead for various forms and levels of separation from the white mainstream.

The Black Panther Party, formed in 1966, was one of these organizations, and soon came to embody these goals. It became the archetype of a Black Power organization in the eyes of the general public and certainly in the media. The Black Panther Party was originally focused on fighting police brutality in black communities through self-defense and self-help, but their armed civilian surveillance of the police, armed protests, and acts of civil disobedience garnered the kind of media attention that made the Party the face of the Black Power movement well past its prime.[3]

Working on the overarching premise that the civil rights movement failed to bring about real social change, Black Power advocates argued for alternative ways of achieving concrete social transformation. Black Power activists were involved in movements for community control of resources, including public schools, local police forces, and social services. They fought for welfare reform, employment opportunities, and housing rights. The movement also focused on prison reform, and worked to end the relentless police brutality that plagued black communities. This latter point is particularly germane in light of the severe police and state repression that the movement faced.[4] Self-help was another primary aim. The Black Panther Party survival programs, for example, provided needed services for children and the elderly that were not being provided by the state. (For detailed accounts of the movement see Jeffries 2006; Joseph 2006, 2007, 2010; Nelson 2011; Ogbar 2004.)

The Black Power movement also gained steam from the international political environment. Black Power activists placed the movement for black liberation in the United States in the broader context of African struggles for independence and anticolonialism movements across the globe. Black Power organizations made both symbolic and real linkages to Africa, often drawing parallels between African colonialism and African American experiences. Organizations like the Republic of New Afrika, for example, argued that as an internally colonized people, black Americans should secede from the United States and occupy the southernmost states as a new African nation.

While Black Power was not one united movement with a single clear ideology that was universally adhered to, it is clear that the movement arose in reaction to lagged progress in implementing civil rights gains and in opposition to the integrationist ideas that dominated the civil rights movement. However, it still retained very significant connections to earlier black radical formations (Marable 1984; McAdam 1999; Van Deburg 1992; Killian 1981; Smith 1981). Despite its many permutations, the Black Power movement at the most basic level advocated for self-help and self-defense in the black community and rejected white aesthetic norms, cultural standards, and values. Self-definition, self-determination, and black pride were central to Black Power (Joseph 2006; Killian 1987; Ogbar 2005; Van DeBurg 1992).

The tactics of the Black Power movement are harder to generalize because they did not follow a dominant pattern like those of the nonviolent civil rights protests. Moreover, many of the tactics of the movement were oriented towards individual and community self-help. For example, the Black Panther Party's provision of breakfast for black children and supervision of traffic stops in the black community were, indeed, movement acts. The movement used acts of civil disobedience as well. College campuses, for example, saw the occupation, takeover, and sometimes destruction of classrooms and administrative buildings as the movement was translated into demands for black studies programs at universities. Scholars have also

TABLE 2.1

	CIVIL RIGHTS	BLACK POWER
GOALS	Access	Self-Determination
DOMINANT FRAMES	Rights	Empowerment
STRATEGIES	Integration	Separation
TACTICS	Marches, sit-ins, boycotts	Self-help, riots, occupation

placed the urban rebellions of the late 1960s within the tactical repertoire of the Black Power movement.

NATION TIME: BLACK FACES IN HIGHER PLACES

There was more to the Black Power movement than the popular image of the movement that dominated television newscasts and COINTELPRO[5] reports. Specifically, there was a strain within the movement that was aimed at dismantling institutionalized racism. In their famous treatise on Black Power, Stokely Carmichael (later Kwame Ture) and Charles Hamilton explicated one of the first social science theories of institutional racism, and made a call for Black Power advocates to work to carve out space in existing institutions and to close ranks in order to build independent black institutional capacity. Carmichael and Hamilton (1992[1967]) define racism as "the predication of decisions and policies on considerations of race for the purpose of *subordinating* a racial group and maintaining control over that group" (4). They argue that racism is overt and covert, as well as individual and institutional. The first form of racism consists of the overt acts of individual whites against individual blacks. "The second type," they contend, "is less overt, far more subtle, less identifiable in terms of *specific* individuals committing the acts. But it is no less destructive of human life. The second type originates in the operation of established and respected forces in the society, and thus receives far less public condemnation than the first type" (4). In other words, institutional racism refers to the kinds of practices and actions that exist within and operate through the existing institutional arrangements of social life.

Their book *Black Power* (1992[1967]) makes the case that black people must build independent institutions. Making the now famous argument that African Americans must first "close ranks" to build independent power, Carmichael and Hamilton state that "black people must lead and run their own organizations" (45). In the face of persistent racism that treated black people as incapable of handling their own affairs, they provide an important justification for closing ranks: "Only black people can convey the revolutionary idea—and it is a revolutionary idea—that black people are able to do things themselves" (45).

They make a key second argument: Black Power can also be gained by carving out space and developing power bases within existing institutions. Carmichael and Hamilton say:

> Black Power means, for example, that in Lowndes County, Alabama, a black sheriff can end police brutality. A black tax assessor and tax collector and county board of revenue can lay, collect, and channel tax monies for the building of better roads and schools serving black people. . . . It means the creation of power bases, of strength, from which black people can press to change local or nationwide patterns of oppression—instead of from weakness.
>
> (46)

They note, however, that this march through the institutions "does not mean *merely* putting black faces into office. Black visibility is not Black Power" (48). There is also a vital distinction between individual uplift and representation in their line of reasoning. What they are really interested in is having black people who would press for institutional change appointed to important positions, rather than the visible placement of black people in positions of power for the simple sake of providing jobs for a couple visible African Americans.

In this way, *Black Power* and similar endeavors provided the blueprint for a generation of new black professionals and political figures who actively worked to develop strategies for gaining institutional power. From the Black Power conferences to the black political conventions and the rise of black mayoral and congressional politics, the Black Power movement profoundly shaped the black political context of the late 1960s and early 1970s. Further, with Black Power as a central ideological force in black life, African Americans who were situated in a variety of institutional settings brought the movement with them. Black people in the United States, informed and inspired by the movement, fought for black studies departments in

American universities, the development of Afrocentric curricula in various educational settings, and representation on the boards of directors of organizations serving black communities. They also sought greater racial diversity and inclusive climates within organizations of all sorts. Though the influence of Black Power on politics has been documented, this particular but essential element of the Black Power movement—the work that African Americans in all kinds of organizations did to bring the ideas of the movement into institutions—is one of the least understood facets of the movement.

Black Politics

Shortly after the SNCC's 1966 call for Black Power became popularized, Harlem Representative Adam Clayton Powell attempted to define it in political terms (Woodard 1999). Calling together a small group of black leaders from across the country, Powell held a small Black Power conference. This meeting in turn led to the creation of a planning committee to put on the first national Black Power Conference in Newark, New Jersey, the following year.

The conference was held between July 20th and July 23rd, 1967—in the wake of one of the bloodiest urban rebellions in American history. Lasting a whole week, from July 11th to July 17th, the Newark Rebellion had left over twenty people dead and at least a thousand injured (Hayden 1967). Despite controversy over whether the timing was appropriate to hold a Black Power conference in the aftermath of the rebellion, more than a thousand delegates and representatives from 286 organizations attended this first national Black Power Conference (Woodard 1999). The conference consisted of workshops and presentations focused around strategies for black community control. In the end over eighty resolutions calling for black power in social, political, economic, and cultural life were passed—some officially and others "in spirit" (Woodard 1999).

The resolutions passed at the conference were a set of wide reaching mandates aimed at "the propagation of self-determination, self-sufficiency, self-respect and self-defense."[6] The conference document opens with this basis for action: "Whereas, the Black people stand at the crossroads of either an expanding revolution or ruthless extermination, it is incumbent upon us to set our house in order." The document continues by arguing that because "Black people have consistently expended too much energy and resources reacting to white definitions, it is imperative that organizational and technical competence develop to initiate and enact new insights, new definitions, and new programs." The more than eighty different resolutions are then listed, some of which were aimed at "closing ranks," as Carmichael would later explicate. Others were aimed external goals, such as gaining power in existing political institutions and carving out autonomous space in historically white organizations. One example was a call for a simultaneous push to "buy black" by supporting black businesses and to exert pressure "against the federal government for the marked ineffectiveness and discrimination of present programs" in order to address black economic development.[7]

The political resolutions are surprisingly "mainstream" for a Black Power conference. Calling for the development of a black lobby in Washington, D.C. and condemning the U.S. government for passing H.R. 421, a controversial anti-riot bill, the political resolutions were generally aimed at reforming existing political formations. This reflects the reality that while Black Power was certainly concerned with self-help and separatism in some cases, there was a strain of Black Power interested in gaining power in traditional political formations and institutions. In fact, several resolutions also called for black control over existing current community resources.

Under the heading of "cultural development," the conference endorsed resolutions to establish an independent black university system, a new black religious philosophy, and the construction of "experimental communities" out of existing black communities. Similarly, the conference recommended the development of a national African American teachers organization and "the formation of new black professional organizations." These new organizations, they argued, should be created with a mind towards "a re-definition of professionality [sic] peculiar to and essential to the Black community."[8]

At the 1969 National Black Economic Development Conference, the final resolutions also focused primarily on building black institutional capacity. James Forman wrote a document that would eventually be called the *Black Manifesto*, which, despite some disagreement over the content, was adopted as the official statement of the conference. The *Black Manifesto*, in short, was a call for a particular form of reparations. It calls on white Christian churches and Jewish synagogues to come up with $500 million to be divided among several endeavors to develop independent black institutions, including the development of a land trust so that black people can purchase or retain land, the establishment of black publishing houses and television networks, and the creation of a black research institute and university.

The Black Power conferences built a power base and organizational vehicle for the development of black political conventions and stronger black presence in mainstream politics. *Ebony Magazine's* annual progress report for 1967 titled, "Political Victories Climax, Year of Strife and Explosion in Nation's Black Ghettoes," opens with a declaration about the year's importance in the struggle for black liberation (*Ebony*, January 1968). It reads, "The events of one day alone—Tuesday, November 7—made 1967 a year of significant political victory for the Negro. On that day Carl B. Stokes was elected mayor of Cleveland, Ohio, the nation's tenth largest city, and Richard G. Hatcher tallied enough votes to become mayor of Gary, Indiana . . . " (118). The article then detailed the Newark Rebellion and the other urban riots of the year, but maintained a hopeful tone when reporting the election of the nation's first black mayors and celebrated the appointment of Thurgood Marshall, the nation's first black Supreme Court justice. The dominant sentiment was that times were changing. African Americans were becoming more integrated into mainstream political formations and there was a feeling that life as it was in America's inner cities could be ignored no longer.

The election of the nation's first black mayors was evidence of African American electoral power in cities with large black populations and coincided with intense racial conflict in those cities. There was an air of hopefulness that black leadership would stall the violence that was tearing across U.S. cities (Biles 1992). However, it was precisely because of the mix of urban violence, Black Power movement building, and the growth of black mainstream politics that the power in American politics was shifting from the urban centers to the periphery with white flight to the suburbs. African Americans were gaining political power in big cities at the exact time that the influence of urban areas was shrinking (Wilson 1980[1978]). Still, black mayoral victories are representative of a strain of the Black Power movement that sought black representatives in existing power structures.

This "black faces in higher places" variety of Black Power was also evident at the National Black Political Convention in Gary, Indiana, in 1972.

In what Manning Marable has called the "zenith of the entire black movement during the Second Reconstruction," this unprecedented collectivity
gathered twelve thousand black delegates from across the country in Gary
to both discuss a plan of action for the National Democratic Convention
coming up later in the year and to strategize about the larger movement
(Marable 1984). Even though the convention was full of conflicts between
individuals and organizations with differing views on what black people
needed and how to go about doing it, the conference brought together
grassroots activists, established political leaders, and multiple ideological
strains all under the umbrella of Black Power. From revolutionary nationalists who advocated armed resistance to recently elected officials, the participants in the largest and widest reaching convention in black history
(Woodard 1999) certainly dealt with the issue of institution building.

In an early reflection on the Gary Convention, Imamu Amiri Baraka
(1972)—who is widely recognized as the single most important leader at
the convention—summarized this joining of the minds of Black Power:

> We need voter registration not because of a Democratic nominee but
> because we need to register Black voters to begin to move toward local self-
> determination. We are woefully under-registered and electoral politics must
> be seen as a legitimate area of struggle if we are dealing for the Black com-
> munity and trying to seize political power where we can. We should not talk
> about world revolution if we cannot even win a councilmanic [sic] spot in
> our very city. The goods and services that accrue to these local elective and
> appointive office must be in the hands of Black people interested in the lib-
> eration of Black community. . .
>
> (47)

The Gary conference was an attempt to pull together the various Black
Power advocates to unify around institution building, with the goal of not
only creating independent institutions but also using black access to existing
institutions and electoral politics as a power base for gaining black liberation.

The impact of the Black Power movement on black participation
in mainstream politics is clear. From the election of black mayors to the
development of the Congressional Black Caucus, Black Power's theme of
building political and institutional power shaped African American participation in U.S. political formations in the late 1960s and early 1970s.

Even Richard Nixon picked up the movement's slogan, though his true political agenda was aimed at co-opting the movement (Kotlowski 1998). Nixon saw an uncontrolled Black Power movement as a major threat to American life, so his administration developed the black capitalism initiative and funded the Office of Minority Business Enterprise as a black capitalist alternative (Weems and Randolph 2001). Though in some ways he was able to subvert the movement, black mainstream political participation continuing into the 1980s and beyond is an enduring outcome of the Black Power movement (Joseph 2010). For example, the historic election of Harold Washington as mayor of Chicago in 1983 was largely a result of black militant support and voter registration drives (Joseph 2010). In fact, Peniel Joseph (2010)—drawing a connecting line between Black Power and black electoral politics, including Jesse Jackson's 1984 and 1988 presidential campaigns—places the election of Barack Obama, the nation's first black president, in the Black Power tradition.

The "nation building" strain of the Black Power movement was not only played out in the political arena. From the rise of black studies programs, the development of black student unions, to the creation of independent black educational institutions, black theaters, and black museums, African Americans used the fuel of the Black Power movement both to carve out institutional space within white institutions and to develop independent black institutions in civil society. This black radical "march through the institutions" (Dutschke 1969), though an important outcome of the movement, has largely been understudied and under-theorized in black power and social movement studies, with significant debate over whether all Black Power-era institution building and business endeavors should even be considered part of the movement at all. (See Warren Hill and Rabig 2012 for several treatments of this debate.) This critique is reminiscent of Rap Brown's response to Whitney Young's 1968 announcement that the Urban League would work for Black Power through black capitalism. Brown retorted that the whole idea of Black Power had been "diluted and prostituted to the point where even the most conservative negroes are now for Black Power" (Brown 1967, as cited in Carson 1981:289). Indeed, in a movement principally remembered for its more radical tenets, for its pushing the boundaries of black movements, and for its staunch critique of capitalism and the existing racial order, these seemingly mainstream elements appear to fall outside of the movement. But there is no single authority by which to answer the question "What is Black Power?" In considering all of the ideological, organizational, and action elements that fell under the tent of Black Power, Michal O. West's (2012) answer to the question of "to whom did the tent belong?" is the only one that makes sense: to "all of its occupants. In sum, Black Power belonged to all who claimed it" (294).

Regardless of the scholarly debates, this phenomenon is important not only because it changed the organizational landscape of civil society, but also because it created important shifts in racial practices in organizations and contributed to the incorporation of the black middle class into mainstream institutions. The rising black middle class of the late 1960s was central to the development of a network of black organizations, which shared a "mood of protest" about racial issues with the working class and poor African Americans—issues that were the concern of the Black Power movement (Smith 1981). This network, radicalized by Black Power to turn the black political focus toward institution building and gaining institutional space in white organizations, led to the widespread development of independent black organizations. Indeed, between 1966 and 1967, Charles Hamilton's speaking and consulting centered on the idea of closing ranks through the creation of black political organizations that would be independent of the white power structure (Smith 1992).

Thus, while Hamilton's influence on the way the general public understood Black Power is undeniable, his influence on black social workers was far more direct. He was invited to speak to black social workers in 1967 and 1968 and his conception of Black Power is central to the way National Association of Black Social Workers emerged as an independent organization. Rather than being formed because of exclusion, as it happened with the earlier generation of such organizations (like those of black doctors and lawyers), the black professional associations that came up in the 1960s saw themselves as "technical support for the black liberation movement" (Sanders, as cited in Smith 1992:435).

Moreover, this importation of Black Power into mainstream organizations contributed to the co-optation of the movement in such a way that its transformatory power would look more like today's diversity initiatives than what it looked like at its most revolutionary—certainly not what Stokely Carmichael had in mind when he and Hamilton suggested that black people take the struggle into institutions. Still, in the extant literature on the movement, very little is known about this process.

3

Black Power Professionals

DURING THE LATE 1960S and early 1970s, greater access to education and employment opportunities for African Americans coincided with the dominance of Black Power politics and ideology in such a way that black people brought the movement with them into a variety of institutional settings. For example, black students' push for black studies departments and the hiring of black faculty on college campuses meant that whole cohorts of African American scholars were entering the academy, as both students and professors, in small but unprecedented numbers. The expansion of Lyndon Johnson's Great Society programs, with their call for "maximum feasible participation" from the communities they served, also led to large numbers of African American social workers and program administrators working in Community Action Programs and other social service agencies.

The increased African American presence in a variety of professions was not just a demographic change in those professions. Rather, by bringing the Black Power movement with them, black workers sought to create meaningful societal change within and through their profession. This motivation was not limited to the Black Power call to carve out space in traditionally white institutions and to build new, independent black institutions. From challenging their profession to hire more African Americans to their push for their work to be more racially aware, Black Power-era professionals were often carrying out movements within their professional lives that mirrored the calls of the larger Black Power movement.

As black professionals organized, they developed caucuses and associations to represent their interests and to serve as a sort of racial conscience within their respective fields. This process was critical to the implementation of the goals of the black liberation movement within civil society. All change is hard work and enacting racial change, given the racist heritage and tradition in American culture, is particularly difficult. Black professionals, who encountered professional structures that were slow in keeping up with the new standards of racial interaction and racial practice that African Americans were setting with the Black Power movement, found themselves having to hold their professions accountable for their work as it related to black communities. As evidenced from the numerous demands, manifestos, and founding documents of some of the black professional organizations that grew out of the Black Power era, black professionals were truly executing a black radical march through the institutions and saw themselves as challenging the racial structure of the United States through their work.

Because of the need to react to urban unrest in black communities during the Black Power movement, social services expanded their reach. And because the black family was under attack in social science literature and popular discourse, the social work profession experienced a tremendous growth in its African American workforce and a rise in the community social work model in general. Social workers found themselves in a prime position to staff the new Community Action Programs, Model Cities administrations, and other private and public social service agencies whose target populations were urban African American communities.

Indeed, urban African American communities were the foremost subjects of numerous governmental and social science research missions. As a prime example, in 1965 sociologist and then-assistant secretary of labor, Daniel Patrick Moynihan published the infamous report entitled *The Negro Family: The Case for National Action*, which came to be known simply as the *Moynihan Report*. In it, Moynihan contended, "At the heart of the deterioration of the fabric of Negro society is the deterioration of the Negro family" (Office of Policy Planning and Research, U.S. Department of Labor 1965). Citing the number of children born out of wedlock and female-headed households, Moynihan inferred that "the family structure of lower class Negroes is highly unstable." Moynihan then goes on to identify a black lower-class culture defined by black matriarchy and the passage of bad values and habits (such as not working) from parents to offspring. This cultural form, he argues, caused poor African Americans live in a "tangle of pathology," which is the real root of black poverty. In concluding the report, Moynihan asks:

> What then is that problem? We feel the answer is clear enough. Three centuries of injustice have brought about deep-seated structural distortions in the life of the Negro American. At this point, the present tangle of pathology is capable of perpetuating itself without assistance from the white world. The cycle can be broken only if these distortions are set right.

He goes on to suggest that any effective government policy aimed at alleviating black poverty should be aimed at providing resources to rebuild the black family.

The *Moynihan Report* was originally intended to be an internal report within the Department of Labor, but it was leaked to the public and had a profound impact on the black community. African American commentators sharply criticized the report and a flurry of published responses followed, it disparaging for favoring "cultural" explanations over structural ones, among other issues (cf. Ryan 1971; Stack 1974).

In July 1967, as a result of continuing urban riots, President Johnson appointed a commission led by Otto Kerner, governor of Illinois, to study the causes of and potential solutions for the racial unrest in American cities. After a seven-month investigation, the *Report of the National Advisory Commission on Civil Disorders* was published in February 1968. In stark contrast to Moynihan's deductions, the Kerner Commission reached the "basic conclusion" that, "our nation is moving toward two societies, one black, one white—separate and unequal." The commission warned that "discrimination and segregation have long permeated much of American life; they now threaten the future of every American." However, the commission also opined that "this deepening racial division is not inevitable. The movement apart can be reversed. Choice is still possible." They argued that their goal was "to define that choice and to press for a national resolution," because "to pursue our present course will involve the continuing polarization of the American community and, ultimately, the destruction of basic democratic values." In the report, the commission also issued a challenge:

The alternative is not blind repression or capitulation to lawlessness. It is the realization of common opportunities for all within a single society. This alternative will require a commitment to national action—compassionate, massive and sustained, backed by the resources of the most powerful and the richest nation on this earth. From every American it will require new attitudes, new understanding, and, above all, new will.

(2)

The commission went on to point out that "segregation and poverty have created in the racial ghetto a destructive environment totally unknown to most white Americans." The writers attempted to reveal the hidden structures of racism for a general public, reiterating that "what white Americans have never fully understood—but what the Negro can never forget—is that white society is deeply implicated in the ghetto. White institutions created it, white institutions maintain it, and white society condones it." This, of course, was a very different conclusion than the one that Moynihan drew.

The Kerner Commission also called for a wide-scale expansion of Johnson's Great Society programs, radical welfare reform, and the development of new programs to alleviate poverty and discrimination. Furthermore, the commission stated, "It is time now to turn with all the purpose at our command to the major unfinished business of this nation. It is time to adopt strategies for action that will produce quick and visible progress. It is time to make good the promises of American democracy to all citizens . . ." They called for massive, wide-reaching programs and policies aimed at "chang(ing) the system of failure and frustration that now dominates the ghetto and weakens our society." "These programs (would) require unprecedented levels of funding and performance," they warned, and that "there can be no higher priority for national action and no higher claim on the nation's conscience." Finally, the commission proposed a massive job creation campaign across the nation, integration as a primary tactic to improve ghetto education, a drastic overhaul of the public welfare system which would require that welfare payments meet the "poverty level" standard, and creating adequate and affordable housing in poor urban areas. Police departments, social welfare workers, and the media are also all indicted for playing a role in creating the conditions under which the riots of the late 1960s took place. While there was certainly controversy around the commission's recommendations, many in the political and policy arenas did buy into the suggestions in the face of such violent resistance in several American inner cities.

Despite the fact that Kerner Commission's report garnered considerable attention and support—in fact, the report was an instant bestseller—its recommendations were largely ignored by the Johnson administration. Urban riots continued unabated, and actually picked up pace after the assassination of Martin Luther King Jr. in April of that year. Black scholars and professionals, however, lauded the *Kerner Report* and used it as a rallying point to call for systemic change. In fact, several of the founding demands of black professional associations call for an adoption of the commission's primary recommendations.

Although the Moynihan and Kerner Commission's reports come to drastically different conclusions, they both join a long line of ethnographic studies of black urban communities and reflect governmental and private social scientific researchers' unrelenting and enduring fascination with the "otherness" of the black poor (see Kelley 1997). This proliferation of studies on the African American experience certainly had an impact on black scholars and social work professionals during the late 1960s. Their activism during the period demonstrates, at least in part, a desire to respond to these studies and to reclaim the black experience from charges of pathology. The Black Power era provided the language and the conditions for these black workers to make such challenges.

Access and Entrance

The late 1960s through the early 1970s saw unprecedented access to education and employment for African Americans. Prior to the Civil War, only 28 African Americans held college degrees. By 1900, the black community in the United States collectively held 2,500 degrees. There were 31,090 graduates by 1936, and by 1970 there were 296,666 black college graduates (Brown and Stent 1975). Similarly, the overall percentage of African Americans aged 20 to 24 completing high school increased from 42 percent in 1960 to 72 percent in 1974. In the same time span, the percentage of the black population in the 25 to 34 age demographic having completed four years of college or more almost doubled from 4.1 percent to 8.1 percent (Smith 1978). Along these lines, according to the National Center for Education Statistics, 68,000 African Americans were enrolled in all U.S.

graduate programs and 20,345 Masters degrees were awarded to African Americans in 1976 (Jewell 2003).

These significant gains in education were paralleled by a change in employment rates for African Americans. The number of employed African Americans increased from 7.4 million in 1964 to 8.4 million in 1969. Unemployment rates also dropped sharply, from a high 10.8 percent of African Americans in 1960 to 6.4 percent in 1969 (Walters and Smith 1999), and the black poverty rate declined from 55.1 percent of the population living under the poverty line in 1960 to 34.1 percent by 1973 (Smith 1978). This massive increase of African Americans in U.S. workplaces during the late 1960s and early 1970s set the stage for the emergence of black professional associations. But African Americans were not only working more in general, they were also entering professions in which African Americans had been previously underrepresented or absent. The growth of African Americans in white-collar occupational groupings over this period was tremendous. While only 16 percent of all employed African Americans worked in white-collar jobs in 1960 (compared to 47 percent of employed whites), by 1980, this percentage had grown to 36.6 percent (compared to 53.9 percent of employed whites) (Jewell 2003). In short, the black middle class more than doubled during the 1960s (Landry 1988).

These increases in access to education and employment can be attributed to gains made by the civil rights movement, which removed onerous legal barriers to schooling and work. Further, the general growth in the U.S. economy had an effect in these gains as well. Indeed, the GNP of the U.S. grew 40 percent during the 1960s. However, the antipoverty policies of the Johnson administration—such as the Economic Opportunity Act of 1964, the Civil Rights Act of 1964, and the Equal Employment Opportunity Act of 1972—were also central to these shifts (Walters and Smith 1999).

The Civil Rights Act of 1964 dealt with discrimination in the administration of voting,[1] in public facilities and services, in federal assistance programs, and in employment. The act also created the Equal Employment Opportunity Commission (EEOC), which provided victims of discrimination access to potential redress through the federal courts (Stryker and Pedriana 2004). Title VII of the act was the first federal legislation to outlaw employment discrimination, and was cited as the most important federal legislation to date when it was passed (Stryker and Pedriana 2004). While the EEOC was severely underfunded and often lacked the resources to carry out its mandated mission, it—along with civil rights organizations

and the federal courts—"significantly expanded legal rights and resources available to minority groups" (Stryker and Pedriana 2004:710).

The Economic Opportunity Act of 1964 was the bedrock of President Johnson's War on Poverty. It created the Office of Economic Opportunity and funded several programs with hundreds of millions of dollars, such as the Job Corps, Head Start, Upward Bound, and Federal Work Study. It also created a provision (with Title II) for the development of Community Action Programs (CAPs). Instituted across the country, federally funded Community Action Agencies were tasked with administrating antipoverty programs (Flanagan 2001). Including social services, education, job training and legal service programs, the CAPs were intended to include the poor in mobilizing resources to fight their own poverty (Flanagan 2001). As I detail later, CAPs would become especially important for incorporating a new generation of black social workers into community agencies and for creating relevant targets for community control movements.

Finally, the Equal Employment Opportunity Act of 1972 was the culmination of several preceding executive orders: Kennedy's Executive Order 10925 of 1961 first introduced the term "affirmative action"; Johnson's Executive Order 11246 of 1965 extended nondiscrimination and affirmative action to government contractors; Johnson's Executive Order 11375 of 1967 prohibited further discrimination based on gender; and Nixon's Executive Order 11478 of 1969 applied nondiscrimination law to all aspects of the employment process and gave power of enforcement to the U.S. Civil Service Commission. The legislation additionally gave the prior nondiscrimination acts some much needed teeth by allowing the EEOC to sue employers for discrimination in federal courts.

Taken together, the gains made by the civil rights movement, an improved U.S. economy, a crucial series of Great Society legislation, and the Black Power movement's ideological push towards institution building contributed to the overall conditions under which black professional associations were created in the late 1960s through the 1970s.

WHAT WE BELIEVE, WHAT WE WANT: THE EMERGENCE OF THE BLACK PROFESSIONAL ASSOCIATION

Large cohorts of black scholars entered several academic and professional disciplines in the 1960s. Their numbers were unprecedented, and they were the immediate products of the civil rights, Black Power, and black

nationalist movements (Pinderhughes 1990). These scholars and other professionals were not satisfied with simply integrating or acting as token representatives of the black community within their respective professions. Rather, they came to their professions with a desire to make changes on behalf of the black community and use their professions as a tool for black liberation and as a vehicle for Black Power. But the professional structures they encountered were recalcitrant to change and steeped in old traditions that were often unprepared for and unwelcoming of Black Power ideas.

Across the country, groups of black professionals, empowered by the legal and social gains of the civil rights movement and inspired by the Black Power struggle, sought to implement the gains of the movement in their professions. Indeed, the national professional associations of black psychologists, journalists, sociologists, economists, social workers, firefighters, political scientists, accountants, and librarians (to name a few) were all formed between 1968 and 1976 (Swartout 2006). All of these organizations explicitly aimed to change their profession for the good of black professionals within their field and to further the goals of the Black Power movement by affecting public policy, legislation, and culture through their work. Cheryl Townsend Gilkes (1982) argues that the "increased mobility of middle-class Blacks in white institutions gave them a realistic view of how larger institutions functioned to exclude and control Black people" (309). Because of this, these caucuses and organizations were simultaneously concerned with having "effective voices within the political activities of these professions . . . and creat(ing) forums for discussing the role of black professional relative to black community needs" (Gilkes 1982:310).

These professional organizations were not the first black professional associations, but they were created under very different circumstances than their predecessors. The National Medical Association (1895), the National Association of Colored Graduate Nurses (1908), and the National Bar Association (1925), for example, were formed because African Americans were excluded from similar white associations and operated as parallel organizations as a result of that exclusion (Hine 2003; Ogbar 2004). As reflected in their parallel names (i.e. the National Medical Association as a counterpart to the American Medical Association), these organizations were not necessarily intended for racial uplift or to create racially exclusive spaces within their professions. Rather, they were intended to create professional structures similar to the ones their white counterparts had privileged

access to. In contrast, the Black Power-era black professional associations were born out of unprecedented access to white ones, and openly strove to implement change and create a space for black professionals within their larger professions (Ogbar 2004). Even black attorneys developed a new organization, the National Conference of Black Lawyers, to reflect the Black Power ethic and to take up the legal issues faced by Black Power activists (Josey 2000). The very different political climate led black professionals to intensely question and demand changes to the role of African Americans within their professions as well as the role of their professions in the black community. As Joyce Ladner (1973) notes, it was a sense of "black awareness" tied to the cultural nationalism tenet of Black Power that inspired and shaped the creation of the black caucuses or separate black associations that developed during this period.

The Black Power influence on these organizations is clear. They all sought to move away from integration as the primary goal of black action in favor of seeking self-determination for black professionals and black communities. Importantly, the founders of these organizations worked in the Black Power tradition of challenging white racism head-on. The removal of barriers was no longer enough. Reflecting Black Power's change in tenor from the civil rights movement, they did not shy away from demanding black representation within the professions, nor did they have any qualms calling out long-standing practices as racist. Moreover, they encouraged identification with the black community (and at times other subjugated communities) over identifying with their professions, which they saw as implicated in the perpetuation of white racism. Another central commonality is that these organizations were not quiet. They took over meetings, issued manifestos, made demands—they insisted. These organizations were formed in and served as the vehicles for protest. Though they propounded the ideas and norms of the larger Black Power movement, their movements happened largely within the apparatuses of their respective profession, such that conventions, committee meetings, newsletters, and professional journals became important sites of contention.

The act of issuing manifestos, demands, position statements, platforms and so forth, was a widespread Black Power movement tactic. The Black Panther Party, for instance, based their movement on their 1966 ten-point program and platform, titled "What We Want, What We Believe." The ten "wants" of the Panthers' manifesto were:

1. We want freedom. We want power to determine the destiny of our Black Community.

2. We want full employment for our people.

3. We want an end to the robbery by the white man of our Black Community.

4. We want decent housing, fit for shelter of human beings.

5. We want education for our people that exposes the true nature of this decadent American society. We want education that teaches us our true history and our role in the present-day society.

6. We want all black men to be exempt from military service.

7. We want an immediate end to police brutality and murder of black people.

8. We want freedom for all black men held in federal, state, county, and city prisons and jails.

9. We want all black people when brought to trial to be tried in court by a jury of their peer group or people from their black communities, as defined by the Constitution of the United States.

10. We want land, bread, housing, education, clothing, justice, and peace. And as our major political objective, a United Nations-supervised plebiscite to be held throughout the black colony in which only black colonial subjects will be allowed to participate for the purpose of determining the will of black people as to their national destiny.

(for full document, see Jones 1998:473–475)

Many of the position statements and manifestos issued by these new black associations reflected similar concerns, but in a way that was translated into their professional context and attempted to balance their concern for the black community and for other black professionals. They demonstrated a simultaneous concern with their status and position as professionals and about the larger black community as a whole: as clients, subjects of research, and members of the same racial community. In their position statements, many black professional associations also drew attention to the social problems that affected the black community that they felt were within the domain of their profession. Several associations also referenced the contemporaneous policy environment, especially highlighting both the diagnoses and the recommendations of the *Kerner Report*.

Psychologists

The Association of Black Psychologists (ABPsi), for example, was formed in September 1968, and presented a series of demands issued to the American Psychological Association (APA). The terms, which were presented at the 1968 annual meeting of the APA, showcase the Black Power ethic on which the organization is founded. In its submitted "Petition of Concerns," ABPsi members presented their complaints with the organization and larger profession:

> The Association of Black Psychologists being urgently concerned about its role and that of the American Psychological Association in the Black People's struggle for dignity and equality in this country recognize the following problems as in need of immediate attention:
>
> 1. The extremely limited number of Black psychologists, Black graduate students, and Black students in the undergraduate program,
> 2. The failure of the American Psychological Association to direct its scientific and professional energies toward the solution of prominent social concerns, particularly the issues of poverty and racism and,
> 3. The fact that the general organizational structure of the American Psychological Association reflects a serious lack of adequate representation of Black Psychologists.
>
> (ABPsi 1968, as cited in Williams 2008)

The newly formed ABPsi goes on to make seven demands, proposing:

1. That the American Psychological Association officially endorse the Kerner Commission's *Report on Civil Disorders* citing white racism in America as the factor chiefly responsible for the present conditions of injustice, inequality, and social unrest so prevalent in the country today.
2. That the American Psychological Association immediately set about the reorganization of its own internal organizational structure so as to provide for greater representation and concern for the Black community. More specifically, we strongly recommend that the membership of all official committees, boards, and other groups within the American Psychological

Association which develop and/or implement policies directly related to the Black community involve Black Psychologists recommended or endorsed by the Association of Black Psychologists.

3. That the American Psychological Association brings to bear its full resources and creative energies to the matter of finding solutions to the problems of racism and poverty. The success of such efforts, however, demand recognition that a significant part of the research emphasis must be shifted from total preoccupation with the ghetto as a source of the problems to a consideration of the institutions, practices, and forces within the larger white community that contribute so heavily to maintenance of the status quo.

4. That the American Psychological Association immediately establish a committee to study the misuse of standardized psychological instruments to maintain and justify the practice of systematically denying educational and economic opportunities to Black youth. Further that pending the thorough review and reassessment of the issue on the highly questionable validity of these measures, a moratorium be directed on comparative testing and evaluation projects.

5. That the American Psychological Association re-evaluates the adequacy of certified training programs in clinical and counseling psychology in terms of their relevance to social problems, particularly in terms of their relevance to social problems, particularly with regard to the problems of poverty and life within the ghetto.

6. That at its October 1968 meeting with the American Psychological Association Board of Directors and/or Council of Representatives recommend that immediate steps be taken to get by whatever means necessary significant numbers of Black students into their graduate and undergraduate programs. That the American Psychological Association immediately transmits this recommendation to each department as a prerequisite for accreditation.

7. That the American Psychological Association in consultation with representatives of the Association of Black Psychologists establishes a funded Ad Hoc Committee to implement and evaluate the progress of the recommendations listed above, and that the regular reports are made in the American Psychologist and at subsequent national meetings of the American Psychological Association.

(ABPsi 1968, as cited in Williams 2008)

And when the newly formed ABPsi disrupted the APA's 1969 annual meeting, they argued that the black community had served as "a research colony" for social scientists. Robert Green alleged that "psychologists and sociologists go into the black community and do research but refuse to specify and push major programs of improvement for the black community." "Do not use us for research efforts any longer . . ." he continued, "help us instead to mitigate the effects of white racism" (quoted in Nelson 1969).

In a perfect example of how black professionals translated the interests of the Black Power movement into the professional context of black psychologists, the Association of Black Psychologists developed an expansive and pointed criticism of intelligence testing for African Americans. In fact, in 1969 the ABPsi called for a complete moratorium on the administration of IQ tests on black children (Williams et al. 1980). The ABPsi asserted that these tests were used to:

1. label Black children as inferior;
2. place Black children in special classes;
3. potentiate inferior education;
4. assign Black children to lower educational tracks than whites;
5. deny Black children higher education opportunities; and
6. destroy position growth and development of Black children.

(Williams et al 1980)

The issues and language that the ABPsi used echoes the discourse and concerns of the Black Power movement in seeking a focus on white racism rather than integration and the discursive comparison of the situation of poor blacks to the situation of global colonialism. Moreover, their concerns indicate a balance of demands aimed at changing the organizational structure of the field, and changing the relationship between psychology as a profession and the black community. These sentiments, ideas, and struggles were mirrored in academic and nonacademic professional associations in the United States during the Black Power era.

Sociologists

Black sociologists also organized at the 1968 annual meeting of the American Sociological Association (ASA) in Boston. Under the leadership of

Tilmon Cothran, black sociologists submitted these resolutions at the conference:

1. The council of the association should always have representation from the black membership; a greater effort should be made to assign black sociologists to membership and chairmanships on standing and ad hoc committees;

2. Black sociologists should serve more frequently as chairmen of sections in programs of association meetings;

3. Black sociologists should always be represented as presenters of papers and as discussants on programs that have major relevance to the black community;

4. Criteria for acceptance of papers for the American Sociological Association journals should be clearly enunciated and publicized so that all members, especially black members, will have equal opportunity for the acceptance of their papers, and

5. Black sociologists be secured as readers and referees of papers for publication in the American Sociological Associations journals.

(Blackwell 1974:352)

While the initial resolutions made at the 1968 and 1969 meetings focused on representation for professional sociologists, the group that would gradually solidify into the Caucus of Black Sociologists (CBS) maintained a dual strategy, also focusing on issues outside of their professional lives. For example, the CBS made statements against the Vietnam War, black capitalism, and political oppression of the Black Panther Party (Blackwell 1974:355). These concerns were, of course, of primary interest to the larger Black Power movement.

The CBS remained a caucus of the ASA until its full incorporation as the Association of Black Sociologists (ABS) in 1976. As a result of CBS pressure, the ASA established a Minority Specialist position, the Minority Fellowship Program, and the Committee on the Status of Racial and Ethnic Minorities in the Profession (Conyers 1992). The caucus also ran a journal/newsletter called *The Black Sociologist* for five years, which provided a publication and communication outlet for CBS/ABS members (Conyers 1992).

Librarians

Black librarians, who had other organizations before the Black Power era, organized the Black Caucus of the American Library Association

(BCALA) in 1969. The Statement of Concern that they presented to the American Library Association (ALA) in 1970 espoused both a Black Power ethic and a balance of concern for the community and black professionals. It affirmed that black librarians "convened in a black caucus for the expressed purpose of addressing themselves to many of the pressing problems and issues facing this country, in general, and the American Library Association, in particular" (Josey 2000:87). Solidifying their position, they commented that "Black librarians are especially concerned about the effects of institutional racism, poverty, the continued lack of educational, employment, and promotional opportunities for blacks and other minorities" (Josey 2000:87). And lastly, they condemned the discipline with a reference to the 1968 *Report of the National Advisory Commission on Civil Disorders*, arguing that, "although these socio-economic ills have been condemned by the Kerner Commission, the Commission on Violence, and many other studies, the library profession has been slow in responding to these problems" (Josey 2000:87). They end by conveying their need to develop a professional association and committing to maintain ties with the ALA to evaluate its progress "in fulfilling its social and professional responsibility to minority groups in this profession and in the nation" (Josey 2000:87).

The first official resolution the BCALA pushed through the ALA council was in response to library practices in segregated schools. BCALA founders expressed concern over the number of private schools that were being established across the United States in order to avoid integration—a fundamental part of the white flight that American cities experienced in the wake of the civil rights movement. They noted that many of the new white schools could not afford their own libraries and were asking local libraries to support them. The BCALA saw this as a prime opportunity to hold the profession accountable for supporting school integration and refusing support to these new white flight schools. After a heated debate, the BCALA was successful in passing the resolution "that the libraries or librarians who do in fact through either services or materials support any such racist institution be censured by the American Library Association, and that the ALA staff give the widest possible publicity to this action" (Josey 2000:86). The BCALA resolution is another prime example of how Black Power-era professionals creatively translated the goals and ethic of the Black Power movement into their disciplinary context.

Anthropologists

The Association of Black Anthropologists was also formed during this period. Starting as the Caucus of Black Anthropologists at the 1968 annual meeting of the American Anthropological Association (AAA), the organization would evolve into the Association of Black Anthropologists (ABA) by 1975. The preamble to the constitution of the ABA certainly reflects the Black Power ethic. It reads:

> It is a known fact that anthropology and anthropologists have identified more with the interests of the colonial powers than with the interests of the colonized people they have studied. Today, the anthropology establishment continues to perceive and to analyze the social realities of these people within the framework of theories which were conceived to justify colonialism and racism. As Black and colonialized anthropologists, it is our duty to provide an organizational framework whereby we will change established approaches, methods and theories and the relationships between anthropologists and the people they study.
>
> (ABA, as quoted in Harrison 1987:18)

The ABA cites its purpose as dedication to "encouraging the anthropology of Black people" and "supporting Blacks involved in anthropological study." They go on to say that "the perspective is international and Third World. To achieve its goals, the ABA seeks to identify Black people in the discipline of anthropology and to foster communication between them on issues of professional interest. It further seeks to monitor developments on the anthropological study of black populations" (ABA, as quoted in Harrison 1987:18).

From 1973 to 1975 the Caucus of Black Anthropologists published a mimeographed newsletter called the *News From the Natives*. The newsletter—which published book reviews, job listings, articles, and promoted the work of black anthropologists (Harrison 1987)—served as a vehicle for the exchange of ideas and communication between members. The name, however, is the most telling piece of information about this publication. By calling their newsletter *News From the Natives*, the Caucus of Black Anthropologists made an unequivocal claim of identification with the objects of anthropological study, rather than with other, privileged members of their profession. This act of claiming subjugated identities within the profession and kinship with black communities and other globally oppressed people is central to many organizations of this period. Throughout their founding documents, the ABA reiterated that the situation of black people in the U.S. was one of internal colonialism. The black radical tradition in the United States had long drawn parallels between the situation of African Americans and other arrangements of colonialism and imperialism.[2]

The Congressional Black Caucus

While the Congressional Black Caucus (CBC) is not a professional association in the same way the preceding organizations are, it was formed in 1971 and is an important example of black organizing during the Black Power movement. Growing out of both the passage of the 1965 Voting Rights Act and the backlash against civil rights by the conservative Nixon administration, the CBC became a formalized organization to coordinate the efforts of African American members of Congress who saw themselves as "congressmen-at-large for black people and poor people in the United States."[3]

Shortly after forming, members of the CBC attempted to meet with President Nixon, and made national headlines when they boycotted his 1971 State of the Union Address after being denied his audience for over a year (Office of History and Preservation 2008; Barnett 1975; Singh 1998). Declaring the boycott, Representative William Lacy Clay wrote in a letter, "We now refuse to be a part of your audience" (Office of History and Preservation 2008). On behalf of the caucus, he affirmed, "we are the elected and legitimate representatives of black Americans and in view of the fact that the opinions of black Americans have not been heard or considered by you, as they relate to the State of the Union for blacks, we conclude that your views on the state of black affairs cannot possibly be accurate, relative, or germane" (as cited in Josey 2000).

The CBC's concerns and methods clearly reflected those of the Black Power movement. Before the organization was formalized, its predecessor organization—the Democratic Select Committee—held an unofficial public hearing on the murder of members of the Chicago Black Panther Party (Barnett 1975). And when they finally met with President Nixon in March 1971 (after fourteen months' worth of requests) to express their agenda, they called for "equality of results" in nine areas:

1. Eradication of racism within the United States and in its dealings with other nations.
2. Earning of a decent living or the means to survive in dignity when work is not available.
3. Decent housing for black families and equal access to the total housing market.
4. Fair and impartial justice and adequate protection against drug abuse and crime.
5. Enforcement of civil rights and other constitutional guarantees through vigorous affirmative action by the government.
6. A fair share of the public funds used to support business and community development and full participation in determining how tax dollars are spent in black communities.
7. The federal governments guarantee of ample health care for all citizens.
8. Protection of federal standards and guarantees in programs financed by federal funds.
9. Full participation by members of black communities in the executive, judicial, and legislative branches of the government at every level.

(Barnett 1975:35–36)

Nixon's reply was simply that he shared some of their concerns. Nevertheless, he made no commitment to action on their proposals. Seeing no action from the president in response to their agenda, the CBC soon developed an organizational structure and went on to sponsor seven national conferences on topics ranging from black health to black business and hosted three public hearings on racism in the military, foreign policy and government lawlessness. The caucus also developed a "Black Declaration of Independence" and a "Black Bill of Rights" (Singh 1998). Because CBC members had ideological differences with the 1972 National Black Political Caucus in Gary and Shirley Chisholm's presidential campaign, the organization retreated from the Black Power spotlight and focused on legislative activities rather than taking a larger role in the broader black political scene (Office of History and Preservation 2008; Singh 1998).

Still, the CBC use of the term "equality of results" is worth particular note because it reflects a key distinction between the ideas of the civil rights and Black Power movements. While it was Martin Luther King Jr. who asked, "What good does it do to be able to eat at a lunch counter if you can't buy a hamburger?" (Garrow 1986), the idea behind the question became a primary motivating force in Black Power. The notion of equality of results rests on the criticism that equality of opportunity is not enough; for real equality to exist, there must be an equality of outcomes. Further, the *Kerner Report* suggested that "if existing disadvantages are not to be perpetuated, we must drastically improve the quality of ghetto education. Equality of results with all-white schools must be the goal." This language reflects the movement's concept of institutional racism, which understood that removal of barriers is not enough to ameliorate racial inequality. This translation of Black Power ideas into the context of federal politics is an important part of the history of the institutionalization of Black Power. That the coordinating body of the black members of Congress produced a set of demands in 1971 that mirrored those of the Black Panther Party and the larger Black Power movement illustrates the overarching power of the black power ideology on black organizing during this period.

Black Power Influence

While the Black Power ideology is observable on all of the organizations mentioned here, not all of the new black professional associations followed the same path to creation. Some started as caucuses while others formed immediately as separate organizations. Some caucuses remained as such while others dissolved into some other form of representation within their traditionally white associations. However, despite minor differences in structure and development, the black professional organizations founded in the 1960s and 1970s aligned themselves with the ideas, strategies, and symbols of the Black Power movement. Even the logos that the organizations adopted reflect this influence. Many of them use red, black, and green for their colors. Some even use the image of the raised fist, which is an iconic black power symbol (figure 3.1).

In general, the focus on race in demanding representation and more attention to issues affecting African Americans within the power structures of their national professional associations reflects the black power ethic. In this way, black professionals turned the Black Power gaze on their respective fields by concentrating on institutional forms of racism within their professional lives.

FIGURE 3.1 The logos of many black professional organizations established during the Black Power movement use symbolism associated with it, such as the raised clenched fist and the colors red, black, and green. This can be seen here in the logos of the National Society of Black Engineers (*upper left*), the International Association of Black Professional Fire Fighters (*upper right*), the National Association of Black Accountants (*center*), the National Association of Black Social Workers (*lower left*), and the Association of Black Psychologists (*lower right*).

Given the Black Power influence and the organizational context in which the black professional associations were founded, many of the black professional associations formed during this period will have at least four elements in common:

1. *Identity work.* The black professional associations of the Black Power era favored an identity aligned more with the black community than the norms of their profession. In other words, black professional associations clarified for themselves, their white colleagues, and other black professionals that their allegiances were primarily to the black community. When the founders of the ABA call themselves "colonized anthropologists" or the ABPsi's Robert Green chides "do not use us for research efforts any longer," they

are making a clear identity statement linking the black anthropologist or the black psychologist with "the people"—with the subjects of research rather than the researchers. "Us" refers to black people rather than the professional community. This both signaled their loyalties for their white colleagues and maintained norms for black professionals. These black professional associations thus served a normative function that worked to relay messages about acceptable black behavior in professional spaces. They also provided as spaces for working out issues around what blackness was and wasn't.

2. *Protest wing.* Many of these organizations served as a protest vehicle within their profession. These organizations would (and, in some cases, continue to) take on actions that the white-dominated professional associations would not. Issuing statements of support, "Dear Colleague" letters, and lending bodies to marches and other demonstrations in the name of black professionals was an important element of the work they did. Many black professional associations took stands on social issues that their white counterparts may have felt were outside the purview of their work as professionals. As a result, black professionals also pushed their colleagues in the white professional associations to take definitive stands on social issues. In doing so, they maintained that a social justice orientation was a relevant, acceptable and even necessary modus operandi in their professional lives.

3. *Professional equality.* Black professional associations during the Black Power era saw themselves as a sort of internal Equal Employment Opportunity Commission, in that they attempted to hold the organizational structures of their professions responsible for the recruitment, training, employment, promotion, and professional development of black professionals. Black professional associations pushed for more representation of African Americans in the field as well as for more opportunities to become involved in professional leadership. For example, the Association of Black Anthropologists had "supporting blacks involved in anthropological study" as a primary goal in their statement of purpose. The Caucus of Black Sociologists' call for black representation on the council of the American Sociological Association is also an example of this. As will become evident in later chapters, black social workers demanded greater representation throughout their profession at all levels.

4. *Monitors.* Black professional associations served a sort of watchdog function within their respective professions. They monitored professional

activities as they related to the black community and tried to hold their profession accountable for their interactions with African Americans and the black community. When the ABPsi called for the APA to investigate the "misuse of standardized psychological instruments" because of their impact on educational opportunities for black students, they were acting in this vein. And the activities of the Congressional Black Caucus clearly exemplify this function in attempting to hold the executive and legislative branches of the U.S. government accountable to their African American constituents.

At the heart of these struggles were the dual issues of access and representation for black professionals and new professional relationships to the black community. However, as the later examination of the National Association of Black Social Workers will show, these challenges also reflected desires to keep up with the new black identity being forged by the Black Power movement and to reject white normative and aesthetic values in a way that was in line with the larger movement. Therefore, understanding the actual process of their movements within organizations is essential. In the act of making a movement, black professionals turned the Black Power gaze on their work lives, focusing on institutional forms of racism within their professions. As Ogbar (2004) notes, these new organizations "declared black people's right to autonomous space within white controlled domains" (144). In this way, they "provide(d) both an organizational base for communicating professional disagreement to white institutions and a social linkage with (other) . . . rebellious professionals"(Gilkes 1982:308). Their focus on gaining representation within institutional power structures confronted the unspoken norm of white leadership in the structures that supported and maintained their professional lives.

SOCIAL WORK

The impact of these processes was particularly acute within the profession of social work. There was tremendous growth in the profession in general during the civil rights and Black Power movements. There were sixteen new masters degree programs established during the 1960s and a remarkable increase in the number of masters students, jumping from 4,900 in 1959 to 11,700 in 1968 (Ehrenreich 1985). By the 1970–1971 academic year, "almost 25% of entering students were members of minority groups" (Ehrenreich 1985:198).

Many African Americans saw social work as a profession that would allow them to work toward social justice, and many African Americans in Masters programs in the 1960s were indeed drawn to the fields of education, public affairs, and social work. The growth in African American involvement in the social work profession, however, was not only at the level of education. Thousands of African Americans entered the profession of social work as paraprofessionals in community agencies during the late 1960s. The development of the Community Action Programs (CAPs), initiated as a part of the Economic Opportunity Act of 1964, was central to this process.

CAPs were required to obtain the "maximum feasible participation" in planning, development, and administration from the communities they served. This was by far the most controversial aspect of the legislation, as Moynihan (1969) pointed out in his book criticizing the program titled *Maximum Feasible Misunderstanding*. Many observers, like Moynihan, objected to this requirement because it was a sharp departure from the status quo—funding for community programming was tied to citizen participation rather than in the hands of local politicians and the traditional social service machine. Yet community members and activists rallied around this element of the act, often using the clause to call for more participation from the communities served and to hold CAP administrators accountable for including community members. The maximum feasible participation concept certainly increased expectations for political engagement among poor communities and the activists in them, and the struggles over community control and maximum participation highlighted the uneven power relations within both new and existing social agencies (Williams 2011). In this way, the "War on Poverty Community Action Program (was) a powerful community action force behind the emergence of an effective movement toward a more participatory democracy" (Cazenave 2007:181). The fact that in many communities today, community participation in local decision making is seen as a right is an important outcome of the CAPs.

The CAPs' maximum feasible participation clause positioned African Americans to play a central role in the Great Society programs, and the social work field was ready to provide that labor force. The maximum feasible participation clause allowed CAPs to hire several "indigenous nonprofessionals" who were primarily African American and Latino (Sauber and Vetter 1983; Schinler and Brawley 1987). By 1969 over a half million black "nonprofessionals" had worked in CAP agencies during the previous five years (Hein 1988). But it is important to note here that while the maximum feasible participation clause was intended to draw participation from the black poor, many of the paraprofessionals hired were among the more well-off members of poor communities, often creating tension among those African Americans working in social service agencies and the poor communities they served.

In fact, conflict around CAPs in various communities was often contentious and may have contributed to the crystallization of Black Power ideas and organizations in some neighborhoods. Benson (1971) argues that militant Black Power organizations and moderate civil rights organizations carried the conflict between black power and coalition politics into the "immediate organizational context" of the CAPs. The struggles for control over these organizations had high stakes: control carried with it "programs, jobs, bases of power and influence" (Benson 1971:333). Further, once CAPs were funded, there was often conflict between the staff and the community itself. For example, there was a continuing tension within the programs around "the extent to which the program would emphasize the delivery of services . . . or, as an alternative, the organization of the poor as a political force to exert pressure upon established institutions" (Benson 1971:333). As Benson (1971) points out these, "conflicts provided a fertile ground for the nurturance of the Black Power ideology" (334). The idea of community control over neighborhood resources fit directly into the Black Power ideology, so the struggle around control over CAPs actually strengthened the Black Power ideals of indigenous control, the building of black institutions, and using institutions to fight oppression. Moreover, the agencies themselves provided a concrete target for action, which allowed those both inside and outside of the agency to sharpen their Black Power chops. In the end, while the relative success of the Community Action Programs is debatable, one thing is certain—it was central to the development of a whole cohort of community activists, organizers, and leaders.

The emphasis on community organization within the profession as a result of the Equal Opportunity Act also motivated curricular changes in schools of social work during the Black Power era. The curricula were altered to reflect a new focus on community organization and social change (Ehrenreich 1985; Popple and Reid 1999). The change was marked: As Ehrenreich (1985) notes, less than 1 percent of all social work students in 1958 were concentrated in community organization and social policy tracks. By 1968, 9 percent of social work students were in these tracks. Many schools of social work also created specific courses on African Americans and other minority groups, some making them a requirement (Ehrenreich 1985).

*   *   *

While the changes in the profession during the Black Power movement were striking, this is not the first period in which social work as a profession has taken up the issues of African Americans. Indeed, there is a long tradition of black social work and the profession of social work has had a long history of interacting with movements for black liberation. From Jane Addams's involvement in the development of the NAACP in 1909 through the unprecedented entrance of African Americans into the profession during the Black Power era and the development of the National Association of Black Social Workers, American social work has had a complex relationship with black liberation.

4

"A Nice Social Tea Party"

THE ROCKY RELATIONSHIP BETWEEN SOCIAL WORK AND BLACK LIBERATION

WHEN FOUR HUNDRED BLACK SOCIAL WORKERS walked out of the 1968 National Conference on Social Welfare, T. George Silcott, their spokesperson, commented to the press that the National Conference was "a do-nothing tea party group which has consistently demonstrated that it will not involve itself in social action."[1] His statement hit at the heart of the balancing act that has defined the social work profession: a tension between the provision of services and engaging in social action has shaped the field's professionalization projects, internal conflicts, and outside criticism of social workers. Indeed, the retreat from social action by the social work establishment just as the struggle for black liberation was radicalizing was a centermost grievance black social workers had against the profession. Let me be clear, however, that—with the exception of the National Conference on Social Welfare—social work organizations maintained an overall commitment to the institutionalized forms of social action they had always used. They wrote letters, testified in legislative hearings, and lobbied on behalf of the issues they saw as relevant to their clients. Yet by 1966, with Black Power on the rise and rebellions raging in America's cities, "paper activism" would no longer count as legitimate social action in the eyes of the most radical social workers.

In this chapter, I contend that during a social movement wave, activism outside of social movement organizations becomes defined by the practices of movements. I make the case that groups like social workers, who straddle the fence between activism and service, are forced to rethink their roles. I further argue that this atmosphere of uncertainty, caused by shifting

movement ideas and practices, created openings for dissenting social workers to seek change within the profession.

THE SERVICE/ACTIVISM TENSION OVER TIME

Social work practice has been characterized by a tension between the delivery of social services and the quest for social change. The history of social
work leading up to the civil rights era can be told through the story of the
shifting balance between the dominance of reform work and individual
casework starting at the turn to the twentieth century. This rise and fall
of the centrality of reform work in social work set the stage for the rise of
black insurgency within the profession in the late 1960s.

The roots of what would become the social work profession in the
United States are found in the charity agencies and the practice of the
"friendly visitors" of the 1870s. Maintaining a distinction between the worthy and the unworthy poor was a fundamental process in these early stages,
and middle-class women visited the homes of the poor to screen them for
charity eligibility and to teach "right living." This individualized approach
was the predecessor to the individual casework approach currently practiced in social work today. But by the 1890s, some charity workers, along
with middle-class college graduates, recoiled at the paternalism of their
work. They came to see the social environment itself rather than individual
maladjustments as the cause of poverty and sought reform through settlement work. In doing so, they discarded the worthy/unworthy distinction
and sought to do preventative social work. In this way, the settlement and
casework approaches developed concurrently.

Settlement workers at the turn of the century—who were generally
middle-class, educated white women—lived with their clients in impover-
ished communities, ran educational programs, and sought reform in labor,
child welfare, and women's rights. They believed that the primary function
of social work should be advocacy, community development, and reform.
Caseworkers, on the other hand, still rooted in the charity tradition, were
confident that it was the individual client who was the cause of his or her
own misfortune, and individual change was the key to solving the individual's problems. While both approaches have always existed within the
profession, the dominance of either model over the other has shifted drastically over time. In the post-Civil War era, the individual change model

was in such ascendancy that settlement workers were hardly tolerated at the National Conference on Charities and Casework (NCCC). Yet in 1909 Jane Addams, respected as the mother of the U.S. settlement movement, was elected president of the body.

The tide had shifted again in the 1920s. As a result of class struggle, the American working class was more fully developed and the casework logic of "I'm of a higher class, so you should listen to me" became ineffective. Professionalization was seen as the key to securing a place for social work in the world by offering a new rationalization: "You should listen to me because I have a special set of skills related to housekeeping, parenting, and so forth." The assumption was that professionalism could secure the trust and respect of lower-class clients as well as convince the upper classes to fund their work as social control agents and determiners of who was fit or unfit for social aid. This drive to develop a professional identity and professional legitimacy was based on a set of codes and qualifications and framed the professional activities of social workers in such a way that would be attractive to elite supporters (Ehrenreich 1985).

The solution was a wide turn to psychoanalytic theory and practice in the 1920s and the mental hygiene movement came to dominate the bourgeoning profession. The thrust of this movement was the idea that personality traits are shaped by our environment—not the larger structural environment, but our individual home environments, and child-rearing practices in particular were essential to determining different adult personalities and behaviors. This shift toward psychiatric social work marked a successful turn in the drive towards professionalization since the medical model they aspired to was already an accepted paradigm for treating the "disorders of the mind." By 1929, social workers were approaching full professional status, complete with organizations, journals, twenty-five Masters programs, and a code of ethics. But as Ehrenreich (1985) notes, "perhaps the surest sign of social work's growing credibility was the formation of community chests, common fundraising and distributing organizations, by social work administrators and local philanthropic elites." Community chests, formed in 1913, saw tremendous growth between 1919 and 1948, going from nineteen in 1919 and surpassing a thousand by 1948 (United Way of America 2007). These organizations (later known as United Way) were the primary fund-channeling organizations in social welfare and allowed local elites control over the allocation of money to agencies whose policies and programs were acceptable to them. This money management ensured the domination of the individual casework model of social work for years. The reliance on community chest funding by settlement houses and other social agencies meant that many of them maintained conservative positions on many social issues (Trolander 1975).

Despite the intense, funding-driven dominance of casework, social work was still divided between those committed to reform and those committed to individual work. Although the division was muted because of the staunch commitment to casework, social worker-reformers did not stand idly by. At the 1926 meeting of the NCCC—by then renamed the National Conference on Social Work—"Jane Addams warned against the danger of looking at social work too steadily from the business point of view." She commented that the new leaders in social work "are the psychiatric social workers. They are the newest and most popular group among us and perhaps we can ask a favor from them: that in time they go beyond this individual analysis and give a little social psychiatric work" (quoted in Ehrenreich 1985). Yet regardless of the commitment of Jane Addams and other reform-oriented social workers to social change, the dominance of the individual casework model continued unabated. In fact, casework journals didn't even mention a social issue as all-encompassing as the Great Depression until at least fifteen months after the Wall Street crash in 1929 (Reisch and Andrews 2001). Moreover, under pressure from the elites who controlled their funding, many settlement house leaders even opposed New Deal efforts at relief and reform.

Even as Roosevelt's New Deal was underway, unrest was in full swing. Wildcat strikes targeted several industries in 1933, and general strikes and rioting across the country burgeoned with the growth of the political left in 1934. This unsettled political mood did eventually lead to an overall support of New Deal policies by social work over time. Criticisms still remained, however, within the profession both on the left and the right. The left denounced tying social work to government because of its intimacy with big business. The right held on to a desire to maintain an individual casework model.

During the turbulence of the 1930s, the Rank and File movement within the profession invigorated the commitment to social reform. In adopting the name that challengers within labor unions used to distinguish themselves from their leadership, the advocates of the Rank and File movement made the claim that they were the equivalent of the foot soldiers in the labor movement (Fisher 1980; Walkowitz 1999). In so doing, they were also equating the social work establishment to the labor establishment—an implicit accusation that social work leadership was upholding the status quo (Fisher 1980; Wencour and Reisch 1989). The Rank and File movement rejected the idea that increased professionalization would lead to greater recognition and higher salaries for social workers, arguing instead that it was an illusion representing the views of social work executives rather than actual practitioners. Operating on an analysis that social workers were a white-collar proletariat and that professionalization mystified the real relationships between managers and workers in social work agencies, between 1935 and 1938 several social workers' unions developed across the country. These new movements within the profession challenging the dominant individual casework model, would together with the large scale poverty of the 1930s return reform to the ideological forefront. The rapid expansion of relief meant that financial assistance was given as a right rather than at the discretion of caseworkers, further leaving the role of casework unclear (Reisch and Andrews 2001; Withorn 1984).

But social work would retreat from social reform work again following World War II as a result of the combination of economic prosperity and Red Scare repression. The 1947–1948 Republican-dominated Congress and the later Eisenhower administration effectively whittled away New Deal programs and the public support for the new type of government it had ushered in. During this same period, African Americans from the South were pouring into Northern cities and whites were seeking refuge in the suburbs and exurbs, taking urban jobs with them. As whites were becoming decentralized, blacks were becoming concentrated in the inner cities. So while the early 1950s appeared to be relatively serene as universities expanded and women were becoming more educated than ever, Northern black ghettoes were growing, and the inner cities in particular were becoming firmly associated with notions of criminality and depravity in the minds of the American public (Coontz 1992).

A central element of the racial dynamics of the period following World War II is that whiteness became synonymous with suburbanization and prosperity and blackness with inner cities, poverty, and crime. The simultaneous subsidization of white suburbanization by U.S. housing policy and the concentration of poverty in American core cities meant that African Americans and Latinos were heavily represented on the welfare rolls, with African Americans making up as much as 45 percent of the welfare clients in cities like New York (Walkowitz 1999). As welfare became associated with blackness, the identity of "social worker" also became associated with whiteness. Despite the fact that African Americans had more of a presence in social work than in most other professions, the shifting racial dynamics of the period created an entrenched symbolism of the field as white intervention into the lives of the black poor (Walkowitz 1999). Compounding this perception was the fact that 1950s McCarthyism made identifying with or taking a particular interest in African American or Latino clients dangerous and unprofessional for social workers (Walkowitz 1999). All of these factors worked to further divorce social work from social activism around racial inequality, all while the United States was on the brink of what has been called "the minority rights revolution" (Walton 1988).

As the direct action phase of the civil rights movement emerged with attempts to enforce the 1954 *Brown v. Board of Education* decision, social work would again find itself called to the carpet. Would the profession live up to the social action legacy of Jane Addams and the settlement movement advocates, or would it remain committed to service provision above all else? The former dedication to social action and the tension it created was evident in the relationship between the one body of social workers most committed to social action, the National Federation of Settlements (NFS), and the civil rights movement. Different social work agencies—such as the National Association of Social Welfare (NASW) and the National Conference on Social Welfare (NCSW)—had different relationships to the movement, so the following analysis cannot speak for the profession as a whole. However, the story of the NFS is illustrative in at least two respects. First, most national social work agencies maintained some level of commitment to social change through social action committees or policy advocacy groups within their organization. The NFS was no different. Secondly, the NFS served as the action wing of the whole profession in many ways. Several social work leaders held leadership positions in both the NFS and the NASW or NCSW either simultaneously or at different points in their careers. So while it is true that the NFS had a stronger identification with the profession's activist legacy, the NCSW also claimed Jane Addams as one of their founding mothers. Despite these overlaps, how the NFS interacted with the movement is central to understanding the larger relationship between the profession and the civil rights movement because it operated as the outer boundary of acceptable social action within the profession. No other national social work body would have a greater opportunity, ability, or ideological impulse to participate in the emerging movement. In this way, the story of the relationship between civil rights and social welfare is the story of how settlement workers and leaders interacted with the movement.

THE RELATIONSHIP BETWEEN THE BLACK LIBERATION MOVEMENT AND SOCIAL WELFARE

Social work was generally receptive to and supportive of early legislative civil rights gains. As one of the most integrated professions prior to the civil rights movement, American social work had long shown a commitment to racial equality. For example, the National Conference on Social Welfare (NCSW) had always ensured that their meetings were held in facilities that did not segregate and in cities that would be hospitable to African Americans. However, urban riots and Black Power created a new challenge for social work, both in the larger political environment and from within. Many practitioners questioned how they would fare in the new political scene while black social workers in particular were adopting Black Power modes of protest as they mobilized. Yet the "by any means necessary" revolutionary tenor of the Black Power movement struck the wrong chord with even the most action-oriented social work bodies. So, despite an early commitment to civil rights and renewed defense of social action, by the late 1960s the Black Power discourse around social action encouraged another retreat, this time behind the ideals of integration and moderation.

Meanwhile, the NFS underwent several reflective moments in regards to their policy and identity around social action. Though the organization was redefining and reorienting itself throughout the civil rights era, there were several serious episodes of boundary renegotiation as Black Power ideas took hold in the black liberation movement. Its first in-depth period of self-reflection occurred between 1963 and 1965, when the NFS needed to address earlier criticism surrounding social action leveled by settlement practitioners in Detroit and areas of the South. Some settlement professionals argued that their national federation was going too far in making social policy statements and Southern houses preferred a "go slow" approach to changing race relations. In this context, the late 1950s and the early 1960s were marked by counterarguments and defenses by the NFS of its long-standing social action policy.

As a response to the dissent, the NFS sought to clarify its position on social action in 1960. Fern Colburn, secretary of the Social Education and Action (SEA) committee, produced a report called *Social Action Methods in the Practice of the National Federation of Settlements and Neighborhood Centers*.[2] She opens by drawing on the organization's activist legacy, claiming that "the National Federation has a proud history in working to alleviate the suffering of men, women, and children in this country and on the other hand to enhance them in their own right, and help each to make his contribution to society." She then expands her scope, not only emphasizing how the federation helped individual cases but also how "all through history settlement people have not only tried to heal the wounds left by society, but have always sought ways to help society improve itself." "In this endeavor," she argues, "settlements have been leaders among all social workers." She proceeds to outline how the NFS practice of social action included engaging in the serious study of social issues; passing resolutions only when there was substantial agreement among the people at the annual meeting; offering administrative consultation; testifying at legislative hearings; and submitting letters and statements "for the record."

Much of what the SEA secretary had to say was aimed at legitimating the federation's practice of "stance taking." In addition to noting that majority consensus has always been necessary for resolution passing, she points out that (1) no resolutions had been passed when there was a significant minority opposition, (2) while there had been disagreement over social work programs throughout NFS history, these originated from one or two dissenters and never out of a general sense of controversy, and (3) "the social action program ha[d] always been non-political and non-partisan."[3]

While there was indeed some controversy over the advocacy work that NFS had long been a part of, an appeal to the federation's legacy was enough to smooth over the ruffled feathers of those who would have preferred neutrality on matters of civil rights. But this defensive posture would soon be challenged by the question of whether they would participate in the March on Washington in 1963. While the leadership was comfortably able to rely on the legacy of Jane Addams to defend their practice of stance taking and legislative lobbying, the prospect of supporting this high-profile direct action measure brought their willingness to be activists into question. This question would mark the beginning of a period of reflection and identity renegotiation that would signal NFS's first real foray into civil rights action.

Civil Rights Actions

When the call to march on Washington was sounded, the NFS paid very little attention. Soon, however, local member houses began asking whether NFS would publicly support and condone the participation of settlement workers in such a demonstration.[4] In other words, these members wanted to know if it was acceptable to attend the march as full representatives of their respective settlement houses. A series of executive committee meetings ensued discussing whether it was appropriate to participate in direct action techniques. In the end, the federation decided that member houses that wished to participate could do so with its support.[5] Nevertheless, some of the official NFS letters sent to member agencies arrived too late for individual boards of directors to approve settlement participation.[6] In response to this confusion around the appropriateness of settlement participation in the march, NFS sent out a questionnaire to all member houses, asking whether they had participated and to solicit any information about their involvement.

Thirty-nine member houses responded to the survey. Of them, only seventeen directly participated in the march. However, several others were very involved in many aspects of the action, including sending members, sponsoring buses to transport neighborhood residents to Washington, D.C., and local settlement houses providing lodging and food to marchers. These settlement houses were clear to point out that their activities were undertaken as citizens and supporters of the community and not necessarily as representatives of the settlement houses and the NFS. In actuality, most settlements were not involved in social action. Some had followed the national organization's lead and taken stances on issues such as fair housing, fair employment practices, and school desegregation, but many workers were interested in participating in more civil rights activities and sought guidance on how to handle these issues.[7] The response written by Benjamin Leonard, the head of the Five Towns Community House in New York City, highlights this desire. After confirming that his agency had participated in the march, he noted that the march had a galvanizing effect on their agency: "One of the significant results for the marchers was that each returned to his home community imbued with the idea that he must do something on the local level." He continued, "The march also revealed to the non-leaders (rank and file) of each community, that there is power and strength in demonstrations. I think this becomes the challenge for the leaders of each community, namely to help keep pace with the urgency of this social revolution of which we are all a part."[8]

Similarly, in a letter to their board of directors, the executive staff of the Mount Pleasant Community Center in Cleveland, Ohio, expressed their interest in being involved in a new association of civil rights agencies, "which was working to eliminate discrimination and segregation of minorities . . . in the city of Cleveland." Asking the board to meet, discuss, and make a decision on this activity, the staff argued that, "social work as a profession and settlement work in particular are being criticized for touching the surface of many problems, but aggressively tackling nothing; that we offer palliatives after the damage has been done; that we are fence straddlers wanting to please everybody, offending none, accomplishing little. That we give information, talk much, meet in committee but have not enough strong convictions to act." They then asserted that they "should become more actively engaged with the enlistment and participation of the 'grass roots' in our Mt. Pleasant area in being seen and heard in the field of human relations and civil rights." Murtis Taylor, the center's director, and her staff perfectly reflected the tension snaking through the settlement endeavor at this critical moment in the civil rights movement: a desire to use the appropriate bureaucratic procedures of their organization to encourage social action, while recognizing that those procedures and structures were often not conducive to these same goals. In this same vein, Taylor briefly remarks in her survey response how the United Freedom Movement (also based in Cleveland) "moves so fast in making decisions for action that further Board involvement has been difficult because there is no time for Board to discuss whether the agency should officially picket this group or that company." She continues, "The community is much aware of the Freedom Movement sweeping the country. . . . Perhaps we can discuss at the May Conference the Civil Rights Movement and the Settlement's role."[9]

The president of the Hamilton-Madison House in New York City expressed a similar sentiment in his response as well. "Since last fall Hamilton-Madison House has faced a series of situations arising from the intensified fight for civil rights which have caused disagreement between our board and staff. The basic issue," he argued, "has concerned the stand which the House ought to take respecting civil rights activities which violate the law; obstructing the construction at Rutgers Housing site and the recent school boycott are two cases in point."[10] He went to say that the board had been confronted with the "need to take a stand for or against an action program formulated and led by strong outside action groups. In each case, we were asked to devote the resources and prestige of our agency and the time of our staff to achieve a goal we approved of through methods we opposed."[11] His concern represents the central issue to this moment of redefinition of identity and renegotiation of boundaries: the desire to support the civil rights movement and participate in direct action methods of social protest, but intense uncertainty about the appropriateness of such tactics for settlements.

In the Goddard Riverside Community Center's response to the survey, Frederick Johnson also addressed the issue of movement tactics. He wrote, "It was my feeling that most of the white people who went on the trip were very happy to have an opportunity to directly participate in a cause that they believed in and yet not have to 'storm the barricades,' e.g. get arrested, sit-in. In short it was a dignified, respectable demonstration."[12] His response reflects the centrality of the discussion around the settlements' commitment to civil rights but aversion to extralegal tactics.

In 1964, after the difficulty of deciding whether to support the March on Washington for Jobs and Freedom, the NFS realized that member agencies were dealing with civil rights concerns in their communities and wished to participate in wider civil rights debates and issues. As a result, they formed a subcommittee on civil rights to provide informed guidance on impending civil rights actions for which their support would be requested, and to direct local houses on emerging civil rights issues.[13] This decision was largely shaped by the sharp criticism leveled at the settlement method of social action, which Herbert Gans (1964) portrayed as marginal and failing in an article published in *Social Work*, and which was under intense fire by Alinsky organizations in various parts of the country.[14]

The need for the subcommittee was underscored by the results of a survey conducted in March 1964. The survey asked member houses to report any involvement in local civil rights efforts, to describe any stands they had taken on civil rights issues, and to let the NFS know if guidance on any policy matters from the larger national organization was needed. Forty-one member agencies responded to the survey and the majority (twenty-nine in total) had been involved in some sort of civil rights effort. Most of this involvement, however, cannot be characterized as direct action. For example, several member agencies reported writing letters and attending meetings, but not much else. The director of the Market Street Neighborhood House in Louisville, Kentucky, wrote, "Please share with us any information you have about ways of taking action, etc. We have only worked with our own club groups, written letters, attended meetings, etc."[15] Many of the requests for guidance indicated a need for direction on how to reconcile civil rights movement activity with the long-established settlement identity and process. When asked where guidance was needed, Shig Okada of the West Side Community House in Cleveland, Ohio, listed concerns about "the use of picketing to bring about desired changes (and) the extent of Board involvement where there is a diversity of views on civil rights." Similarly, Denis Dryden of the Stuyvesant Community Center in Brooklyn, New York, said that "sensitizing and activating Board members (and) (a)ctivity without losing settlement character—that is rent strikes, sit-ins," were areas of concern.[16]

Settlement professionals interested in participating in the civil rights movement were forced to ask themselves: Is this really what we do? Can we march on Washington and still be who we are? Does participating in direct action mean we are becoming something different than what we have always been? Does refusing to participate mean we are not who we say we are? To know the answer to any of these questions the NFS had to first answer the most fundamental question of all: "Who are we?" This was not a simple query. It called into question their legacy as activists. Even further though, it held their brand of social action up against the efforts of activists risking their lives in the Selmas and Birminghams of the civil rights movement.

In many ways, through these multiple surveys and extensive conversations around civil rights activism, the NFS was putting their finger on the pulse of the movement to see where they should go. It represents a wider complicated navigation of rapidly shifting political norms and values created by the intense uncertainty of the period. "Real activism" became defined by what the movement was doing rather than just its stances, and the question for NFS soon became "Where do we fit?" By 1965, the federation was beginning to find its way in the new political terrain and was prepared to stake a claim in the new politics. In Executive Director Margaret Berry's[17] report to the board of directors in January 1965, she asserted, "We meet at a time when change is in the air in this rich country. We are irrevocably part of one world. We have finally made the great leap forward in civil rights legislation. There is hope we can turn our generosity and compassion on the dark spots in our own country. Settlements are an important part of this effort."[18]

How to deal with the civil rights movement, especially as the federal government was moving forward with civil rights legislation, was certainly a central concern for settlements. Whitney Young, then executive director of the National Urban League, delivered an important speech to the 43rd National Conference of the National Federation of Settlements in San Francisco. He commended the settlement movement for its work with African Americans in urban centers: "I am proud to say that most of the settlement houses of this country have stayed and fought when neighborhoods changed. In remaining behind, they forged ahead. In responding to new challenges, they created new opportunities."[19] On the other hand, he pointed out that the problems these new populations faced were different than those confronted by the European immigrants who settlements originally served. Citing the loss of manufacturing jobs, lack of adequate housing, and deteriorating urban neighborhoods, Young argued that "your settlement houses stand in the crucibles of our greatest challenge—the neighborhoods in which there is the greatest hardship, the greatest discrimination, the greatest poverty, the greatest disorganization and the greatest despair." Such a situation, he contended, called for "an all-out, massive, coordinated assault at the neighborhood level by philanthropy, local, state, and federal governments, civil and non-sectarian religious groups, and civil rights agencies working together."[20] His address spoke to the same concerns Berry previously addressed at the board meeting just months before.

In October of that same year, Loma Allen, the secretary of the Social Education and Action (SEA) committee, gave a speech to the Delaware Valley Settlement Alliance detailing the role of settlements in civil rights. Attempting to offer some much needed clarity on the issue, she maintained that settlements could serve three purposes in the new movement. First, they could be a "builder of bridges over chasms,"[21] serving as a link between local neighborhoods and the wider community, between people who have and those who have not, and between those with light skin and those with dark skin. She contended that the settlement "spans the gullies and the ditches that isolate people from one another."[22] Secondly, she said that the settlement could be the central location for information on what's going on in the world, a kind of "radar station" to the entire community. Finally, Allen argued that the settlement should be a working demonstration of people of different racial, ethnic, and economic backgrounds involved together in finding solutions to the problems that affect them all.[23]

Allen also emphasized the historical roots of settlement work in creating meaningful social action. She reminded the audience that the origins of settlement work were rooted in the abolition movement, and of the role of Jane Addams, for example, in the creation of both the NAACP and National Urban League. She then claimed that integrated settlements were neither new nor radical for the profession, citing the steady growth of working with black populations during the first twenty-five years of the settlement movement. On the basis of this historical background, she offered this guideline to the leadership and activities that settlements should participate in: "the primary function of a settlement, as such, is not that of aggressive leadership in the application of pressure, but that such a position does not preclude a wide range of possible choices in defining areas of cooperation in complementary action with organizations for which this is a primary role."[24]

Moreover, she stated that settlements had a responsibility to provide opportunities for interracial participation. In the era of Community Action Programs that required maximum feasible participation, many communities were demanding more and more representation on settlement boards and staffs. In this context, Allen noted that

> where tensions have been high within predominately Negro areas, agencies may find themselves under attack for having white persons on their board and staff. They may sometimes find themselves under pressure to increase the minority representation to the point where the interracial nature of the team would be destroyed. However there can be no compromise on the principle of maintaining an interracial board and staff . . . which provides an ideal situation for expressing commitment to the goal of integrated society.

Lastly, she pointed out that the NFS was seeking support for a project in Mississippi and for a race relations study. These two projects would become the federation's primary intervention into civil rights action and would allow them to lay claim to an activist identity for at least a while.[25]

Race Relations in a Time of Rapid Social Change

In 1964, following the March on Washington and the ensuing discussion about civil rights, the NFS sought funds to study the particular role of settlements in the shifting racial and political climate and on race relations generally. They hired St. Clair Drake, coauthor of the book *Black Metropolis* (1993[1945]) and professor of sociology at Roosevelt University, to carry out the study in that following year. He and his research assistants surveyed executives of 142 agencies in fifty-nine cities. His report, completed early in 1966, covered issues ranging from the racial composition of boards and staffs to whether member agencies allowed black groups to use the facilities. He concluded that while the end of segregated cities was a long way off, integration must remain the long-term goal. Settlements thus had to resist the urge to create all-black boards and staff as that would compromise the integration ideal. Moreover, he argued that settlements should not make aggressive leadership for integration their primary function, and should instead concentrate on building bridges between the ghetto and other parts of the city and between blacks with whites. He contended that, "the white volunteer must continue to be used," and agreed with Loma Allen that "there can be no compromise on the principle of maintaining an interracial staff." He finished with another reminder of the settlement movement's historical roots, noting that "settlement houses had played a major part in moving immigrants into the mainstream of American life and they should play a similar role for Negroes."

Drake's report, titled *Race Relations in a Time of Rapid Social Change*,[26] was published in 1966 and distributed to each member house as a guide to race relations. It reflected the organization's unwavering commitment to integration as well as its resolute disapproval and fear of separate black activities. The *Drake Report* was widely publicized as the NFS's big contribution to helping member agencies deal with race relations. One of the primary outcomes of the report was a restatement of the organization's overarching belief that integration was good and Black Power was bad. The choice to hire Drake itself has been characterized as "unfortunate" (Lasch-Quinn 1993) as he was a staunch integrationist, therefore precluding any consideration of how to engage the emerging radical movement in the settlement tradition.

The *Race Relations* project not only reflected the desire of the National Federation of Settlements to insert itself into civil rights politics, but also the deep confusion around racial issues for member houses. Moreover, the *Drake Report* was a clear attempt at keeping their activism within the bounds of the settlement movement. The NFS's second civil rights project would do the same.

The Mississippi Project

In 1966, the NFS was active in the struggle to get the Office of Economic Opportunity (OEO) to reconsider its decision to withdraw funding to 121 Head Start centers run by the Child Development Group of Mississippi (CDGM). As a result of the pressure, OEO did renew funding and the NFS saw this as an opportunity to support the activities of the Freedom Neighborhood Centers (which were closely connected to the CDGM and other Mississippi movement organizations) to further promote the self-determination of black Mississippi communities. Upon announcing the project, Loma Allen remarked that "progress towards justice and equality in Mississippi depends on the success of the self-help community programs conducted in these centers."[27] This was an ingenious decision on the part of the organization, as it recognized its expertise in supporting local community centers as an important contribution to the Southern civil rights struggle. It made perfect sense, so much so that the Stern Family Fund provided a grant to support the project.[28]

The key concept that the NFS rallied around in proposing and maintaining their support of the Mississippi Project was "self-determination." In an exploratory study of Freedom Centers, Herbert Brunson, a researcher hired by NFS, reported that though the programming at the centers varied, the core was structured around meeting community needs. For the most part, they were created as places for people to be able to hold conversations "with some assurance of freedom of expression." He also made clear the centers' relationship to the rest of the Mississippi Freedom Movement, noting that they generally housed the CDGM Head Start programs, held literacy classes to support voter registration drives, and were central to the development and support of the Mississippi Freedom Democratic Party

(MFDP).[29] Brunson recommended that the NFS employ a consultant to the community centers, arguing that there was a clear need for guidance so that the centers did not fail for lack of skilled leadership. He further proposed that the consultant should live in and be familiar with the area they served due to the rapidly changing social conditions. Moreover, he felt that the consultant should be explicitly identified with the Freedom Movement and accepting of "involvement in the political realms."

The NFS followed through with Brunson's proposals. Two African American field workers from Mississippi, Al Rhodes and Coleman Miller, were hired to provide technical assistance to the two hundred Freedom Centers in that state, which were struggling to maintain their funding and programming. Margaret Berry recalls interviewing Rhodes and Miller in an airport, as there was no other place for a white woman to safely meet with two black men in Mississippi's racially hostile environment.[30] Both men had been active with CDGM and other Mississippi movement organizations.

The work the consultants carried out in Mississippi was by far more political and movement-oriented than other NFS activities. The Mississippi workers were involved in boycotts, organized students to protest against police brutality, and helped in the MFDP's struggle to replace the state's Democratic Committee.[31] They maintained relationships with the National Association for the Advancement of Colored People (NAACP), the Student Nonviolent Coordinating Committee (SNCC), the Southern Christian Leadership Conference (SCLC), the Council of Federated Organizations (COFO), and many other well-known social movement organizations.[32] Al Rhodes ran for state representative in 1967 with the permission of NFS to do so while still on the organization's payroll. Rhodes, who stayed on with NFS after Coleman Miller left in 1968, was also involved in Charles Evers's successful mayoral campaign in the town of Fayette.[33] By 1969, he was facilitating a relationship with the Republic of New Afrika, a radical organization, to buy land to support a housing project for poor families.[34] The work that the NFS carried out through their Mississippi Project even earned them surveillance by the Mississippi Sovereignty Commission,[35] which was detailed in records released in 1998.[36]

The Mississippi Project is a largely untold story of the history of settlement houses, and social welfare history in the United States. The federation's strong financial and ideological support for the Southern civil rights movement between 1966 and 1970 sits in contrast to the uncertainty—indeed, at times outright resistance—that it had toward black organizing in Northern and Western states and cities. Two factors help to explain this puzzle. First, there were no official, NFS-affiliated centers in Mississippi and very few in the South generally.[37] This created a space for the NFS to answer only to the needs of the Freedom Centers and the communities they served. There were no long-seated boards with conservative white members or old settlement heads who were worried about the implications of social action to contend with. Therefore, the national office could freely act on their desire to support civil rights without fear of repercussion. Secondly—and more importantly—the Southern civil rights struggle represented something very different than the Northern struggle in the NFS's perspective. The movement in Mississippi was still struggling for enforcement of integration policies, for fair democratic representation in local and federal politics, to be allowed to take advantage of the franchise, and for the elimination of the insidious brand of racism that made safe travel impossible for interracial groups. The Northern struggle, however, was associated with a rejection of white norms and white liberalism, separatist sentiment, militancy, race riots, and the emergent Black Power movement.

CONCLUSION

A tension between the task of providing social services and the desire to tackle and change the larger social conditions that make their services necessary in the first place runs through the history of social work in the United States. The rise of the civil rights movement had found the profession sitting comfortably on the fence that separates service providers and activists. But as the movement took hold, the idea of what it meant to be an activist became less flexible and more clearly defined by the practices of the burgeoning social movement. Social work found itself at a crossroads. Even the National Federation of Settlements, undeniably the most activist-oriented of the national social work organizations, was forced to rethink its role in the "social change" arena. Was it possible to maintain a claim on social action when the definition of activism was moving the picture of an "activist organization" further and further away from what they actually were doing, all while both insiders and outsiders were challenging that identity? This question led to two major moments of identity and boundary renegotiation in the association. With the rise of direct action in 1965 and 1966, the federation reflected on its policies and then took on two projects that signaled their foray into civil rights action—the Mississippi Project and the *Race Relations Report*. The second moment came as the tide of black movement organizing radicalized during 1967 and 1968. The NFS turned to a discourse favoring integration at any cost and advocated for policies and methods that valued the power of establishment as a way to eschew conflict tactics or anything that smelled of separatism. Taken together, this period of uncertainty within the organization created an opening for the rise of internal black dissent, which would become a full-fledged movement that paralleled a larger black movement within the social work profession as a whole.

5

"We Stand Before You, Not as a Separatist Body"

THE TECHNI-CULTURE MOVEMENT TO GAIN VOICE IN THE NATIONAL FEDERATION OF SETTLEMENTS

EVEN THOUGH THE NATIONAL FEDERATION of Settlements inserted itself into the political arena of the civil rights movement, the organization would distance itself from the emerging Black Power movement. This process of "setting apart" set the stage for the next period of reflection and renegotiation of the organization's values, practices, and identity that would occur as black dissent rose within the federation in 1967.

How to respond to militants became the question of the day, and settlement workers across the country were asking for guidance on how to deal with Black Power. The result was a discourse that allowed an out from the complex puzzle of activism vs. service. Because the new "militant mood" became increasingly associated with separatism and confrontational tactics, the NFS could retreat behind a commitment to integration and embrace their position as an "established" institution by formalizing their opposition to extra-institutional tactics. In other words, as the black liberation movement radicalized, the NFS was able to take a moderate position on civil rights and reclaim its activist identity while simultaneously rejecting new Black Power ideas—sort of a "radical flank effect" at work in decisions about social activism (Haines 1988). Black settlement workers, however, were not willing to accept this position. Their movement within the social work profession, combined with Black Power challenges to member agencies across the country, proved to be an emotionally charged conflict lasting into the early years of the 1970s.

BLACK DISSENT

The first concrete sign of black dissent within the National Federation of Settlements (NFS) surfaced in May 1967 at the Central Lakes Regional Board Conference in Detroit. The basic grievance leveled by black settlement workers then was that the NFS staff was completely white in composition and that the NFS board was not representative of the communities they served. Black social workers within the federation were more concerned with representation rather than access (which they already had) and about the importance of participating in direct action. This first step marked the beginning of black confrontation in the organization, and in many ways their dissent challenged the core value of integration and equal access that NFS had developed during the early part of the movement. Black confrontation within the profession as a whole would continue to mount, and it would play out on a national stage at the National Conference on Social Welfare conferences in 1968 and 1969.

The 45th Annual Conference of the National Federation of Settlements—held in May 1968 in Houston, Texas—was overwhelmed by black organizing and the "black question." The meeting was on fire with Black Power. "This is jivin'," one attendee remarked, "these cats packed their troubles and brought 'em here."[1] The conference report reads, "Clearly, racism, militancy and America's inability to move fast enough on its urban problems dominated the talk." Indeed, black social workers had brought their troubles to Houston. What's more, they intended to have them heard and demand action and change from the federation.

At the scheduled Black Power workshop the attendees canceled the planned paper presentations and caucused to come up with a list of demands and proposals to change the NFS's social policy platform for 1968. It issued a set of thirteen resolutions, the first of which was that NFS support a special conference for black settlement workers to come together. They also demanded that member agencies investigate whether their boards were representative of their clients and that NFS require sensitivity training for its staff and for member agencies "to help them become more aware of problems, including minority history and the contributions of minorities." Similarly, they recommended that "agencies develop programs to educate and motivate supporting communities, challenging whites to take risks and make sacrifices." Two other major calls were that the national federation "set a national policy on the hiring of Black people or any other minority group for executive positions," and that it move its headquarters from New York City to Washington, D.C. "because NFS has either been unaware or has not addressed itself to the decision making process in this country." Even more importantly, they demanded that a "black staff member be hired to develop coalitions with big businesses, political groups, labor, and other pressure groups" in order to "more effectively influence important legislation and programs which reflect the interest in work of member agencies." Lastly, they asked that, "member agencies withhold dues" until this staff member was hired.[2]

A second set of demands was produced by the Black Caucus at the federation's Conference on Inner City Violence held in Chicago later that year. It began:

> We, the Black members of the conference on Inner-city Violence feel that the conference has systematically failed to deal with the issues or genesis of the racist and fascist tendencies encountered by the communities in which we function, and we further believe that we who are Black have to effectively deal with the developing direction of our Black Communities. We therefore must demand some definite support and credibility by our national sponsoring agency, National Federation of Settlements."[3]

The fourteen specific mandates reiterate and extend the Houston resolutions. They demanded that "all agencies accept the existence of conflict and violence and support efforts of staff in dealing with this phenomenon on the community level." They also asked that NFS support a separate black conference; that boards, staff, and committees be representative of their communities; and for both black professionals and community residents to be placed in decision making positions. The Black Caucus also insisted that the NFS take a stand against the Vietnam War; recommended that highest priority in funding by community chests, United Fund, and other social service funding agencies be given to agencies dealing with "real social conflict"; and that the NFS should secure funds for agencies dealing with social and economic conflict and the "amelioration of white racism, individual, group, and institutional." The Inner City Violence Caucus document also addressed the subject of white activist involvement in the movement, stressing "that white social workers in settlements work with white racism in the white communities." Along these same lines, they wanted the NFS to "plan programs with themes . . . that promote the level of Black consciousness" that " should be conducted by Black people." To provide for this programming, they made the case that the NFS should "secure funds and immediately employ, and if necessary, train Black staff members competent to be sent into settlements in consultant capacities." The Chicago demands were signed by fifty delegates, who declared their commitment "to the reconstruction of systems to make them relevant to the needs of Black Communities and are therefore pledged to do all that we can to bring these things about by any means necessary."[4]

These two sets of demands reflect the broader concerns of the larger Black Power movement. Black settlement workers were seeking a move away from issues of access and toward a greater focus on representation, empowerment, and institutional leadership within their profession. Further, black settlement workers were calling attention to white racism by asking that white social workers deal with white racism and allow black social workers to conduct programs in black communities. They also drew attention to the need for real resources—more that just ideological commitments—to support black communities.

It was after the Chicago demands were put forward that real, sustained negotiations between the Black Caucus and the NFS began. The Black Caucus formalized their position in a series of meetings with the newly formed New Directions Committee. This committee, formed between late 1967 and early 1968, was tasked with exploring new directions in settlement work, primarily those related to race relations and the black liberation movement. Overall, it was largely a response to both Black Power challenges to the settlement movement and black dissent inside the organization, the latter of which served as a sort of exclamation point to more general critiques that the settlement tradition was outdated. Throughout the New Directions process, conferences and meetings reflected the tension between black dissent and attempts on the part of white settlement workers to understand and assist with racial change at times, and at other points to resist that change.

Through this process, the Black Caucus prepared a formal position paper on "New Directions for Settlements." It opens with the understanding that "settlements, like every other major institution in the inner-city, are faced with the tedious task of self-confrontation." The Black Caucus further acknowledged that "the very nature of the dynamics flowing through the inner-city compel the settlements to reflect on what use [*sic*] to be, to dwell on what is, and to ponder the contents of a dream to efficiently face the realities of tomorrow. As we dwell," they warned, "it is evident that we cannot be tomorrow that which we are today." They then posed a potent metaphor, describing victims and settlements as "dwarfs" fighting the "giants" of white and institutional racism through ineffective programs intended to "soothe the victim" and prepare them for the next blow since neither the victim nor the program possessed the tools for a definitive victory. The Black Caucus also presented a definition of racism similar to that of Stokely Carmichael and Charles Hamilton, which was attuned to the idea that white people do not believe themselves to be racist and that this belief is sincere because "institutionalized racism means that many whites do not discriminate in any direct, overt way." In other words, the Black Caucus position statement contends that most whites do not have to personally participate in overt discriminate for discrimination to exist. Rather, they cite Lee Rainwater in arguing that white America employs a number of "dirty workers"—such as policemen, teachers, real estate agents, slumlords, and social and welfare workers—to do the discriminating for them, enacting social control over blacks. They are clear that these dirty workers can also be black—what characterizes them is not their race, but that they "control black people as quietly and unobtrusively as possible."[5]

In addition to demanding that NFS sponsor a conference to hammer out these issues, the Caucus ultimately focused on three specific points:

1. The need for NFS to seek large grants to be distributed to local groups based on their ability to develop programs based on certain criteria. In particular, these grants were to go to agencies that "deal with real social conflict and its resulting violence."

2. The need to restructure the NFS board. Redistribution of funding and services could not be done in the NFS's current arrangement. Specifically pointing to trends to hire indigenous workers in the field and in leadership as well as an adherence to the standard of maximum feasible participation, they argued that many new sources of funding, including earmarked grants from big foundations, required black representation on boards and staffs.

3. The need for black male leadership to "direct the course of settlements in the 1970s." This issue was framed as "symbolically important" both to secure funding and to model forward racial thinking and practices.[6]

The Techni-Culture Conference and Representation

Following the demands from the black delegates to the Inner City Violence Conference and the formalized "Black Caucus Position," one main focus of black organizing became the development of a separate conference for black settlement workers. The intent was to gather black settlement workers together to work on increasing representation in the NFS and to bring about "community control" at the local level in order to create strategies for neighborhood change.[7]

Opinions among the NFS leadership about holding the conference were varied. There was an overall tentative sense of support for the conference, but many still expressed reservations. The results of a survey of executive board members show that 78 percent voted to approve the conference. Some who disapproved or those who had doubts argued, like Janice Forberg, that it was "a luxury [they couldn't] afford." Yet many did disapprove on principle, such as board member Andy Brown, who was concerned that the black group was not united and those who disagreed would shun the gathering and be in a position where those at the conference were speaking on their behalf without their approval. He drew a parallel between the request for a Black Caucus conference and what the Detroit Revolutionary Union Movement (DRUM)[8] was doing to the United Auto Workers (UAW) union at the Chrysler plant in Detroit. He argued that UAW's reaction had been "to permit no split of the organization, and not play into a separate organization, but to respond immediately to the real needs." Loma Allen, then a board member and former secretary of the Social Education and Action committee, added that a separate conference, "negates the whole philosophy of NFS—that people of every creed and color work together with neighbors of every creed and color." She also made the case that a separate conference could not deal with the dismantling of "white racism," which had been a major point by the black caucus. Mrs. G. F. Gannon questioned the division that may come from such a meeting considering that settlements have always worked toward integration.[9]

Even some who approved the conference expressed reservations. For example, Lea Taylor voted to approve it, but only if "the financial funding of such a conference be the main responsibility of those proposing it and that in no way shall the responsibility of the financing be a burden on the national staff and the member agencies' support the of the national program." Lester Glick pointed out that he was "seriously concerned about the separatist implications in [the] demands." While these responses reflect the NFS's commitment to integrationism, they also reflect how the integrationist philosophy was used not only to challenge Black Power but also to rationalize their resistance to the movement for community control of local agencies both from black settlement workers and from the larger movement.

The top leadership at NFS was publicly supportive of the conference, writing to board members and executives that they "warmly endorsed" such a conference. Behind closed doors and in discussions amongst themselves, however, they often took a sarcastic, belittling approach. In a letter to then-NFS president John Austin in January 1970, Margaret Berry writes that she wants to update him on the upcoming Techni-Culture Conference, adding derisively, "they are *bound* to call it that" (emphasis in original). After touching on some other pieces of NFS business, she ends, "I just hope that the Techni-Culture Conference turns out marvelously. It has certainly taken time, and some of the things I'm sure they're going to 'demand' [quotation marks in original] are things which we would have been working on in the same time we were trying to get the money for the conference."[10]

While the conference was initially planned as a coming together of black settlement workers, conversations and experiences at the 1969 National Conference on Social Welfare in New York led organizers to adopt a multicultural frame, resulting in a shift in the conference focus. When the Black Caucus of the NFS reconvened at this meeting, other people of color also voiced their discontent with the organization. A series of meetings and conversations moved the Black Caucus to organize around a coalition with "brown, red, and yellow brothers and sisters."[11] They decided that it should be a gathering of all settlement workers of color, dubbing it the "Techni-Culture Conference" (TCC), a name that played on the term "Technicolor."[12]

The new statement of "rationale for the conference" reflected this shift, declaring that "the racist attitude which dominates American life is destroying the physical, social, and psychological growth of minority people." As a result, "To overcome the negative impact of white racism, minority people recognize their need to meet, discuss, and determine their own agenda for the growth and development of their community life." Again arguing that national coordination of local programs was necessary, the statement goes on to "call together on a national level all neighborhood and settlement people of minority background to convene for the purpose of establishing a plan for the development and operation of such organizations serving minority people."[13]

Importantly, the conference was intended for minority settlement workers specifically, "in order to help them identify how they can more effectively relate to the neighborhood issues of self-determination, racial identification, and financial resources of both the public and private sectors." The organizers saw its most significant contribution as relating "pragmatic approaches to dealing with current urban issues" and offering a "comprehensive . . . examination of the internal and external pressures that affect settlements' and community centers' relationships with the residents of the neighborhood." The very first objective on a list of five was the "reorganization of settlements in predominately minority communities to effect community control."[14]

The decision to move toward a multicultural organizing model presented multiple challenges for TCC organizers and created an opening for criticism by the NFS leadership. Five days before the conference, Antonio Tinajero, a Latino leader in the settlement movement from San Antonio, raised a flag of concern when he personally called John Austin. "The gist of his complaint," Austin reported to Margaret Berry, "seemed to be that matters have been very inefficiently handled" and "necessary parties to the conference, particularly in the other minority groups, have not been contacted with the result he was seriously considering whether he should attend the conference at all."[15]

The conference was held on February 11th through February 13th, 1970, in Chicago. While official recollections of the conference are few, by all accounts it seems that it did not go as planned. There were more registrations than could be handled efficiently, and many sessions were cancelled in favor of several caucuses, both scheduled and impromptu. In particular, over two hundred women caucused, and a youth caucus drew considerable attention as well. Interestingly, the multicultural nature of the group meant that the black leadership found themselves being challenged. Margaret Berry reported that a Puerto Rican attendee shouted to Halloway "Chuck" Sells (one of the leaders of the Black Caucus), "We're walking with you, not behind you!"[16]

But the conference did garner several successes, such as the creation of a sustained attempt at creating permanent structures to give voice to the various racial groups within the NFS and gain representation in NFS's board and leadership committees. Specifically, the Techni-Culture Committee (as it came to be known) presented Margaret Berry with three concrete demands after the conference in February. First, the Techni-Culture Committee (TCC) demanded that, at the upcoming May 1970 NFS conference, all of fifteen vacancies on the thirty-member NFS board "be allocated to Indian, Asian, Hispanic, and Black Technicultures, in order to begin the process of equal partnership, participation, and representation in the decision making process." Secondly, the TCC further requested that one of those slots be "designated for youth representation." Finally, they raised concerns that the NFS national staff did not reflect the people of color who were a part of the settlement movement, recommending that the national office take steps to assure staff representation. To facilitate this, they suggested that, as someone who was in line with the views of the caucus, "Mr. Henry Reid be designated the status of permanent staff member with the title of associate director."[17] The TCC's overall stance was that much, if not all, of the other changes they were interested in making within the settlement movement could be accomplished by inserting "black faces in higher places" within the organization.

These demands were made to the NFS board shortly after the TCC conference and they planned to continue to press for these goals at the May 1970 NFS conference in Cincinnati, where black settlement workers vowed to use "modified disruption" tactics to have their voices heard.[18] The interaction at the Cincinnati conference is indicative of the interplay between the NFS establishment, which continued to contrast the "power" frame of settlement dissenters to their own "integration" frame. At the annual business meeting held there, two statements regarding the Techni-Culture Conference Committee were to be heard.

Dr. Arthur Logan, a black physician and president of United Neighborhood Houses of New York, urged whites in the NFS to not "assume the burden of guilt which white America properly bears because of the centuries of injustice . . . and do not expect to be able to atone for those sins by your performance in relation to your minority brothers in this room." He continued by asking them to "not be intimidated by the appearance of, or by the statements of, or the performance of any person here who happens to have a somewhat different ethnic background." Logan went on to directly warn the Techni-culture group against separatism, pleading for them to use "cerebration" rather than emotion, and to use the established mechanism for nominating boards and committees to create change through and within the system. He ended by saying, "If you don't get the recognition you want, do not leave the NFS—continue, instead, your efforts for greater acceptance within the framework of this organization." The "establishment of a new body, ethnically oriented, may appear to be desirable," he argued, "but know that the truly productive future for those in whose interests you work—the consumers, the neighbors of settlements—lies in your traveling down the road toward one world really inclusive of all people rather than traveling down the road toward a separate organization built on the false sands of ethnic exclusivity."[19]

Halloway "Chuck" Sells responded by saying, "The Techni-Culture Committee states now is the time that techni-cultures translate their similarities of color, their social bondage, their repression into a untied action for change. We stand before you, not as a separatist body." He then mentioned that a comprehensive program for the Techni-Culture Conference had been developed after their consultation and meetings with all Techni-Culture groups. Making it clear that "these proposals (would) be carried out regardless of the outcome of the meeting," the program included a plan to develop a substantial communication system for neighborhoods; fundraising; staff development and training programs to draw people "indigenous to the community" into the agencies; and a request to "the board and staff to develop a philosophy that programs of the national federation must have as an integral part of the specific purposes of such programs basic factors that will contribute to the elimination of the institutional racism and poverty."[20]

While the issues covered by Sells were the background and foundation of the TCC concerns, the concrete demands at the meeting were focused more on representation. They were pressing for 50 percent representation on the NFS board, or to fill the existing fifteen vacancies with "Black, brown, red and yellow" people.[21] This demand was met. When NFS delegates left Cincinnati, 62 percent of the board was comprised of people of color, as compared to 30 percent just days earlier.[22]

The rest of the "modified disruption" at the conference laid the groundwork for a concerted effort and sustained dialogue between the TCC and the NFS establishment, one that mostly focused on representation on the board and committees. Central to black settlement worker demands for representation at all levels was that the NFS recognize the TCC as a standing, regular committee of the federation, and that the newly created associate director position be filled by a black man.[23]

A Black Associate Director

The TCC had requested that a staff vacancy be elevated to associate director, and that the position be filled by a black man. The board and Berry agreed to this and she started to contact potential candidates she had identified. Two candidates stood out for her. TCC leader Halloway Sells considered one candidate unacceptable—Walter Smart was the other. In relating his qualifications for the job, Berry focused not only on his work experience but the fact that he was a courageous and "absolutely straight human being." She spoke about how he had "suffered his share of humiliation in the South," having had "the experience of his home being burned in Georgia." "But," she continued, "he has worked out these feelings and is quite comfortable in relating to others—of any hue."[24]

As Berry was researching and contacting candidates that she was interested in, the TCC wrote her with a new list of candidates and she scheduled an interview with Morris Jeff, a central figure in the TCC movement and someone the caucus suggested. However, after the Techni-Culture Conference in February 1970, the TCC informed Berry that they had decided as a group to only back Henry Reid. Choosing a single candidate was a strategic move to pressure Berry into hiring someone that would be in agreement with the TCC. After the caucus settled on a single candidate, Jeff withdrew himself from consideration.[25] Berry made it clear that she was not interested in hiring Reid, though never clearly expressed why in writing, and wanted to go ahead with Smart. The TCC group did not take her position lightly. In a presentation to the board, Sells detailed the resolutions that came out of the conference, including that

> Henry Reid be designated the status of permanent staff member with the title of associate director. The majority group has always controlled our community. It is now being asked to give some of it up. We object to a majority white board and all white staff selecting someone to represent our interest. We feel the time is now that Techni-Cultures black, brown, red, and yellow focus on accountability. We believe it is the responsibility of Techni-Cultures

to work to prevent whites from using Blacks, Browns, Yellows, and Reds for their own purposes without our consent. We call upon the NFS Board to act upon these priorities today.[26]

It was not enough. In the end, Margaret Berry asserted her right as executive director to choose her associate director and hired Smart. Sells and the rest of the group were livid. The TCC publicly accused Berry of impropriety in handling the situation. Smart tried to be sensitive to the fact that there was conflict around the position and delayed accepting the post until Berry felt she had exhausted all options. He came in under circumstances that were unwelcoming at best. White settlement workers were bitter about the rise of black leadership in the organization, while the TCC group was upset that their choice was not respected. Yet the fact that Smart was neither chosen nor endorsed by the core black activists in the NFS but was a black man nonetheless in many ways worked to silence the TCC group. In a way, they fell into a trap in the representation frame that Carmichael and Hamilton warned against when they argued "black visibility is not black power."

Smart replaced Berry at the helm of the NFS in 1971 after she resigned to assume the presidency of the National Conference on Social Welfare. With Smart in place as executive director, 62 percent representation on the NFS board, and Betti Pittman, a black attorney newly elected as president of the organization, the TCC disbanded within two years of their first conference. Smart did work with and sought to be accepted by black settlement worker activists, but they never fully saw him as one of their own.

Nonetheless, Smart really did change the face of the organization. By 1972, he was characterizing the NFS as "the Nation's oldest organization fighting for *people of color*" (emphasis mine),[27] and claiming that "the National Federation of Settlements continues to believe that our highest priority should be the elimination of racism in America."[28] He also wrote a column that appeared in major black news outlets like *Ebony* and *Jet*, and generally tried to forge a new identity and a fresh public face for NFS, central to which was work with people of color generally and in black communities in particular. For example, in 1974 the federation ran a public relations campaign in magazines across the country where the bulk of the page was taken with a picture of a black child, one version with a boy and one with a girl. The large lettering across the top of the boy's picture read,

"When I grow up, I wanna be a pimp like the guy next door." Underneath the photo, ran seven short paragraphs of text: "Kids take their heroes where they can find them. When a boy growing up in the ghetto sees a pimp, he sees a big, beautiful block-long car. A girl sees that hookers have fancy clothes. Numbers runners have money, pushers have cool." The rest of the text is about what neighborhood centers can provide, "from a part-time job to a free breakfast." At the bottom of the ad were the words, "National Federation of Settlements: The Other Heroes on the Block."[29] The "blackening" of the federation's image is clear. However, despite the shifts Walter Smart ushered in, the Techni-Culture fire had undoubtedly dimmed as the activism within NFS subsided in the face of this ironic victory.

Smart's directorship of the organization was also part of a larger trend towards black male leadership in social service agencies around the country. An outcome of the rise in educated black professionals in the post-civil rights era and of concerted movements of black social workers within the profession, this shift was an uneasy transition to say the least.

CRISIS OF RELEVANCE

By the time black settlement workers and the Black Power movement launched a wide scale critique of settlement endeavor in the late 1960s, the National Federation of Settlements was no stranger to criticism. The challenge came on the heels of severe criticism, as early as 1939 and as late as 1965, of the settlements themselves from Saul Alinsky and Alinsky-style organizations.[30] The Alinsky strategy was to go into communities and draw on indigenous leadership, create concrete targets, help them set attainable goals, and then leave them organized and prepared to fight on their own (Alinsky 1971). The disruptive tactics he and his organizers used, however, were in direct conflict with the settlement way of doing things, which emphasized speaking and organizing *for* the communities they worked in and operated on the idea that educated, well-spoken, and influential settlement workers were best suited to actually make changes *on behalf of* their neighbors. Alinsky's basic critique of settlements was that poor people did not need someone to speak for them, but needed to be given the tools to speak and fight for themselves, and he often chose settlements as targets for action in communities he organized. The various assaults on settlements leveled by Alinsky led the NFS to pull together a series of news articles, scholarly articles, settlement opinion papers, and various working papers clarifying and denouncing the Alinsky method, which was distributed to all member houses.[31]

The attacks continued in 1964 when Herbert Gans published an article in *Social Work* entitled "Redefining the Settlement's Function for the War on Poverty." He accused settlements of being outmoded and advised settlements to "fight for the social and economic policies necessary to reduce poverty and racial discrimination" (Gans 1964) rather than seeking to imbue poor people with middle-class values. Margaret Berry's response to the article defended NFS's commitment to integration arguing:

> The settlement has always taken an inclusive view of society, and believes that segregation by religion, race, or economic condition is unhealthy for democracy. It has believed that "consensus is better than warfare," and has seen progressive social programs emerge when people were in communication. To become only a "protest agency of the poor" seems to imply a segregation of the poor and a kind of class warfare that cuts off opportunities for the evolutionary development of social reforms.
>
> (Berry 1965)

These critiques of settlements were about both content and practice. Both Alinsky and Gans argued that settlements should no longer press for integration nor should they try to impart middle-class values to poor people. Further, though, they stated that settlements were behind the times in terms of the *practice* of seeking social change in how they sought to speak for poor communities rather than supporting them in speaking for themselves and how they worked to change people in communities they intended to help rather than the oppressive social policies affecting them. They argued that settlements were outmoded and irrelevant in a protest era characterized by calls for self-determination and community control by any means necessary, tenets that were central to the Black Power challenges to NFS both from black settlement workers inside the national organization and from the black communities where settlements were located.

During the late 1960s and early 1970s, social workers everywhere were grappling with the issues raised by the Black Power movement. Settlement agencies were often located in urban neighborhoods that were rocked by riots and had to deal with communities that wanted greater control over the institutions in them. Settlements in Northern cities in particular were also

struggling to serve young people who strongly identified with the movement. Many settlement workers and leaders conceived of themselves as
being on "the front-lines" and sought guidance from their national office.[32]

In Philadelphia, for example, the Houston Community Center found
itself negotiating with the local black youth it served. In 1965, the center
had fired a black part-time worker who worked closely with the teens in
the neighborhood for his "difficulty accepting agency policy against serving the black community exclusively."[33] Many of the teenagers protested
his firing and submitted a petition to the director. In 1966, the center
hired a program director who taught a black history class at the center and
quickly became very popular with the youth. Eventually, that relationship
too became strained and he resigned after being placed on probation with
the center. This time, the teenaged clients of the center insisted that he be
rehired. Harry Freeman, recalling these events, characterized these protests
as being under siege. To resolve the conflict with the neighborhood youth,
the Houston Community Center hired another adult worker to co-teach
the black history class. In all, these events forced the center to reflect on
their role in "militant politics."

As a result, the center produced an informational packet on their *Dialogue with Black Power* as a learning tool for other settlements. They raise
the point that Black Power "is unsettling to social welfare practitioners
who see these alternatives available to them: ignore or resist Black Power
and watch it grow into rebellion; or respond and work with it and possibly
antagonize the white power structure which controls the finances for much
social welfare." They continue, "We believe that any agency operating in
the Black community these days must face the challenge of Black Power
and its militant advocates." They conclude that their "role within the neighborhood [had] to be a broker between conservative and militant, bringing
them together to act in areas of agreement, rather than use their energies on
intra-neighborhood conflict."[34]

Along these lines, Eleanor Hardy and the Community Work Department of the Philadelphia Friends Neighborhood Guild wrote a working
statement on "Rendering Settlement Services in a Predominately Black
Community." Hardy and her colleagues were responding, in part to the
police repression of student protests at the Philadelphia Board of Education offices on November 17th, 1967. After a discussion of the emergence
of the Black Power movement and a summary of what happened at the

student protests and the subsequent suppression, the Friends Neighborhood Guild asks itself, "What shall be the role and contribution of the third primary institution: Welfare, of which our settlement is a member?" The answer: "the Guild must support the momentum to make the Black community believe in its own ability and self-respect."[35]

In the wake of these sorts of community control challenges, the staff and leadership of the NFS received several inquiries about how member agencies should respond to militant groups seeking control over "agency policies, programs or personnel."[36] They issued a statement and provided guidelines on community control, reaffirming that "the role of a settlement is one of building a creative partnership among peoples of all races and economic levels for the purpose of creating a society of equal justice and opportunity for all." They acknowledged the "need of excluded minority groups to band together for self-help and mutual aid," but went on to reassert the belief "that settlements must press for a society in which differences are not the basis for exclusion or special privilege, but are cherished as part of the vast human mosaic." The following guidelines were based on this settlement philosophy:

1. Settlements and neighborhood centers are best comprised of people who have vital and deep roots in the neighborhood, together with people of the wider community who have a concern for the neighborhood and its importance and who can translate neighborhood needs to the larger community; and
2. The current urban crisis demands an immediate and massive response by individuals, private organizations and government at all levels to fulfill now the American promise of equality and the right to a decent life.[37]

Obviously, the issue of community control was a particularly relevant one for settlement workers. Operating community and neighborhood centers meant that "neighbors" seeking community control sometimes targeted settlement houses. Outside specialists also echoed the call for community control to the NFS leadership. When Tom Gwynn of the National Urban League addressed the NFS board at an October 1968 Board Training Institute, he focused on how to handle rising demands for community control. He discussed the "myth of the melting pot" and emphasized the "new pride in difference" and the "need to recognize individual and specific needs." He advocated a new thrust towards community control and urged agencies to be agents for change. This entailed helping communities develop their own power and resources, dispersing the decision-making process, supporting communities with their own goals, and acting to "get rid of the dead wood on the board."[38]

The speakers at the Urban Crisis Conference in October 1968 addressed the issue of Black Power and white responses to it. Edwin C. Berry, then-director of the Urban League of Chicago, opened the second day of the conference with an appeal to end white racism and specifically dismissed the idea that Black Power was simply black racism. He countered that this response was a "distortion of the legitimate aspirations of black power," which "many whites are using as an excuse to cop out." And in a direct appeal to white social workers, he consoled, "I know it's tough to hang in, seek to work constructively under the epithets of 'honky,' 'Whitey, get out,' and others. To the honest, whites, I say, you must hang in—work as equals. We blacks must expect of you the kind of heroism, for a little while, that you have routinely demanded of all blacks for all the years since the emancipation proclamation." "The future of our country," he ended, "can settle for no less."[39]

The push for community control hit hard on the most sensitive spot for settlement leadership and old-timers in the movement. At the contentious 1968 NFS national conference in Houston, where black dissent in the organization really took hold, Margaret Berry addressed her executive speech to the issue at hand—community control—and the challenge it presented to way things had "always" been. "This is the first time in the history of the settlement movement that our accepted values are being seriously challenged," she claimed. "Our trust in the peculiarly American paradox of freedom with control," she argued, "has been shaken with the awareness of deep cleavages and we have a sudden fear of continuing violence because of the shattering of concepts which seemed to hold us together." Berry then warned that "the fact that neighborhood groups now say: 'I want to do it myself,' that they want to 'take over,' spells the end of any conscious or unconscious patronizing. Now we are moved into an unsentimental appraisal which challenges the very values we live by." Finally she counsels, "No agency today can rest in the sluggish backwater. Each agency must ask: Do we use our whole strength, our establishment— for useful social purposes?"[40]

There was a very real sense among many on the NFS staff and among local and national settlement leadership that the settlement philosophy itself was under attack. When the New Directions Committee met with representatives of the Connecticut and Rhode Island agencies, for example, the conversation reflected a larger theme in the organization's discourse during this period: that NFS should not participate in conflict tactics, but remain committed to their role as established institutions. At this meeting, Mr. Wattles of the Hartford Community Centers said that he had gone to the Conference on Inner City Violence in Chicago a few weeks earlier to learn to deal with urban violence. Instead, he said, he discovered "whites in a minority and under attack from the blacks."[41] The way he saw it, racism became the major theme and transformed the social work conference into a Black Power conference. He spoke about the demands that the Black Caucus presented, "which in essence recommended that the settlement movement move from the middle-of-the-road position in the area of conflict and violence."[42] He admitted that he was not prepared to do this and that he saw a "continuing role of settlements in the gray areas of racial conflict and tension." The rest of the conversation settled in around the idea of being the "establishment." Mr. Tyson of the Southfield Neighborhood Center in Stamford, Connecticut, noted that the real question was, "Who are we, agents of whom? The establishment, people doing for others?" As a way of wrapping up the establishment discussion, Mr. Ganter of the Hartford Community Centers asserted, "Many of us are too old for the militant confrontation that the extremists promote and which are tearing our nation apart. It may be that this is the only way to change a racist society. Some of us should seek other alternatives for dealing with the problems, which are more consistent with our history and value orientation.[43]

A delicate dance around the fear, resentment, and defensiveness was occurring behind the process of heading in new directions. Many white social workers took particular umbrage at perceived attacks on established white liberals. Richard Peters, chair of the Executive Committee, suggested at an April 1968 meeting that there was "nothing wrong with being part of the establishment,"[44] as it suggested "a heritage of which we can be proud, and it means that we have arrived, have resources and ties." At the May 1968 meeting of the committee, Mrs. Kirshbaum responded to criticism that boards did not reflect the communities served by settlements by mentioning the "reluctance of some Negroes to participate on boards because they are afraid of being tagged as establishment."[45] She went on to say that agencies could not let this affect their legitimacy by abdicating leadership. "One must face the fact that power lies in the establishment—it has money, jobs, political ties," she avowed.

From the very inception of a black caucus within the National Federation of Settlements, there were strong and differing reactions from white settlement workers and leaders. In a 1969 NFS newsletter column, Margaret Berry wrote, "The existence of a Black Caucus within the settlement movement brings different reactions. Some support the idea. Some oppose it on idealistic grounds, believing that it condones the very racial segregation that we have been striving to eliminate. Some white people, who have fought effectively for inclusiveness, now feel hurt or betrayed when they are excluded." Berry goes on to claim that she welcomes a black caucus and takes it as a show of faith in the settlement movement. She reminds settlement workers that "the Federation is an inclusive organization and is committed, in the words of the Executive Committee, to the goal of a 'society in which differences are not the basis for exclusion or special privilege, but are cherished as part of the vast human mosaic.' The settlement movement has given many of us the opportunity to find friends and co-workers in diverse groups and to learn for ourselves that common human impulses transcend race or religion. We value this experience."[46]

But the response by the settlement establishment to the movement within the NFS and the larger shift to community control and rise in black male leadership at all levels speaks volumes about the process of shifting race relations during the tumultuous transition period in U.S. race relations in the period following the civil rights movement. Moreover, these interactions between black activists and the established white leadership of the National Federation of Settlements reveal the centrality of emotional dynamics in social movements.

Social movements scholars, rejecting the collective action literature that focused on the irrationality of crowd behavior in the early part of the twentieth century, have until recently ignored the function of emotion in social movements.[47] However, as Jasper (1998) points out, emotions are an "integral part of all social action," and as such, "affective and reactive emotions enter into protest activities at every stage" (404). Operating on this realization, studies on the emotional nature of social movements have focused almost exclusively on the emotionality of movement participants.

Indeed, as Aminzade and McAdam (2001) point out, scholars have yet to explore the emotional dynamics of the "complex interactive processes that mobilize the emotions of [actors outside of movements]" (15). Therefore, where emotions have been studied, the focus has been on the emotionality of challengers—not the emotional responses of power-holders. But it is logical to assume that the prospect of losing power or power sharing would bring with it intense fear, resentment, bitterness, and other negative emotional reactions. These "complex interactive processes" are difficult to understand without recognizing the emotions underlying them. The difficulties of understanding emotion in retrospect notwithstanding,[48] it is clear in this case that the response of elites within the NFS cannot be understood without exploring the emotional content of their reactions.

Judith Trolander (1987), writing about the tension between professionalism and social change in the settlements, characterizes the general shift to black male leadership in settlements as a root cause of the movement's decline. Her argument borders on outright racism, expounding that "Blacks as a group seemed to have more difficulty with administrative matters, such as dealing with boards, raising money, and writing grant proposals." She continues to lay the blame on the promoted black leaders, saying "in part, this situation may have resulted from a reluctance to accept white help, perhaps because of the danger of white control." "Yet," she argues, "by themselves, Blacks sometimes lacked the necessary administrative skills and influence" (209). She also describes the resentment and hurt feelings that white settlement workers felt as black social workers "took over" and neighborhoods continued to insist on "community control" over their institutions, without any comment on the white racism that these grievances were rooted in.

Observing that "the black ascendance to leadership was accompanied by a corresponding departure of a generation of whites from the settlement house movement," Trolander contends that the "general white settlement leaders' reaction was 'to hell' with the blacks" (211). "The abrupt black takeover was a slap in the face to many whites," she argues (211). Though this fear of being pushed out was central to the response by white settlement people, so was the patronizing and belittling attitude present in Trolander's more contemporary reflections. The outpouring of support and sympathy Margaret Berry received after the charged Cincinnati conference is revealing of the sense. John Austin wrote:

It was interesting to me to observe the events as they unfolded at Cincinnati on one weekend and to come home and following Tuesday week (election day) see almost the identical thing happen in Berkeley where an outstandingly fine liberal white congressman of 12 years longevity in Congress was upset in the Democratic primary by a young black city councilman. These wrenches and steps in new directions forward take a terrific toll of existing talent. And I suppose only time will tell whether the personnel casualties are over-balanced by the personality pluses.[49]

She received another letter from Mrs. Anderson Page, who wrote to congratulate her on "practicing what [she] preach[es]." Page also mused "that was quite a meeting we had. I hope that now the Techni-culture Conference have gained the seats they will use their new found 'power' [quotation marks in original] for the general good and not for power alone. Many I listened to were impressive but some were beguiled by their own rhetoric—and so I guess is true of many of us old white ladies."[50]

Ousted board member Gordon Herstslet wrote John Austin after the Cincinnati meeting as well. He expressed his surprise at "how far the Techniculture group had gone," referring to the number of board and committee leadership positions they had secured. He went on to exclaim, "It will be interesting to see how this 'palace revolution' turns out." But he also added, "At the moment, I feel that the Techis have been guilty of overkill. They will eventually discover that the Establishment—whether you like it or not—has a vital contribution to make."[51] This combination of resentment at being pushed out and looking down on the movement of black workers runs throughout many of the responses by white settlement leadership.

The response by the NFS's leadership (and established white membership) showcased the ongoing strain between trying to keep up with the times of social action and new norms of racial interaction while maintaining that what they were doing—indeed, had been doing since Jane Addams's reform days—was still useful and effective. For example, Executive Director Margaret Berry's address to the May 1968 NFS conference in Houston highlighted the "reform potential" of settlements and how to mollify the loud demands for community control. She made it clear that the sentiment of the day was that they had to get with the program being demanded by black social workers. "But," she asked the audience, "can we use our establishment for useful social purposes?"[52]

Berry was a prominent player in shaping the direction that NFS would take on the administrative end of the black movement within the organization, and sat at the center of this conflict in her own thinking. Her reaction made it clear that she that she fully realized that the NFS couldn't keep on with old ways and had to respond to the black movement within their ranks. As *Cincinnati Enquirer* reporter James Adams observed at the Cincinnati conference, "Miss Margaret E. Berry, spunky executive director of the NFSNC, is learning yesterday's rebel can be today's establishment symbol."[53]

However, she maintained a strong desire to hold on to both the organization's and her own personal legacy of social change work, and would not allow a blanket indictment of their previous work towards social change. After a New Directions Committee meeting in June 1968, Austin sent Berry a little note: "I hope that none of the discussions made you feel defensive because you have no reason to. The Federation has always kept pace with the times and right now some new direction is indicated, and that's what all the flack is about."[54] She responded by saying that she felt like the meeting was useful and that all the issues were dealt with but that her "human reaction" was to be ambivalent. "On the one hand," she disclosed, "I'm the first to say that we can't go on as we are, and when I fully realized that last fall I pushed for this New Directions process. I really welcome new directions intellectually, and emotionally. What is hard is to hear newcomers make statements as if they were general truths, which belittle true accomplishments . . . you can half kill yourself though, and all you get is blame because you didn't accomplish the impossible."[55]

This personal exchange between close colleagues and friends reveals a highly emotional process that must have been central to the transitions in racial understandings and interracial relationships in all sorts of organizations during the Black Power era. It seems particularly so for those white and interracial organizations that considered themselves advocates of racial equality. It couldn't have been easy for Berry and her contemporaries to have black colleagues telling them to move aside in favor of black leadership of the organization. Still, what accounts like Trolander's do is to justify "white bitterness" at black struggles for leadership without attempting to understand a context in which power sharing with whites seemed impossible given the entrenchment of white leadership and the perception that those white leaders were doing more harm than good in the black community.

Berry maintained a firm commitment to integration in general and in the NFS especially. She wrote to Austin just before the 1970 Cincinnati conference that "the words 'restructuring the Federation' which is used constantly and is listed for one of the Cincinnati workshops being arranged by H. Sells, really means an all-minority board and staff." She then notes that this demand "is also based on a perception which is false—the neighborhoods served are all minority. If that were true there could be the usual charge that all whites are leftover do-gooders and should retire from the scene."[56] She also defended her personal commitment to racial justice by calling on her own work in black communities. In an interview on-site at the Cincinnati conference, she's quoted as saying, "As an old revolutionary, I'm perfectly willing to defend the role of the federation," and, "I spent 10 years in Pittsburgh's Hill section in the vanguard of racial justice. The Settlement House movement may not be perfect but at least we didn't desert the inner city."[57]

These responses reveal a visceral emotional reaction: resentment at being asked to step aside and defensiveness at being told you haven't done enough. These emotions go beyond the clear political and philosophical commitment to integration and established ways of doing neighborhood based social work, reflecting a deep hurt and personal confusion. Being charged with irrelevance clearly hit on a sore spot for settlement workers. Looking back on the settlement movement in a July 1976 article published in *Social Work*, Bertram Beck—director of Henry Street Settlement in New York City—proclaimed, "Fortunately, the settlements were not untouched by the events of the 60s" (268). He argued that the community participation trend of the decade increased the number of minority persons on the settlements' staffs, governing boards, and directorships, thereby reducing the gap between settlement leadership and its constituency. What happened, "during the sixties," he reasoned, is that "the old role of the settlement leader as social spokesman had been further diminished by the evident ability, willingness, and desire of the people who suffered the social problems to speak out and bear witness themselves" (Beck 1976:269). This caused settlement leaders to "gain a new humility in their relationship to the participants" (269). This new humility, however, was clearly resisted, accepted defensively, and was ushered in by the Black Power movement within the settlement endeavor.

CONCLUSION

In the archived papers of the National Federation of Settlements, I found an undated document with no author attributed to it. It looks like a flyer or a leaflet someone would have handed out to people at a meeting. Across the top, in all caps, it shouts, "BULLETIN: THE FACT IS THAT NFS MUST CHANGE! THE RUMOR IS THAT THE EXECUTIVE DIRECTOR OF NFS WILL TENDER HER RESIGNATION IN BEHALF OF THE NEW DIRECTIONS CONCEPT!!"[58] The author goes further: "And that she will encourage all the little old white ladies to resign from the board; that the Board will reflect the 80% Techni-Culture constituency of NFS; that the Executive Director's ties with the 40's and 50's concept of NFS rendered her impotent to deal with the institutional racism of the 60's; that we went through the 60's with an all-white staff; that we entered the 60's in a financial crises and the outlook for the 70's is dim; that the fact is if NFS continues with white domination it will limit our opportunity for securing needed outside resources."[59]

From where I sit, as a twenty-first century researcher, I am most struck by the frank way in which they talked about the racial issues at hand, and by the "directness" of all of the organizing that was going on within the NFS. Their style clearly reflects a black professional ethic of "telling it like it is," as shaped and culled by the National Association of Black Social Workers and other emergent black professional associations during the 1960s and 1970s. But more than that, it opens a window into the uneasy transition to a different way of "doing race" in America—post-civil rights, but not quite.

Black social workers were demanding things like greater representation within their professional structures and calling for things like community control in black neighborhoods, but they were also demanding their right to speak out and make claims about the racial inequality they witnessed and experienced in their professional lives. This was met with some defensiveness among the white establishment against whom their challenges were being leveled. This interaction is central to the tumult of changing racial relationships and rules in the Black Power era, which Robert Smith refers to as an "intervening period" between the civil rights and post-civil rights eras.

Central to the context, of course, is the Black Power movement. The Techni-Culture Movement drew on Black Power frames, ideals, and identities in their activism. However, the specific power frame they used was translated into a simpler call for more black representation, which was further transformed into a relatively disingenuous call for multicultural representation. In the end, they certainly accomplished their goal of minority representation in the NFS. There was a black executive director, a black president, and a 62 percent representation of people of color on the board. And that was it. The "representation" frame didn't stretch much further. In other words, once representation was achieved, the movement was over. But it wasn't enough. These were symbolic victories, the most ironic of which was the appointment of a black man deeply distrusted by the TCC group as associate director. In other words, the directorship went to a black man who shared the same race with the activists but did not share the group's vision of black progress.

The case of the Techni-Culture Committee of the National Federation of Settlements in many ways stands in contrast to the rise of separate professional associations during this era. By maintaining an explicit commitment to gaining representation within the organization rather than creating a separate organizational structure, they operated on a different interpretation of the Black Power movement frames. Moreover, by making an ahead-of-their-time kind of move towards multicultural organizing, the Techni-Culture Movement offers an interesting point of comparison for the better-known National Association of Black Social Workers.

6

"We'll Build Our Own Thing"

THE EXIT STRATEGY OF THE NATIONAL ASSOCIATION OF BLACK SOCIAL WORKERS

THE WALKOUT OF FOUR HUNDRED black social workers from the 1968 National Conference on Social Welfare (NCSW) annual meeting was a powerful scene and remains a central element of the NABSW's narrative history.[1] However, it was not the first plan of action for confronting the National Conference, nor was it the preferred one.

In the April preceding the 1968 NCSW forum, a black caucus organized at the National Association of Social Workers' (NASW) National Social Action Workshop on the Urban Crisis, held in memory of Martin Luther King Jr.[2] The Urban Crisis Conference (UCC) invited a powerhouse group of activists and radical scholars to speak, including Charles V. Hamilton, Alvin Poussaint, and Richard Cloward.[3] The event was marked with numerous demands for greater activism on the part of NASW.[4] Throughout the conference, the national organization was pushed to support the upcoming Poor People's March on Washington, and a march was organized by several social workers along with a seven-point platform.[5] They wanted to proudly take a stand as social workers to call for action on the *Kerner Report*, to push for legislation on a guaranteed annual income, to eliminate the welfare freeze, to immediately pass open housing legislation, that negotiations to end the Vietnam War begin immediately, to cease the riot suppression bills, and to support the poor people's campaign.[6]

Black social workers played a prominent role in the workshop's activism. The social workers who came together at the Urban Crisis Conference in Washington, D.C. represented several groups of black professionals who had organized separately in 1967: the Black Social Workers of Detroit;

the Associations of Black Social Workers of New York City, San Francisco, Los Angeles, and Pittsburgh; the Catalysts and the Afro-American Family and Community Services of Chicago; and the Alliance of Black Social Workers of Philadelphia (Jaggers 2003; Johnson 1976). The black participants of the conference were called together by Audreye Johnson in response to their anger about the lack of black leadership and representation at a conference on the urban crisis (Johnson 1976). Black social workers at the conference were incensed when a memorial service was held for Martin Luther King Jr. in the garage of the hotel—just three weeks after his assassination.[7] At the caucus meeting, they formed a tentative national association called the National Association of Black Catalysts, came up with an organizing plan to recruit other social workers, and decided to caucus again at the NCSW meeting coming up in May.[8] Core organizers decided to meet with NCSW leadership to discuss a list of demands they had put together.

When they arrived in San Francisco on Sunday, May 26, 1968, the word was already out that black social workers would be meeting after the opening reception to talk about the development of a separate national organization. They found their planned meeting room was locked, so they decided to meet the next day. On Monday, in the absence of a meeting room, the group met in a hotel suite. The room was overflowing with people and energy. The discussion was "hot and heavy" with lots of disagreement and intensity, but the group reached an agreement in the end. They appointed a steering committee and individuals who would arrange to meet with NCSW leaders. Despite many attempts, however, the Executive Committee of the NCSW refused to meet with the steering committee of the Catalysts. Nor would they allow time on the conference program for black social workers to discuss their demands.[9] It seemed their hand was forced by unresponsiveness and resistance.

Tuesday, May 28 was a working day for the group. They collaborated in small groups to generate a list of concerns, which were then compiled into a larger position statement. Preparing a unified statement from such a wide range of social workers from all over the country was a difficult process. Doug Glasgow recalls it as a tense but exciting time: "It was a period of great strategy in the sense that made it possible in two days. By the second day, we finally said that at the opening session plenary session we want all blacks to walk out and come across to Glide Memorial where we are going to discuss an agenda that the black community needs."[10] In those two days, the decision was made to take over the meeting, present the demands, and walk out. The position statement was hammered out and photocopied to be distributed the next morning. After they delivered the position statement and walked out, the group re-convened at Glide Memorial Church. Between Wednesday, May 29, and Thursday, May 30, the group appointed an official steering committee and decided on an organizational structure.[11]

The discussions at Glide were intense. Participants not only decided on a formal position statement, but they spent a good deal of time discussing what they wanted to be moving forward. They addressed questions of whether to be a caucus or a separate organization. They dealt with issues of identity—should they call themselves "black" social workers or use "Negro"? Should it be an exclusively black organization, or could it include white social workers? Social workers involved in working with and organizing with black communities from across the United States articulated their visions for the nascent organization's direction.[12]

The organizing that occurred at the 1968 conference was only the beginning of the organized national movement of black social workers within the profession. In the year that followed, the newly formed National Association of Black Social Workers would pursue a dual strategy of negotiating with the NCSW and NASW leadership and "closing ranks" to work on their own organization. They held their own meetings and conferences, and were hard at work setting the agenda of the organization.[13] While they would come back together with the NCSW at the 1969 meeting, black social workers' actions at the 1968 annual forum changed the trajectory of social welfare and was a part of a much larger context of social protest during this era.

In many ways, the 1968 annual forum of the National Conference on Social Welfare was caught in the crosshairs of numerous movements (actual and ideological) taking place around the country. The organizing of black social workers at the conference was but one of many challenges to the social welfare profession at this time. The Poor People's March on Washington took place that very week, and welfare rights organizers were represented at the forum. California fruit workers were also striking as student uprisings flared up on campuses across the country. And less than two months earlier, the Kerner Commission had published its report, which called out social welfare as a part of constellation of institutions that created the conditions for urban riots. There was also a general air of criticism of social welfare coming from all corners (Vasey 1968).

Even though the 1968 forum saw protests from fruit workers, black social workers, peace protestors, and welfare rights organizers, it is the 1969 NCSW annual forum that has been characterized as the most tumultuous in conference history.[14] John C. Kidneigh recollected "the tone of social action and social change permeated every session." The 1969 New York conference was certainly more contentious than the initial demonstration in San Francisco, in part because of a strengthened alliance between NABSW and the National Welfare Rights Organization (NWRO), who had planned to disrupt the meeting. The NWRO, a radical organization of welfare recipients and allies active in demanding changes in social welfare during the late 1960s and early 1970s, took the lead early on, and in fact garnered the bulk of the attention for their disturbances.[15] Before the opening session started, the NWRO took over the registration area, demanding free registration and donations from conference attendees.[16] "As soon as the opening session had been convened at 7:30 on Sunday evening," wrote Margaret Berry, "the platform and microphone was taken by a group of welfare mothers and George Wiley, national direction [sic] of NRO [sic]."[17] The NWRO demanded a total of $25,000 from the audience in addition to a direct donation of $35,000 from the NCSW to them, and informed NCSW participants that no one would be allowed to leave until the money was collected.[18] From their perspective, the NCSW was filled with professionals profiting from work with the poor without genuinely seeking to change their dire situation. The group's logic was to force financing for social action by demanding money from the very social workers they called "fat cats," "racist pigs," and beneficiaries of "white imperialistic society."[19]

The crowd did not, however, passively accept these accusations or demands. Participants yelled back and many tried to walk out, but like the disruption at the 1968 meeting, members of the NWRO and the NABSW blocked the doors.[20] People were physically stopped from leaving the ballroom during the demonstration, so the tensions were high.[21] Eventually, the staff of the Hilton Hotel intervened and removed a temporary wall so people could leave.[22] The police were called in and at least six people were arrested for unlawfully detaining people from leaving.[23] After a brief statement in the morning, the NWRO left the conference to march on Sears, which they claimed was discriminating against welfare recipients in granting credit.[24] Their departure, however, did not bring an end to the disruptions. The NABSW soon took over, and as Margaret Berry wrote in her recollection of the events, they "emerged in force."[25]

As the organization's annual business meeting began on Tuesday evening, the NABSW took over the stage and read their demands.[26] The demands presented in writing were similar to those presented in 1968. Black social workers and the NWRO reiterated their belief that "the present structure, policy, and functioning of the social welfare system is racist, inadequate, and unresponsive to the needs of black and brown colonized people in this country."[27] More specifically, NABSW demanded greater representation of "black and brown people" throughout the boards and committees of the NCSW; that the 1970 meeting be focused on white racism and poverty; that the NCSW hire lobbyists to work on issues of race, poverty, and national welfare policy in Washington, D.C.; that the NCSW work with the Council on Social Work Education to completely overhaul social work education in order to develop curricula "relevant to the urban crisis and minority groups"; and, lastly, to give African American social work professionals greater access and control over admissions, financial aid processes, and faculty appointments in social work schools and agencies.[28]

The NCSW leadership's lukewarm response was that they agreed with the spirit of the demands and planned to look into them.[29] Though the NABSW abdicated the stage in the face of this seemingly positive response, actions were already underway that would change the course of their organization. The new organization had decided to give the national leadership only one more chance to respond to their demands. If they did not, the NABSW would stop negotiating for any increased inclusion in favor of organizing for change within the profession and within black communities through their own separate organizational body (Jaggers 2003).[30]

While the organization had decided to make an attempt to negotiate with the NCSW, NABSW leader Howard Prunty made an executive decision to give the NCSW an ultimatum to respond by noon on May 27, just a single day after receiving them.[31] It was a move that had only partial support from the NABSW membership. Garland Jaggers (2003), who was a part of the founding group and published an account of their movement, characterizes the issuance of a twenty-four-hour ultimatum as a "tactical mis-step" (52). However the decision was characterized, it was a key turning point in the group's move to focus on their own organization and mobilize against the profession as a sort of "outsider within." "This was the last time that

NABSW sought dialogue with NCSW," wrote Audreye Johnson (1988:13). As Shirley Better put it, "We were looking to be a caucus until then, but then we decided to move on and become our own organization."[32] "This," Jay Chunn added, "was when we said, 'we'll build our own thing.'"[33]

CLOSING RANKS

This idea of closing ranks was also evident at the first national conference of the Association of Black Catalysts, which later would become the NABSW. On August 30, 1968, the Chicago Catalysts hosted the first national conference of the fledgling organization in Chicago over the weekend. More than two hundred black social workers participated in the conference, dubbed the "Confab in Black."[34] Both Charles Hamilton, coauthor of *Black Power* (1967), and Charles Ross, then on the Metropolitan Welfare Council, delivered keynote addresses to the group.[35] The overarching theme of the conference was "Unity-Survival," which manifested in discussions about the role of the black professional in the liberation movement.[36] The invitation detailed that the "confab will revolve around such questions as: How can the Black Professional participate in the current revolution? What are the present dilemmas facing the Black professionals? How can Black Professionals create their own power base? What new roles and linkages does the Black revolution demand of the Black Professional?"[37] Much of the conversation revolved around maintaining black identity and loyalties even while working among whites. Ross, for example, talked about a system in the United States that had produced "a race of colorless men and women— who have Black skins and white minds and grey loyalties."[38] He pointed out the gap between the "brother in the streets" and the "brother in the office" who had been "whitewashed" through his subjection to the system in the colleges and graduate schools."[39]

The workgroups that met the second day of the conference agreed on a set of goals and justifications for the organization.[40] The items reveal a self-conscious consideration of the role of the black professional in relation to the larger black community, emphasizing the necessity for black professionals to "unite Black people regardless of status to work toward relationships directed toward their mutual survival," to "play a supportive role in assisting groups, offering expertise in the planning needed or asked for by groups," and to "embody a code of ethics relevant to Black people."[41]

In describing their purpose, they stressed that the new organization must "concern itself with connecting Black [sic] of all descriptions (light, brown, tan, Black, non professional and professional, pimps and Ph.D.'s etc.)."[42]

This self-evaluation and self-conscious commitment to affirming a black identity and connection to the black community is also clear in the code of ethics produced for the conference. The introduction to the Catalysts' *Code of Ethics for Black People* defines the codes as the "take-off points to help develop awareness about our current state of Blackness and to look at the relevance of what it may take to improve our total participation in the Black Revolution. They are designed to help us confront ourselves."[43] The first point reads: "We must recognize that the traditional role of the Black Leaders has been to act as a buffer between a hostile and unsympathetic white community and our oppressed Black Brothers and Sisters. As Black People, we must determine that this is a condition that we cannot and will not tolerate this any longer."[44]

The rest of the codes develop a set of standards for black professionals in relationship to the larger liberation movement. "We must," they claim, "make it absolutely clear that we are totally committed to the Revolution."[45] They underscore that their commitment is to the black community and not white employers with codes like, "We must view all issues only from the vantage point of what is best for Black People," and, "We must be responsible for using our acquired skills to wipe out the obstacles which prevent Black People from achieving maximum realization of their innate potential for social economic and political growth."[46] Many of the codes also address how to use their position as professionals responsibly. For example, they argue, "we must take advantage of our unique relationship to the system and 'TELL IT LIKE IT IS' at every opportunity" (capitalization in original). Moreover, they maintain that black professionals "must use our skills to initiate programs for the Black Community based on information collected and interpreted by Black Researchers" and "take advantage of every opportunity to use the system in whatever fashion that is beneficial to Black People."[47] Others make statements about the responsibility to hold all social workers accountable for their actions in the black community. For example, one code reads, "We must demand excellence from anyone serving the Black Community,"[48] and another that "We must demand that the same level of goods and services be placed into Black communities that is taken out." And still another reads, "We must demand that the same level of excellence in service be extended to Black People that is extended to whites."[49]

This rhetoric was clearly embedded in the ideology of Black Power. In his January 1973 editorial of the *NABSW News*, William Greene discussed the organization's growth. He drew attention to some of the forces that gave impetus to the NABSW's formation, such as the "failure of integration efforts and the visibility of a separate Black America and white America; the velocity of the Black Power revolt that was penetrating the very fabric of American life; [and] the Black revolution and solidarity that would provide power and increased opportunity."[50] Yet while the NABSW activists obviously placed themselves within the Black Power movement, it is clear that their gaze was primarily inward. Both the Confab and the code were as much about who they must be or what they must do as black professionals as they were about what they must demand of their profession and the institutions they were a part of. The focus on the development of a black identity that supported the "Black Revolution" and the commitment to use their skills for the benefit of the black community call on the Black Power frames of self-determination and self-help rather than the civil rights rhetoric of access and integration.

What both the "Confab in Black" and the *Code of Ethics* reveal is that black social workers were critically evaluating their role as professionals in a rapidly changing society and in a black political environment that was shifting to a focus on working-class identities rather than the middle-class sensibilities of the earlier civil rights movement. As new professionals, as members of a rising middle class, as MSWs, as degree-holding African Americans—what was their role in a movement for which the economic question was central and the primary representative image was the inner-city working-class rebel? Furthermore, and perhaps more importantly, they were struggling with the question of how they, as a part of a profession implicated in the oppression of African Americans, could use that same position in the service of gaining greater economic, social, and political power for black people.

This act of claiming a place in the Black Power movement would manifest itself in an internal movement within their profession to make their home base live up to the promise of the Black Power movment and create a mold for black professionalism that would mesh with emergent Black Power identities. Their movement was paralleled in other professions, and

their collectively forged black professional identity would draw a blueprint
for being black and professional in a way that remained committed to the
ideals of black liberation.

THE NABSW MOVEMENT

Reflecting on the organization's past twenty years, Audreye Johnson (1988)
wrote that

> accountability to the Black community was and continues to be the
> focal point of NABSW, it is the heart and soul of the organization. For
> NABSW there has been the need to understand and cope with racism in
> social work which is carried out in the social welfare arena in the delivery
> of social work services, whether in administration, education, or profes-
> sional practice.
>
> (11)

Shirley Better, when recalling the conditions that gave rise to the movement, spoke of arriving in the Watts neighborhood of Los Angeles, California in 1966 when the community was "still smoldering" from the riots, and
finding that social work agencies were not playing an active role in needy
black neighborhoods. She was shocked at the few benefits the poor black
community accrued from the civil rights movement and came to the conclusion that "every social institution in [the] community served the white
establishment and not [the community]."[51] Though the War on Poverty
policies meant that more social workers were in low-income communities,
Better felt that they weren't helping the conditions in the black community.
As a black social worker herself, she observed that the social work profession "continued to suggest that the poor minorities were to blame for the
dismal state of their communities," and was keenly aware that the professional education black social workers received taught them to be "gatekeep-
ers" rather than "advocates for change." Further, she astutely commented
that "faculty in the schools of social work continued to make money and
get tenure doing research on us."[52]

In fact, all of the NABSW founders I spoke with pointed to the urban
rebellions of the 1960s as important junctures in their own thinking about
their work in black communities. Garland Jaggers recollected how he and
his colleague Louis Bates had formed a small organization of black male

social workers early in the 1960s. They were primarily concerned with the treatment that their black clients received in social welfare agencies and their own position within the profession. "So we decided to do something about it," he said, "so we set up a meeting with other black social workers— at first only men. So we met at my house and organized the Association of Black Social Workers in Detroit." "But," he continued, "it was after the rebellion of 1967 in Detroit, that the organization really picked up steam. After that, social workers gravitated to the organization looking for ways to counter the destruction in their community."[53]

Douglas Glasgow, one of the founders of the NABSW and former dean of the Howard School of Social Work, had a similar story about working with the Sons of Watts in Los Angeles while he was a doctoral student. The Sons of Watts, an organization of young men from the community who were involved in the rebellion, became a community improvement organization of sorts. He cites this experience—witnessing the ineffectiveness of social welfare to deal with the kinds of issues that Watts was facing—as a part of the impetus for developing the organization, both for him personally and as a whole. He also remembered that when black social workers arrived at the pivotal 1968 NCSW conference in San Francisco they immediately noticed there was nothing on the program that dealt with the current situation of African Americans.

> We came into San Francisco that year. It was a year in which, of course, King had died—had been killed. Bobby had been shot. The cities had been burning. Some 80 cities in the United States went up in flames, you know—uh, were put up into flames, I should say. Uh, and we came into San Francisco at this national level conference of social welfare and they had the usual agenda. . . . It had no relationship to the reality of what America was facing because America's cities were burning. America was in total shock at the death of both King and Kennedy and wondering what is going to happen in this country. So we walked in to this conference, we looked at the agenda, and we said, "They don't even talk about the cities, the urban cities," um, and I think that's what propelled us.[54]

All of these founders' observations point to three major categories of grievances that black social workers leveled within the profession, all of which echo Johnson's depiction of the NABSW being a challenge to racism in social work administration, education, and practice: (1) Black social workers were treated as second-class citizens within the profession, and that white leadership did not value their perspectives and implemented racist interaction styles; (2) the institution of social work was racist at its core, as the structures for obtaining jobs and promotions were racist in character, the processes by which profession-level decisions were made unfairly benefited white social workers, and the curricula of social work schools were racist in scope; and (3) white social workers in black communities were carrying out racist practices, and simply providing services without seeking social change and action in the communities they served was inherently racist.

While the NABSW movement extended beyond the profession to issues such as state proposed welfare reform[55] and other local matters affecting the poor and black people,[56] here I focus primarily on the work the NABSW did to bring about changes in administration, education, and practice within their profession. I find that their tactics were both constrained and enabled by the profession they were seeking to challenge. Therefore, although we might commonly think of social movement tactics in terms of marches and pickets, movements in organizations need to be considered in context. In the case of black mobilization within social work, their various campaigns were played out in the conventions, schools, journals, and committees rather than on the streets.

Black Marginality in the Profession

Black social workers had multiple concerns about job opportunities and security. For one, black social workers, especially those who dealt with issues of race or concerning African Americans, were often marginalized and ghettoized within the profession. This often made it difficult to find opportunities to publish and get their white colleagues to take their work seriously. Because of this marginalization, African American social workers often faced difficulties being promoted in both academic programs and in social agencies.

When I spoke to Dr. Sokoni Karanja (formerly Lathan Johnson), a social worker during the civil rights era who was an activist in the profession and who attended the founding conference of the NABSW, I asked him to state some of the primary grievances expressed during that time. He offered his time at an agency in Cincinnati as an example:

I was the assistant director—[another social worker] who was white ran it. And you know, I consider myself to be a man of average intelligence and [this guy] was about half as smart as me. (*laughter*) But he would try to treat me as though I didn't know anything. There was a black lady too, worked with us, who he also tried to treat like she was stupid. We had to stop them from thinking they were special—these folks were not like Jane Addams. These were ordinary white folks who wanted to treat us like we were "less than" . . . Yeah, we dealt with a lot of white rejection and looking-down-the-nose type behavior.[57]

Garland Jaggers related a similar point in a conversation he had with Louis Bates when they founded of their organization in Detroit. He recounted, "I talked about one of my white classmates who graduated with us and became a director of minority relations. Whoa. And I had been told by my supervisor it would take me ten years to become a supervisor."[58]

This sentiment is echoed throughout the movement, and it was certainly an overarching theme at the first conference of the Association of Black Catalysts in Chicago in August 1968. In addressing the gathering, Hamilton said that "Blacks working in the midst of whites are subject to compromise and coercion or rejection" and that "in the conflicts of interests, white ones will, in the majority of cases, prevail."[59] And in discussing his interest in organizing black male social workers in Detroit, Jaggers (2003) recalls that he and Bates "bemoaned the fact that there were very few Negroes in key positions . . . in Detroit's social welfare system," and how he observed white fellow graduates fast-track into publication and new positions while they struggled for promotion, and were often not even made aware of opportunities for promotion in the first place (13).

Indeed, the idea that black social workers were marginalized within the profession was the primary impetus behind the creation of the *Black Caucus Journal* in 1973.[60] The journal, Audreye Johnson (1988) wrote, "offered to African American social workers something which had not been readily available to them in the past, an opportunity to publish their work" (14). Indicating the difficulty of publishing research on African Americans in the mainstream journals, Johnson (1988) asserted that "there was no need to apologize for the focus of the work upon Blacks" in the NABSW journal (14). As a result, she argues, "the publication opportunities within NABSW pushed white dominated social work publications to be more responsive to publishing African American authors" (14).

Concerns over the employment of black social workers in the field were also at the heart of this grievance. As Shirley Better put it, when asked about the problems they had with the profession, "Well, our jobs was another thing. We always had to be worried about our jobs."[61] She talked about the sense that black social workers were always in a tenuous position in universities and agencies alike. Her impression was certainly echoed in the situation at the Berkeley School of Social Welfare (BSSW) in 1969. On May 19, 1969, several students from the program issued a list of demands regarding the program. The list was not addressed by the school's faculty or administration.[62] These same students were among the actors who addressed the conference at the contentious 1969 NCSW meetings in New York, and they worked with the nascent NABSW to put pressure on the BSSW.[63] In the NABSW's position statement, two of the specific complaints against the BSSW drive home the point about the marginality of black social workers in the profession and in their respective workplaces. First, the NABSW observed that "the U.C. Berkeley School of Social Welfare sent 15 white faculty members to the NCSW conference with expenses paid; the request of two Black faculty members to have their expenses paid was denied."[64] The second criticism pointed to a specific faculty member whose reappointment had been threatened. They claimed "because Ron Lewis, as a Black faculty member has been working on behalf of Black students and the Black community, the white members of the school's evaluation committee are threatening the repressive action of recommending not to reappoint him."[65] The NABSW went on to demand the charges of discrimination at the BSSW be investigated. This case is illustrative of the overarching anxiety over employment experienced by many black social workers as a result of racism within the profession.

Institutionalized Racism

The second grievance addressed the inherent racism they saw within the profession. They repeatedly argued that racism was institutionalized into the structure of the profession. This racist core began in the nation's social work schools, as was evident in numerous complaints about the practices there. Dr. Glasgow recounted that the profession was trying to develop programs and curricula that were important to black communities without any consultation from black people themselves. So, he says, they started intervening "in the normal processes of CSWE and NASW and NCSW who were doing business without blacks. And so then we said that blacks must be in every area."[66] He spoke specifically about the problems in social work schools. At UCLA, for example, black social work students needed to confront the school of social work and the whole social sciences division in order to bring more black faculty in the university on tenure lines, as it had been normal practice to bring in black faculty as adjuncts and part-time instructors who "came and went, and came and went."[67] He also high-lighted the concerns black social workers had with how few black students were included in schools of social work around country.

The list of demands at the 1969 National Conference on Social Welfare included a sharp indictment of social work education, and called for "schools of social welfare become more relevant to the Black and Brown communities, and minority groups, especially by a marked increase in the number of such persons on the faculty and that the schools employ more of such persons with tenure."[68] To work toward this aim, the NABSW suggested that "the schools of social work should work toward specific quotas of fifty percent of Black and Brown personnel on their faculty and administrative staff."[69] But the demands did not stop at just representation on the faculty level. They proposed that "schools of social welfare should launch positive recruiting programs that will open up new post-high school educational opportunities for Black and Brown and minority groups students. Such students and faculty should participate actively in developing admission and financial aid policies and supportive services for these programs."[70] They further contended that schools of social welfare should do more to provide more field placement for minority students and communities, and that there should be more "black and brown field work supervisors." They end their statement with a critique of social work curricula, pushing for schools to "move diligently to develop curricula that relate to the urban and rural needs of Black and Brown and minority group students, faculty, and the community, as well as the understanding by the white community of their participatory role in the disfunctioning of all groups of people."[71]

In general, black social workers' arguments about the institutionalized racism in the profession stemmed from the overt and covert racism that they saw pervading the system that educated social workers. In addition, they argued that the national organizations of social workers utilized racist practices. In the first list of demands presented to the NCSW at the

1968 meeting, they claimed that the NCSW was a "white institution" whose board and planning committee did not reflect the "ethnic composition commensurate with its expressed concern."[72] They also demanded that NABSW representatives be appointed to the "powerful committees" of the NCSW. During the follow-up protest at the 1969 NCSW meetings, they continued with the same line by demanding that "there be a sharp increase in the representation of Black and Brown people and minority groups, minority groups includes Indians and Asiatics [sic], at all levels of the NCSW, including the National Board, staff and all committees."[73] Implicitly, this set of demands goes beyond concerns for job security and reflects a desire to move beyond simple demographic or descriptive representation. In other words, black social workers were not demanding some sort of symbolic representation that would be fulfilled by inserting any black faces into the NCSW power structure. Rather, they sought substantive representation. They wanted to be represented by black social workers who would represent the interests of African American social workers as the NABSW articulated them.[74]

CURRICULAR TRANSFORMATION

By all accounts, American social work had reverted to a white-centered focus by the 1920s, following an earlier focus on pluralism among at least settlement workers within the profession. But in response to pressure from the NABSW, African Americans and other people of color throughout the profession in the 1960s, the Council on Social Work Education (CSWE)—the accrediting and standards-setting body of the profession—eventually adopted standards mandating content on race, racism, and people of color (Potocky 1997).

Social work made huge strides in the recruitment of people of color into the profession and in making curricular change in social work education as a result of internal professional activism. The CSWE had nondiscrimination mandates in place much earlier than many professions. In fact, CSWE had implemented a standard prohibiting discrimination in the selection of students and faculty for schools seeking accreditation as early as 1954 after the *Brown vs. Board of Education* ruling (Pins 1971; Trolander 1997). But the pressure black social workers exerted on the profession—both through NCSW and within other arenas, including CSWE—led to the adoption of relatively aggressive recruitment standards for students and faculty of color and to the creation of diversity-related curriculum standards in the early 1970s.

By 1965, the CSWE nondiscrimination standard was revised to require accreditation reviews to incorporate details on how schools deal with discrimination in admissions, their overall program, and in recruitment and retention of faculty (Trolander 1997). The standard was further revised in 1968 to mandate schools "demonstrate the special efforts it was making to enrich its program by providing racial and cultural diversity in its student body and staff" (CSWE 1971). This made the CSWE the "first among national accreditation bodies to have an affirmative action standard" (Trolander 1997:120). When it was formalized as Standard 1234 in 1971, review teams were tasked with assessing promotion and tenure policies for faculty of color, discrimination within field placements, and internal procedures for handling discrimination complaints in programs (Trolander 1997). They also launched several special programs to aid schools in attracting, developing, and retaining more students and faculty of color (Pins 1971). Standard 1234A, added in 1973, would specify that "a school must make special, continual efforts to enrich its program by providing racial, ethnic, and cultural diversity in its student body and at all levels of instructional and research personnel and by providing corresponding educational supports" (CSWE 1973:1). As Jani and colleagues (2011) point out, this was also the first time CSWE guidelines "explicitly suggested that the curriculum should reflect knowledge of racial and ethnic minority groups" (286). The primary purpose of Standard 1234A, according to CSWE (1973), was "to achieve the incorporation of knowledge of racial, ethnic and cultural groups, their generic components as well as differences in values and life styles, and the conflicts these generate in the configuration of American Society" (1).

Standard 1234A was largely a reflection of internal pressure. Responding to activism by people of color within social work, the CSWE organized task forces to increase the numbers of faculty of color in schools of social work. These task forces were convened for American Indians, Puerto Ricans, and Chicanos in 1970, and later for African Americans and Asian Americans in 1971. The CSWE Black Task Force grew out of a June 1970 CSWE workshop titled "Problems and Needs of the Black Community—Issues, Development, and Perceptions: Implications for Social Work Education." The workshop called for the CSWE to identify and develop curricular content on African Americans, as well as find ways to increase the numbers of African Americans in social work programs, at both the graduate and undergraduate levels (CSWE 1973). The Black Task Force was charged with answering this call. It was made up of fifteen black social workers and nine liaison members from black schools of social work. NABSW members were an important part of the process. Both Jay Chunn and Charles Sanders served as liaison participants at the Howard University and Atlanta University Schools of Social Work respectively.

The task force concluded that the absence of black content in the social work curriculum was a result of pervasive and persistent racism in the United States. They made the case that the lack of black social work educators was directly tied to this lack of curricular materials. So, while it acknowledged that recruiting and retaining black faculty was important, the task force focused its report on curriculum reform. Pointing out that "many white social work educators continue to view the inclusion of Black content as a non-scholarly endeavor," the task force asserted that "an endeavor of this nature must have the commitment of the total social work education community, adequate funding and minority staffing" (CSWE 1973:2). Overall, the Black Task Force's curriculum suggestions proposed heightened attention to the role of institutional racism in the lives of African Americans, and made particular recommendations for the three major areas of study in most schools of social work: human behavior and social environment, social welfare policy, and services and methods/practicum.

In the CSWE curriculum policy, human behavior content was defined as the "body of content relating to human behavior that is designed to contribute the student's understanding of the individual, group, organizational, institutional, and cultural contexts within which human behavior is expressed and by which it is significantly influenced" (CSWE 1969, as cited in CSWE 1973). The Black Task Force insisted that for social work students to understand black behavior in context, they must account for the distinctiveness of the black American experience marked by a history of slavery and exclusion. Therefore, the curriculum should "consider the Black experience in the United States as unique, not to be compared to any other immigrant group" (6). They further asserted that "social work education must recognize that societal-economic forces and the resultant institutional racism may be a major factor that creates stress in Black communities and limits the realization of potential in Black individuals" (6).

This focus on institutional racism was also central to the Black Task Force's recommendations for curricular changes in the social welfare policy and services sequence. The CSWE instructed social work programs to provide a way for "all students to acquire knowledge of the general policies, conditions, legislative bases, institutions, programs and broad range of services relevant to social welfare in contemporary society" (CSWE 1969, as cited in CSWE 1973:7). The task force pointed out that while social work education does look at the history of social welfare policy, it had not considered the failure of these policies as they related to black communities. They argued that social work "has not acknowledged that the nation's preoccupation with power, profit, and privilege has been a primary determinant of American social welfare policy" in a way that institutionalized discrimination against African Americans in social welfare (6). They went on to suggest that this sequence of the curriculum "must include historical documentation of the fact of racism in American life and, in so doing, direct scholarly attention to its solution" (7).

The Black Task Force also provided an outline of educational objectives and underlying assumptions as a guideline for adopting their suggestions. Their object was to help the student to develop:

1. An understanding of how the economic, social, political, and class forces that determine social policies are implicitly influenced by racism;
2. An ability to analyze how social policy is formulated by legislation, by the courts, and by government bureaucracies, and how this formulation is influenced by racism;
3. An awareness of the impact of institutional racism on Black Americans and other ethnic minorities with a particular reference to the distribution of societal resources and the patterns of delivery of educational, health, and social services.

(8)

The task force based these objectives on three basic underlying assumptions: that "racism in combination with poor-law thinking is dysfunctional and inhumane in our current society"; that "the persistence and viability of institutional racism is incompatible with the goals of social justice"; and, finally, "social problems such as poverty, unemployment, and ghetto living require basic structural changes rather than remedial, incremental reforms" (8).

Recommendations were also made for the practicum and methods area of social work curriculum, which the CSWE defined as "the area of the curriculum designed to help the student learn and apply the knowledge and principles of social work practice in accordance with the values and ethics of the profession" (CSWE 1969, as quoted in CSWE 1973:9). They point to three areas of basic knowledge that they believed social work students would need to develop in order to work with African Americans: the history of black people, especially as it relates to culture, religion, and family development; the political and economic systems that affect African Americans; and a perspective on "human growth and development . . . that recognizes the oppression of Black people and evaluates behavior with regard to the societal forces that depersonalize and reject Black people" (CSWE 1973:10).

Taken together, this was a harsh critique of social work education, but the task force also offered a way forward. Their suggestions were reflected in the new CSWE diversity curriculum standard. The first curriculum policy statement by CSWE in 1952 stated that social workers should consider all social, cultural, and spiritual influences on an individual's development. By 1962, the curriculum guidelines mandated that social work curricula help students to "recognize, understand, and appraise, 'human behavior in the light of personal and cultural norms and values and varying conceptions of effective social functioning and well-being'" (Moore and Dhooper 2000:7). The 1973 guidelines for implementing Standard 1234A went even further, suggesting that "effective responsible participation in the helping professions in a diverse society requires that opportunities be provided to incorporate the understanding that is based on direct interaction and involvement with different groups in the broader society" (CSWE 1973). By 1983 the curriculum policy statement advocated for the inclusion of diversity content and required the curriculum to pay attention to "patterns and consequences of discrimination and oppression," and "the experiences, needs and responses of people that have been subject to institutionalized forms of oppression" (CSWE 1983, sect. 7.4, as quoted in Moore and Dhooper 2000:7). This shift towards a focus on institutional racism is a clear reflection of the black movement within the profession.

In addition to changes in the CSWE guidelines, black pressure within social work resulted in other important developments: new courses with diversity content were offered at schools of social work, new textbooks were developed that dealt specifically with diversity issues, more articles were published in the discipline on the subject of race, and there were modest increases in the number of students and faculty of color in social work. By the 1970–1971 academic year, almost 25 percent of all incoming first-year MSW students were students of color: about 14 percent of first-year students were black, and 4.3 percent were Chicano or Puerto Rican, reflecting a 2.5 times increase in the total number of students of color that entered in 1968 (Pins 1971). A year later in 1972, there were 1,226 black first-year MSW students, almost 15.8 percent of the incoming class of Masters students (CSWE 1972).

LICENSURE

While the general demands were for greater inclusion and representation in the national organizations and changes in social work education, the institutional racism grievance might be best illustrated through an examination of the NABSW's campaign against licensure for social workers early in the 1970s. In 1969, the National Association of Social Workers approved a resolution to start requiring the regulation of social work practice through licensure at the state level (NASW 1973). The NABSW vehemently opposed this measure, seeing the proposal as racist both in intent and outcomes. The licensure system, as proposed, would only be available to those holding Masters or doctorate degrees; black social workers largely practiced with undergraduate degrees or as para-social workers, without degrees. Secondly, the NABSW expressed concerns about the tendency of certification boards to use discriminatory testing (Johnson 1975). The long history of bias against blacks in standardized exams, both inside and outside the profession, did not inspire much confidence that licensure exams would be any different (Garcia 1990).

The NABSW saw this potential for widespread exclusion of black social workers as incredibly problematic. Since many of those receiving social work services were black and poor and there were already limited numbers of African American social workers, the licensure system would lead to an even greater mismatch between service providers and their clients. To NABSW, the licensing proposal would further entrench a system in which whites "intervene, plan for, set values, define needs, and intimidate Black folks in the name of 'social work.' They claimed it was a 'catastrophic insult to a whole race of people for whites to attempt to institutionalize these racist, condescending, missionary, [practices]" (Johnson 1975).

Moreover, they insisted that the licensing proposal was made in response to massive internal dissent—a sort of sanction for challenging the profession. In his statement to the New York State Legislative Higher Education Committee on licensing, Phillip Berry, vice coordinator of the New York State Association of Black Social Workers, targeted licensing in particular as an ineffective way to deal with the identity issues the profession was trying to resolve. He contended that the questions around which services should be provided to whom, by whom, and for what purposes should (and could) not be dealt with through the licensing of practitioners. "Licensing under the guise of an attempt to answer and address these issues," Berry argued, "is deceptive, elitist, non-functional and inadequate."[75] "This is an unequivocal drive to diminish and/or undermine progressive and reform seeking practitioners and organizations committed to viable social change, like the NABSW."[76]

In all, the idea of requiring licensure for social workers reeked of elitism and racism for NABSW members, and it was perceived as a desire to promote professionalization over the needs of clients. In the official position paper against licensure, the organization lambasted this "diabolical scheme" as intending to weed out new professional minorities who had struggled to achieve Associates and Bachelors of Social Work degrees. It was, they believed, meant to drive the profession "back into the passive, conservative, clinical, and white middle class characteristics of the past." The official statement concluded with an allusion to Malcolm X: "the National Association of Black Social Workers serves notice to all advocates of this racist and class oriented scheme that we have mobilized to fight the implementation of this proposal through any and every means necessary."[77]

They did rely on several means, playing out their campaign against licensure within the context of their profession. One tactic they used was coalition building. They built a particularly strong coalition with the Radical Alliance of Social Service Workers (RASSW),[78] who wrote their own position paper against licensure.[79] The NABSW also testified before the New York State Legislative Higher Education Committees on Licensing and lobbied at both the state and federal levels.[80] They also published articles on the "absurdity of licensure" in numerous social work newsletters and journals.[81] But even after a long and concerted opposition, the NABSW and their supporters lost the battle. The American Association of State Social Work Boards was created in 1979 to coordinate the regulation efforts of state boards and by 1990 all fifty states regulated social work practice in some way.[82]

The opponents of licensure had little chance of winning this battle. Operating in an era of the rapid growth of American universities (Jacoby 1987) and the increasing academization of social work practice, it would be difficult to imagine arguments against licensure gaining any real ground. Proponents framed licensure as the last step in securing real professional status for social workers. It was, in many ways, the final tool in creating an exclusive, skill-based profession.

Yet the NABSW's concerns with institutionalized racism in the profession are reflected in the licensure battle. And while they were not able to change how the profession would use licensure on the path to professionalization, they were more effective in making curricular innovations and in increasing diversity in the profession.

Racism in Social Work Practice

Another major grievance was related to the ways in which the profession's racism was projected onto black communities. As shown in the *Code of Ethics* produced by the Catalysts, there were serious concerns about the quality of goods and services in the black community. Moreover, the idea that social work—and the NCSW in particular—just was not meeting the actual needs of black communities was closely connected to what the NABSW saw as the profession's lack of political involvement in the racial issues in the era. In an essay about the emergence of the NABSW, Jay Chunn—the official NABSW's first president—wrote, "in 1968, when America was burning down—Chicago, Detroit, Cleveland, Watts—the white folk were still building the role and function of case work, looking at intrapsychic conflict and the like."[83] Also, recall T. George Silcott's depiction of the NCSW as "a do-nothing group which has consistently demonstrated that it will not involve itself in social action."[84]

In an interview with Dr. Chunn, I asked him what the major conflicts were with mainstream social work during this uncertain time. After correcting my use of term "mainstream"—it would be better characterized as "white social work," he said—he answered: "irrelevance to the struggle, irrelevance to liberation, to community development, the black community, crime and joblessness. I mean, it was almost completely oblivious.

You have to keep in mind that social work organizations at that time were designed to strengthen the profession as opposed to strengthening the community."[85] Shirley Better had a similar response: "Social service agencies did not operate in a way to meet the needs of poor black people. They mainly went along with the social welfare system—punitive, stigma—all that. Social work wasn't standing up to issues. They just went along with the status quo."[86]

One of the earliest statements by the national body of black social workers—made at the Urban Crisis Conference—did not shy away from criticizing this institutional obliviousness and apathy, and openly declared: "The NASW has been, and is now, irrelevant to meeting the needs of Black people. We feel that the NASW is not committed to system changes in the interest of Black folk."[87] And in the list of demands circulated at the 1969 NCSW meeting, they called on whites to confront their own racism and for "Black Experts (not white experts who heretofore acted as experts) to speak to the issues confronting the Black community."[88] Along these same lines, Audreye Johnson, one of the founders of the NABSW, argued that "social work agencies and institutions were found to be non-responsive and non-reflective of the needs of the Black community and of the Black perspective" (Johnson 1975).

The association's most well-known battle—the fight against transracial adoption—grew out of this particular grievance. In 1972, the NABSW issued a statement opposing transracial adoption on the grounds that the preservation of black identity and black culture can be best accomplished if a black child is placed with a black family. The association charged adoption agencies with not putting enough effort into the recruitment of black adoptive families, and alleged that agency policies discriminated against black families who might otherwise be interested in adopting. They insisted that "Black families can be found when agencies alter their requirements, methods of approach, definition of suitable family and tackle the legal machinery to facilitate inter-state placements."[89] But overall, they maintained that the desire to place black children in white families was due to the shrinking numbers of white children available for adoption, such that interracial adoption was chiefly about filling the needs of white people who wanted to adopt to the detriment of the black family. The NABSW says as much in their statement: "We fully recognize the phenomenon of transracial adoption as an expedient for white folk, not as an altruistic humane concern for black children. The supply of white children for adoption has all but vanished and adoption agencies, having always catered to middle class whites, developed an answer to their desire for parenthood by motivating them to consider black children."[90]

In the statement, the NABSW also pointed out several alternatives to transracial adoption, which included exploring and supporting options within the child's extended family and changing standards to make adoption more feasible for interested black families. The NABSW contended that if there were viable options within the family, those would be preferable, even if the family members required financial support. They also observed that adoption agencies' "emphasis on high income, educational achievement, residential status and other accoutrements of a white middle class life style eliminates black applicants by the score."[91]

In addition to bringing the issue into the national spotlight, the association created adoption assistance programs for black families, lobbied for the creation of subsidized adoptions for black families, aided in the growth of black-run adoption agencies, and published numerous articles on the issue.[92] Between 1971 and 1973, for example, the New York State chapter of the NABSW was actively involved in a campaign to start their own foster care and adoption agency.[93] While they were unable to raise the necessary funds for this endeavor, they did start a counseling and referral service for black families interested in adoption.[94] The service advised prospective adoptive families on the "requirements, procedures, and policies" of child welfare and adoption agencies.[95] In their announcement of the service, the New York chapter of the NABSW claimed, "Our goal is to recruit as many homes as possible for the thousands of Black children who need the warmth, love and security of a loving Black family."[96]

The transracial adoption struggle certainly did not end the practice altogether. However, the NABSW was exceptionally successful in changing the debate around the practice. Despite the fact that there was no law banning transracial adoption, by 1973 the Child Welfare League had changed its adoption standards to say that same race adoptions were preferable. These were the same standards that had been revised only in 1968 to be more favorable towards interracial adoptions. And by 1973, transracial adoptions had slowed to a trickle, reversing a slight upswing (Silverman 1993). And even with the rise in international adoptions to the United States since then, domestic black/white adoption rates have remained low.

Any way you look at it, the transracial adoption issue has never been the same. The central issue in the debate moved from the value of decreasing barriers to interracial families (the dominant discourse between 1968 and 1972) to preserving black culture and identity in a way that mirrored aspects of the Black Power movement and worked to challenge the notion that families should be colorblind. Whatever individuals may believe about transracial adoption, the work that the NABSW did ensured that, whatever the outcome, the best interest of black children (however conceived) would be at the center of the conversation, and that the idea of white families wanting to adopt black children could be problematic was integral to the discussion.

Professional Identity and Style as Resistance

The NABSW movement clearly focused on issues affecting the black community, but the development of a new professional style—a new way of being in the professional world—was also a central resistance strategy for the NABSW. The organization collectively developed a professional identity that would reflect a commitment to black liberation, which was increasingly defined by the practices of the larger Black Power movement. The professional norms they developed required not only maintaining and demanding a commitment to a high standard of practice in black communities, but created standards for interacting with one another, advocating values such as not "back-stabbing" and supporting the endeavors of other black professionals. Furthermore, there were clear principles for interacting with white coworkers and bosses, including adherence to rules like always "telling it like it is"[97] and calling out white racism. They also developed a basis to make racial claims to expertise on "black issues." Central also to the emergent identity and interaction style was the idea that activism was essential to racial loyalty for African Americans and to racial progressivism for whites.

In his editorial for the Fall 1970 issue of the *Black Caucus Journal*, Charles Sanders observed that several traditionally white journals had attempted to increase black representation since the birth of the publication. So he issued a challenge to both black and white social workers:

> As we mirror ourselves against our white and black world, we see additional roles for both as vital to our mutual welfare. Many of our black brothers are

not motivated to write for black journals, even when it has been expressly created for them. The black brothers will run vigorously to the opportunity to get published in white journals, because these are more prestigious, highly developed and circulated. Again this is a reflection of the self-hate, cynicism, discontinuity which constrains real blackness. To these brothers we say, "Are you really committed to creating and developing viable black institutions?"

(8)

Sanders challenged the "blackness" of black social work professionals who chose not to publish in the *Black Caucus Journal*. It is a clear example of a professional norm growing out of Black Power-era professional associations—that in order to be *authentically* black, you are required to support the professional endeavors of other black professionals.

His challenge to white social workers was related: "To our white brothers we say, 'Yes, competition is a major reality of our social system.' But if we are truly to replace newer values for our older ones, and vitally concerned with the black quest for developing viable institutions in the black community, then your technical assistance, not competition, is appreciated in this venture" (8). As he sets a standard for black professionals to be authentically black, Sanders is simultaneously explicating a standard for white social work professionals who claim to "be down" for the cause—assist, don't compete.

This new professional style grew out of both self-reflection and through their mobilized interaction with the white social work establishment. It was an identity and approach that would reflect their desire to merge the sometimes conflicting roles of activist and professional. Former NABSW president Cenie Williams, in his Fall 1969 "Message From the President," emphasized the necessity for African American social workers to identify with the black community over their profession. Existing social agencies "perpetuated dependency," he argued, and "black professionals have an obligation to confront (those) institutions," and to make their "own innovations" (9). He writes:

This identification with blackness and with the plight of our more unfortunate brothers and sisters draws us all closer together in these critical times. In the past, many Black professionals believed that the best way to survive in America was to disappear completely, leaving no trace of our African heritage. We were under the assumption that the only way we could be citizens was to acquire all of the Anglo-Saxon values and patterns of behavior, in short, to "ape" whites. History has proven the fallacy of this logic.

(9)

Williams continued, "Black social workers have an obligation to attack, discover and expose all the pathological social ills that retard and destroy our people. These ills are mainly economic exploitation, political impotence, and social degradation." Though social workers were not political or economic experts, they could work through community organization and group work to "create vehicles for technical assistance" to deal with the many issues affecting the black community. "The Black social worker," he argued, "must cease serving as a buffer or peacemaker for the establishment" (9).

Williams also made it clear that his primary goal as president of the association was to "provide a structure through which all Black social workers can become actively involved in helping Black people regardless of their philosophies." He chided that "we can't afford to spend long hours and months debating about which philosophy, program, or approach is best for Black people. In my opinion the only question that should be raised is simply 'Is it good for Black people?'" He ended by saying that "the Black community has no need for 'suitcase-carrying intellectuals' who just sit around and talk about problems without ever becoming involved." Black social workers were encouraged to "do" rather than just "talk," and that an activist orientation was required in order to be "authentically black" (Williams 1969).

This set of norms was characterized by a professional style that valued closing ranks in the most literal sense of the term by (1) maintaining a commitment to black-only organizing, (2) defining commitment to Black Power ideals as the only way to truly be black, (3) shunning (at least rhetorically) interracial relationships and those African Americans who were in them, and (4) rejecting white aesthetic norms. In many ways, it was also built on a conception of blackness that privileged men and masculine ways of being in the world.

The NABSW's code of ethics, which was written in 1968 and remains unchanged, begins: "In America today, no Black person, save the selfish or irrational, can claim to be neutral to the events taking place in our society. Therefore, this is a statement of ideals and guiding principles based on functionalism and not professionalism, given the context of pain in our daily lives as Black Americans practicing in the field of social welfare."[98] This opening reflects the sentiment that their organization was central to their ability to function or survive in their role more than it was a statement on how to behave as professionals. Moreover, it made a clear claim that in order to be truly black one had to take a stand on the issues facing black people in America.

Members are asked then to commit themselves to the interests of the black community by subscribing to seven statements:

> I regard as my primary obligation the welfare of the Black individual, Black family, and Black community and will engage in action for improving social conditions.
>
> I give precedence to this mission over my personal interest.
>
> I adopt the concept of a Black extended family and embrace all Black people as my brothers and sisters, making no distinction between their destiny and my own.
>
> I hold myself responsible for the quality and extent of service I perform and the quality and extent of service performed by the agency or organization in which I am employed, as it relates to the Black community.
>
> I accept the responsibility to protect the Black community against unethical and hypocritical practice by any individual or organizations engaged in social welfare activities.
>
> I stand ready to supplement my paid or professional advocacy with voluntary service in the Black public interest.
>
> I will consciously use my skills, and my whole being as an instrument for social change, with particular attention directed to the establishment of Black social institutions.[99]

The code of ethics embodies three of the functions I propose that Black Power-era professional associations serve: identity work, operating as monitors on racial issues, and acting as a protest wing. From the get-go, it formalizes the professional norm of identifying with the black community over a professional identity. The NABSW founders were explicit in their expectation that black social workers were black first and social workers second. In her twenty-year retrospective on the organization, Audreye Johnson wrote that the organization "served as a cohesive agent not only for Black social workers, but recognized the unique relationship which exist [sic] between

African Americans whether they are providers or consumers of service."
Secondly, the professional norms laid out in the code point toward a sense
of responsibility for monitoring, shaping, and changing social work practice with black communities. Lastly, in claiming that members use their
"whole being" for the purpose of social change—especially establishing
black institutions—the architects of the organization declared its function
as a protest wing of the profession.

In some ways, the focus on black social workers and the development
of a professional identity and black professional standards were primary to
the NABSW's founding. Johnson (1975) recalls that, at first, the "NABSW
had moved toward a recognition of its heritage in social work, and would
later address issues which were germane to the African American community."
Indeed, much of black social workers' activism was about the confirma-
tion of a new black identity, which in part meant demanding respect based
on an unapologetic blackness and identification with a black community
as opposed to white social work. For example, in announcing they had
formed a national organization at the 1968 Urban Crisis Conference, they
listed their goals as (1) "to reinforce Black identity," (2) "to act as a vehicle
for united action for Black folks," (3) "to provide a vehicle for communica-
tions on a Black basis," and (4) "to reconstruct systems to meet the needs
of Black folks."[100]

Many times these demands came about as explicit appeals to black mas-
culinity and the supremacy of men and their ways of being in the world. For
example, when Detroit social workers organized their national organization in 1967, it was created for black *male* social workers (Jaggers 2003:14).
I also asked key informants about the relationship between men and
women in these organizations, and each echoed the idea that the sentiment
of the time was for men to lead the way. This seems to have been a matter
of respect. In confirming an identity based on unchecked blackness, men
would be best suited to project a sense of "unapologeticness" around racial
issues. Social workers' mobilization, like many other Black Power-related
mobilizations, occurred in the aftermath of the 1967 *Moynihan Report* and
other social science attacks on black men and families. This led to a conscious desire to reclaim and project a strong image of black men and to take
control over a public redefinition of black manhood. When I asked Dr.
Karanja the question, we beat around the bush for a while until he eventually interrupted me: "Let's be clear—we were a bunch of chauvinists—in

fact, I'm a recovering chauvinist to this day." He admitted that they had a tendency to "devalue women's involvement and commentary" then, and that the organizations "could have been stronger had [they] been more engaging of women."[101] Certainly, not all black men who were social workers during this period would agree with this characterization. But he is not alone in his sentiment as it relates to the organizations of the period.

While the gender dynamic of Black Power-era organizations has already been well documented and thoroughly debated,[102] the dominance of men in the NABSW was particularly peculiar because of the predominance of women in the social work profession. It was an oddity noticed by outsiders as well as insiders. Reporting on the 1968 conference for *The Monitor*, a Catholic newspaper in San Francisco, Will Connelly noted first that while men were increasing in numbers in the profession, they were still in the minority. Nonetheless, he observed that "the males, still vastly in the minority in this kind of work, did most of the hard talking at NCSW's most muscular convention in almost a century of its existence."[103] Audreye Johnson retrospectively addressed the issue by saying that women made up the majority of the NABSW and had served in all leadership positions except as president of the organization. In recounting the "positives and negatives" of their movement, she mused, "Will they question the pattern of leadership everywhere but at the top?" (Johnson 1988)

The centrality of men to the movement also revealed itself in homophobia and antifeminist sentiments within the movement. Poet Cheryl Clarke (2005) recalls that the national director of the NABSW was given a standing ovation for these remarks during a speech given at the 1979 annual conference of a regional chapter of the organization: "Homosexuals are even accorded minority status now. . . . And white women too. And some of you Black women who call yourselves feminists will be sitting up in meetings with the same white women who will be stealing your men on the sly" (34). Clarke saw this construction of competition over black men as a tactic that "many Black men use to intimidate Black women from embracing feminism" (35).

The gender dynamic between black activists in the profession (the most visible of whom were men) and white social workers (many of whom were white women) was thus fraught with a unique tension. The decidedly masculine tone of black social workers' organizing was often perceived as angry and attacking. This, as is discussed later, is a central trope in American racism: painting black men as angry and white women as victims. Here, this dynamic was on display.

In Audreye Johnson's (1988) retrospective, she said that the NABSW conferences "have provided respite and renewal where members could speak and act Black." She says "this was acceptable and expected behavior which members enjoyed." What speaking and acting black meant, however, was taken for granted, and it was constructed in a very particular way. The movement put together a space and language that not only excluded whites, but also those African Americans who maintained intimate relationships with them or strayed too far to the white end of the black/white spectrum they had formed. The movement's push for "black consciousness" and to "free our minds" was presented in contrast to thinking or acting "white." There is a picture of a woman with an afro who attended the Association of Black Catalysts conference in 1968. The caption reads: "Naturals were very much in evidence at the ABC confab. This sister . . . is typical of the movement of professional Black women away from white concepts of beauty and toward a glorification and appreciation of their own natural selves. 'The first step in Black liberation is to liberate oneself from the honkified [*sic*] concepts we have been saturated with,' she says."[104] Also, recall Charles Ross's charge that black men and women who had been socialized into educational and religious institutions "have Black skins and white minds and grey loyalties."[105] Black men who had white girlfriends were said to "talk Black and sleep white."[106] Language like this promoted an idea of blackness that was free of white influences.

In that meeting at Glide Memorial Church, there was also much discussion about naming between those who felt like the term "black," as rooted in the Black Power movement and as a term of empowerment, should be used and those who still argued for the use of the term "Negro."[107] But underlying this debate was a discussion over still-developing definitions about what "black" was and who fit that description. Garland Jaggers recalled that "there was a struggle in the 60s in terms of whether or not you were black. It was 'Who is black?' And the blacker you were, the faster you would move up, and we had no definitions of blackness, but everyone was throwing it out there."[108] This identity work—deciding who is black, what black is and isn't—was essential to the NABSW movement, even if the definitions were unclear.

All of the language, norms, and expectations of being black in the space of the NABSW reflected the dominant Black Power ideology of closing ranks, then being championed by Stokely Carmichael and Charles Hamilton. It was in sharp contrast to the rhetoric and norms of the civil rights movement, which valued integration and movement closer to the "mainstream." Another way closing ranks operated is through claims to legitimacy and challenges to the social work establishment based on the idea that black social workers were better suited to deal with black communities because they were black. This sentiment—an almost strictly racial definition of expertise—is echoed in both the struggle against licensure and the transracial adoption issue. But this process also parallels what the literature on professions says about the process of professionalization in many ways. Expertise is central to professionalization, serving as the foundation to authority in the work that professionals do. Certain skills, tasks, and competencies are defined as uniquely theirs, thereby creating a basis for the profession's existence. As Abbott (1988) argues, professionals claim to have the jurisdictional authority to classify a problem, reason about it, and take action. Black social workers were clearly a part of the profession of social work and thus were "insiders" in the field's professional practice. However, their intra-organizational movement challenged the collective expertise of social work professionals by claiming that African American social workers had specialized knowledge, skills, competencies, and sensitivities that white social workers did not and could not have, making them experts on black communities. This was a challenge to the institutional logic of the profession, which held that expertise came exclusively, or most importantly, from training and not one's race or other characteristics.

Yet, this professional identity was shaped by black social workers "outsider within" status as well (Hill-Collins 1986). As nonwhite people socialized into the logic of a profession that operated on white assumptions, valued white ways of thinking, and was demographically dominated by white people, African American social workers had a unique vantage point from which to view the profession. This position allowed black social workers—who both understood the logics, conventions, and norms of the discipline but were simultaneously rooted in the black community and the logics, conventions, and norms of the Black Power movement—to place themselves at the intersection of professional and movement understandings. These professional norms and their issues, framings, strategies and tactics are a sign of this positionality.

The rise in the number of African Americans in white collar jobs also coincided with the Black Power movement in a way that shaped the very meaning of black professionalism. This new professional style—marked by a commitment to the larger movement above their profession, a commitment to high standards of practice in black communities, an ethic of sticking together, a commitment to call out racist behavior, and a move towards closing ranks around all black organizing—set a standard for being an "authentically black" professional. This standard was further defined against a white professional identity and other "inauthentic black" identities. Moreover, it created the foundation of black professional associational life in the 1960s and beyond. These newly forged identity and professional standards represented a new class of black professional organizations, which would facilitate what Bayard Rustin (1965) called the transition from "protest to politics" as well as the institutionalization of Black Power within the professions.

CONCLUSION

Black social workers, along with other black professionals who made movements within their professions, drew primarily on the identities, ideas, and strategies of the Black Power movement. They worked to adopt a new black identity and affirm black values, black aesthetics, and black interaction norms and apply them in their profession. The assertion of the right for black communities to have control over the institutions in them was also central to their movement. At its heart, black social workers were standing up for a new blackness and claiming a position of power and control over the destiny of themselves and the larger black community. They were also developing and operating on a sophisticated understanding of institutional racism, one attuned to the idea that racist intent was not always necessary for racist outcomes to occur and that seemingly race-neutral policies and practices could have a disparate impact on people of color.

The popular and scholarly understanding of the Black Power movement is that it was largely a tool of the black masses and only at times embraced by the black intellectual. The black middle class has been almost universally characterized as falling into the assimilationist, accomodationist, or the moderate camp of the black liberation movement. But these black middle class workers were organizing around Black Power frames and strategies and their enduring efforts would shape the way we think about racial politics in the workplace and professional well into the twenty-first century. While black social workers and other black professionals clearly were not among the most radical or revolutionary elements of the larger movement, how they employed the movement's content firmly places them in the Black Power tradition.

To be clear, though, their mobilization was not some sort of romanticized utopian movement. In many ways, by adhering to a strict racial definition of their issues, they worked to reinscribe and confirm existing gender and class lines. In resorting to claims to power based on a forceful male leadership, the respect they demanded emphasized male respect, or respect based on a manly form of being in the world. Doing this actually bought into the domination of women. Additionally, the dominant tactic of making racial claims on expertise on the black community, while rooted in a desire to subvert white patronization and imposition, reinscribed a class hierarchy in which "we," a decidedly middle class of African Americans, are perfectly capable of making claims and decisions for a poor black community. Many of their arguments seem rooted in a claim that the black middle class, rather than the white elite, is the rightful guardian of the black poor. Moreover, while it's hard to assess the extent to which mobilized black social workers spoke for all social workers, it is apparent that on some level they did not. Not every black social worker walked out that day in May 1968. There were also black social workers of the era who did not join the up-and-coming NABSW because of fundamental disagreements about issues or tactics.[109] Though this mobilization represents a dominant trend among black social workers—and indeed, black professionals of the era writ large—it is important to recognize those black social workers who stood in opposition to the movement.

Still, without a doubt, their movement had a profound impact on the profession and practice of social work. One of its greatest triumphs is forcing a review and interrogation of the curriculum in schools of social work. A complete transformation is still elusive, but most social work education does reflect the less pathological representation of black culture and black communities that black social workers struggled for. Furthermore, the inclusion of Afrocentric visions of social work practice is a direct outcome of their efforts. Their work has also forever changed both discourse and practice around transracial adoption and black family policy, and the

NABSW should be credited for the focus on kinship care programs and familial support in the black community.

Another extremely important, though less formal, outcome of the movement is changed interaction styles and expectations for black professionals. Black professional organizing in the Black Power era demanded respect and pushed for new ways of talking to and interacting with black colleagues. Moreover, as professionals they created space for making racial claims to increased representation on committees, in leadership positions, and in hiring by black professional workers. Their organizing undeniably laid the groundwork for a new way of being a black professional as the 1960s drew to a close. Their claims were new, surprising, and shocking to white colleagues. When I spoke to Shirley Better, she told me that their white colleagues were "startled" at the claims they were making. Early NABSW members went even further and worked to create organizations that validated and justified demands about the professional place of African Americans in the field.

By making a tactical decision to withdraw from negotiations with the NCSW, the NASW, and any other white social work organizing body, the NABSW movement was at the forefront of a larger movement of black professionals seeking to organize as "technical support for the black liberation movement" (Sanders, as cited in Smith 1992:435). There is evidence that many of the Black Power-era professional associations emerged in similar ways. Many initially confronted the white-dominated professional organizations at national conferences somewhere between 1968 and 1970 followed by a series of negotiations. However, closing ranks and creating separate organizational structures was not the only way that black professionals inscribed the Black Power movement within their career worlds. On the contrary, as the earlier discussion of the Techni-Culture Movement within the National Federation of Settlements revealed, some organized black workers were successful at changing existing organizational structures and dissolved their temporary organizing structures as a result. A comparison of these two movements both highlights some important theoretical concepts in the study of social movements and sheds greater light on how the movements worked together to exact change in the social work profession.

7

Exit and Voice in Intra-Organizational Social Movements

EMERGENT MOBILIZATION FRAMEWORK

BOTH THE NABSW FOUNDERS and the social workers central to the Techni-Culture Movement acted on the perception of rising opportunities for change due to an atmosphere of uncertainty within the profession created by the gains of the civil rights movement and the rise of Black Power politics. Civil rights victories meant that by 1966, when these movements of black professionals began, legal segregation had been defeated, removing some of the obstacles to access. But the context of Black Power ushered in a new sort of ambiguity in the profession because it disturbed the racial norms and rules at a different level. The Black Power movement's calls for community control, power to the people, black pride, and the rejection of white norms and values created a sense of confusion around how black and white people would move forward together into a post-civil rights America. The movement of black social workers is just one manifestation of the contentious negotiations that characterized this era.

Doug McAdam's (1999) emergent mobilization framework attempts to explain the processes by which mobilization materializes. Recall that first, an external shock caused by broad changes destabilizes previously stable social and political relations, creating an atmosphere of uncertainty. This in turn leads everyone involved to try to make sense of the new environment, which creates space for dissidents to rise up if they perceive either an opportunity or threat. They then either appropriate existing structures or establish new mobilizing structures to carry out innovative collective action.

TABLE 7.1

	CIVIL RIGHTS	BLACK POWER	NABSW	TCM
GOALS	Access	Self-determination	Self-determination and black representation	Self-determination and multicultural representation
DOMINANT FRAMES	Rights	Empowerment	Empowerment / Social action	Empowerment / Social action
STRATEGIES	Integration	Separation	Internal bureaucratic insurgency / Exit	Internal coup / Voice
TACTICS	Marches, sit-ins, boycotts	Self-help, riots, occupation	Meeting takeovers, issuing statements	Takeovers, making statements, conference

Table 7.1 shows how the two intra-organizational social movements (IOSMs) under examination compare to the Black Power and civil rights movements in goals, frames, strategies, and tactics. While there were differences in strategy and goals, both sets of organizational activists clearly placed themselves in the Black Power tradition. I see these differences as primarily related to critical decisions made by the leaders of the two IOSMs and the organizational identity of the targets. Moreover, I argue that differences in tactics between the larger Black Power movement and these IOSMs stemmed more from the constraints of their organizational context than their ideological differences with the movement.

My analysis of the development of the National Association of Black Social Workers (NABSW) and the Techni-Culture Movement (TCM) shows that they follow closely the path McAdam suggests. The urban rebellions of the late 1960s, the *Kerner Commission Report* that implicated white institutions in urban violence, the assassination of Martin Luther King Jr.—all worked together with civil rights gains and the rise of Black Power to create instability and uncertainty within the profession. Ironically, white social workers' attempts at addressing urban unrest also contributed to the widespread dissent within the profession, as black social workers often perceived these attempts as disingenuous, half-hearted, and wrong-headed. As a result, both the NWBSW and the TCM perceived an opening within the profession to create concrete and meaningful change. In addition, both organizations were organizing within the same profession, drew on highly overlapping activist pools, and employed the language and frames of the Black Power movement. Yet in the end, the TCM appropriated existing structures while the NABSW constructed a new organization from which to mobilize.

The TCM fought from within the committees, conferences, and the board of the NFS. Not only did their action originate within the structure of the organization, but they also mobilized those structures for their own means by demanding black representation, a greater commitment to social action, and a move towards community control in local settlements. The NABSW also got their start by voicing their demands in the apparatuses of the target organization by taking over conference sessions and demanding audience with the NCSW leadership. However, these black activists withdrew their mobilization from inside the organization very early on, and created their own organizational structure for action. Still, even though the NABSW organized from outside, they did not completely withdraw from the profession or other social work professional associations. They still relied heavily on the existing structure of the organization for their actions.

But what factors explain why these two groups took different paths to activism within the profession? Why did one eventually appropriate existing structures and the other create a new one? What might the answer to this question reveal about the conditions under which groups in similar contexts would appropriate existing structures or construct new ones for mobilization? I contend that contrasting organizational identities combined with differences in leadership and key decisions that were made at crucial turning points best explain the divergent outcomes.

ORGANIZATIONAL IDENTITY

Organizational identity is defined as "that which is central, enduring, and distinctive about an organization's character" (Albert and Whetten 1985). These identities are considered to be relatively durable, so much so that the central features "are presumed to be resistant to ephemeral or faddish attempts at alteration because of their ties to the organization's history" (Gioia et al. 2000). However, the fact that organizational identities tend toward stability does not mean that such identities are not complex. They are created and maintained through the interaction between outsiders and insiders, and are susceptible to changes in interpretation and translation over time and by different actors (Gioia et al. 2000).

Related to the idea of organizational identity is organizational legitimacy. "Legitimacy is a generalized perception or assumption that the actions of an entity are desirable or appropriate within some socially constructed system of norms, values, beliefs, and definitions" (Suchman 1995:574). In other words, organizational legitimacy is the sense, by both inside and outside stakeholders, that an organization is doing the right thing. "Doing the right thing," then, is tied both to the identity of the organization and the norms of the larger culture. In both cases here, the organizational legitimacy of the target organizations—the National Federation of Settlements and the National Conference on Social Welfare—was challenged by black insiders on the basis of not living up to the value of social action and racial progressivism central to many organizations in the shifting political climate of the 1960s. This charge was less relevant, however, to the NCSW; their organizational identity did not rely on being perceived as committed to social justice and action like that of the NFS. In this way, the challenge to the legitimacy of social inaction within these two organizations was received differently by the target organizations.

The different organizational identities of the NFS and the NCSW not only shaped the structures black social workers encountered (and thus the outcomes of their movements), these identities were also manipulated by activists in their attacks. The TCM employed the strategy by accusing the NFS of failing to live up to the activist roots and legacy it prided itself on, and/or arguing that its particular style of activism could no longer suffice in comparison to the direct action central to movement politics. The NABSW activists focused on exposing and challenging the NCSW and its "unwilling[ness] to involve itself in social action," when social action was the order of the day. By appealing to the past heritage of social work in social action, these activists were pointing out and manipulating target vulnerabilities (Jasper and Poulsen 1993) very much created by the intersection of the profession's history and the historical moment at which the movements within these organizations rose up. Emerging on the heels of the civil rights movement and with Black Power ideas and riots in full swing, the TCM and the NABSW were able to exploit the idea that only social action would do—not only because black social workers said so, but because the times dictated it.

The allegation of irrelevance runs through much of the language that black social workers used during this period of organizing. This was a particularly challenging charge for a profession with such a rocky road to professionalization. The professionalization of social work was in many ways a constant struggle to stay relevant—to stay necessary and as a result continue to be seen as a legitimate profession. But as African American social workers gradually gained more power, they used evolving definitions of relevance to the advantage of their movement. In an earlier period, irrelevance may have been defined by answering the question "What do they do anyways?" Black social workers, however, attempted to redefine the idea of relevance in terms of race, asserting that in order to be relevant the profession needed to be concerned with racial justice and with trying to change the social world of their clients. For example, when black social workers accused the NCSW of being unresponsive and inadequate in their dealings with "black and brown" people, they were in essence advocating for this new racial justice definition of relevance and appropriateness in the field.

The different organizational identities of NFS and NCSW also clearly shaped their response to internal black dissent. The NFS responded with some actual concessions and recognized that times were indeed changing, so it entered a phase of serious reappraisal as reflected in the New Directions process. On the other hand, the NCSW was slow to act and maintained their ostensibly neutral position on social issues.

Because the NFS was publicly and centrally committed to social action and racial justice—or at least racial integration—they were open to the Techni-Culture Movement demands for representation. Despite the defensiveness of NFS leaders, it is clear that the Techni-Culture Movement affected them at a fundamental level. They often drew on their legacy as activists—and on the memory of Jane Addams, in particular—to figure out how to respond to the TCM's demands or to defend the work they were doing. Settlement leaders seriously grappled with accusations that they were not living up to their identity as activists and social change agents. For example, when interviewed about racial conflict within the NFS, Margaret Berry defended herself by pointing to her previous work in Pittsburgh's Hill district, a historically black neighborhood in the city. Declaring she spent ten years "in the vanguard of racial justice" there, she attempted to reclaim and reassert her identity as an activist in the face of allegations that the settlement movement had strayed too far from its activist roots.

On the other hand, the NCSW was not affected in the same way by the NABSW's demands because of their formalized stance against social action. For black social workers to challenge the NCSW, it had to be on different grounds. Rather than asking the organization to live up to its identity, these activists had to go a step further and argue that the organization's identity was wrong. This was a very different tack, but in short, the push for social action was received differently by an organization that claimed an activist identity than one that explicitly disavowed one, meaning black challengers in the NCSW had to use other tactics and lines of argument than those used by the TCM.

Finally, the different racial traditions of the National Federation of Settlements and the National Conference on Social Welfare contributed to the different outcomes of black organizing. Because of the NFS's involvement in the civil rights movement and the influence of Jane Addams's memory on the settlement movement, black social workers within the organization could call on a stated historical commitment to racial equality that settlement people felt more obligated to respond to. For example, Jane Addams is remembered as the mother of activist social work and was involved in the founding of the NAACP, which made the settlement movement an heir to the history of African American uplift. Black settlement workers explicitly drew on this past and asked contemporary settlement leadership to live up to this legacy. But the NCSW did not have this have this same storied history, nor did it or its members identify with its legacy. Accordingly, this organization did not respond as well to charges that it had not kept up with the racial times. Identity and legacy, however, were not the only factors in explaining the divergent paths of these movements.

LEADERSHIP AND STRATEGIC DECISIONS

Morris and Staggenborg (2004) consider social movement leaders to be "strategic decision-makers who inspire and organize others to participate in social movements." They also point out that a central issue to the study of social movement leadership is "the extent to which the characteristics and actions of leaders, as opposed to structural conditions, matter." In synthesizing established knowledge about social movement leaders, Morris and Staggenborg find that leaders operate within structures, influence and are influenced by movement organizations and environments, are found at different levels and perform various tasks, and sometimes pursue their own interests and maintain organizations at the expense of movement goals. They also note that different organizational structures produce different types of leaders.

The role of leaders in strategizing and framing definitively shape the course of their movements. Snow and colleagues (1986) explain that collective action frames work by diagnosing the problem, proposing the solutions, and motivating participants to be effective. Social movement organizations must thus engage in highly skilled frame alignment work. But as Morris and Staggenborg (2004) point out, the role of leadership is under-theorized in frame analysis since "social movements often emerge within indigenous institutions and organizations and social movement leaders often have prior lives that are imbedded in community institutions." So for Morris and Staggenborg (2004), analysis of leadership must take into consideration both the extent to which leaders shape and are shaped by their environment.

Understanding the way that leaders are shaped by their environment is essential to comprehending the different paths that the TCM and the NABSW took toward change. The leaders of these two movements had dissimilar relationships to the black political movement ideologies that were present at the time, and this influenced the strategic decisions they made and the frames they employed in the movement. Their decisions mark critical junctures in the trajectory of these movements, which Mahoney (2000) defines as "characterized by the adoption of a particular institutional arrangement from among two or more alternatives. These junctures are 'critical' because once a particular option is selected it becomes progressively more difficult to return to the initial point when multiple alternatives were still available" (513).

In comparing these two cases, one particular strategic decision is especially helpful in explaining why one movement lead to a separate organization while the other resulted in black incorporation: Howard Prunty's decision to provide and follow through with an ultimatum to the NCSW. Clearly, this is not the only important decision that was made, but it was a key tipping point in the NABSW organizers' withdrawal from negotiation with NCSW to focus their energies on independent "institution building." The other critical strategic decision that helps explain this puzzle is Halloway Sells's decision to transition from a black organization to a multicultural one. Though the TCM was primarily multicultural only in discourse, it laid particular expectations for the group that diverged from the separatist ideology of the Black Power movement.

By the time the 1969 NCSW forum came around, Howard Prunty had been named president of the NABSW. It was at that forum that black social workers presented a series of demands with an ultimatum that they be met by the following day. Not all of the members of the organization agreed about issuing a deadline, but Prunty was unmoved by any dissent.[1] He felt that they had been dealing with NCSW long enough and that it was time that the other side made some concrete moves. So when NABSW submitted their demands on May 26, 1969, the document's last sentence drew the line: "these demands are to be responded to by NCSW Executive Committee by Noon, Tuesday, May 27, 1969."[2] When NCSW leadership failed to reply in time, the NABSW saw two available options going forward: to show weakness on the ultimatum, or cease conversation and focus on their own organization. Following Prunty's lead, they decided on the latter.

This was by no means the only possible outcome of their mobilization. The NABSW movement started as a general desire for greater black representation and commitment to social action within the organization. It was originally conceived as an internal organization of the NCSW, in that they envisioned themselves as insiders who would push for changes from within as a black caucus of social workers. However, that view unavoidably changed after limited receptivity to their demands and, most importantly, after the failed ultimatum.

Halloway "Chuck" Sells, who emerged as the leader of the TCM, has been characterized as "somewhat of an integrationist,"[3] to the extent that people wondered how he ever came to lead a "militant" group.[4] Some felt that his "integrationist" tendencies made him more amenable to expanding the vision of the black caucus to a multicultural movement because it separated them somewhat from the feared Black Power movement. Whether this allegation is true or not, Sells's integrationist vision certainly shaped the Techni-Culture Movement's commitment to working within the NFS. In contrast to the NABSW, the TCM never seriously considered becoming a separate organization.

The move towards a multicultural frame—a model that sought the representation of all people of color on a larger scale—may have precluded the development of a separate organization. While the Black Power model of organizing clearly encouraged separate organizations, the ideas around what a multicultural organization should look like were more amorphous. But it is also important to note that the multicultural model did not work particularly well for the TCM. Although they maintained an ideological commitment to multiculturalism—and by all accounts, Sells really believed in the model—in practice black demands took precedence over all others and the leadership of the group remained black. This mismatch between the stated ideal of multiculturalism and the actual practice of the organization, which favored black interests, certainly opened the group to criticism from other people of color and the NFS leadership. This had the effect of delegitimizing the organizational model. But more than this, the TCM commitment to multiculturalism, shaky as it was, didn't offer the same sort of blueprint for building a separate organization as a commitment to black power organizing would have.

A CONCEPTUAL MODEL OF INTRA-ORGANIZATIONAL SOCIAL MOVEMENTS

Fundamentally, these movements within existing organizations were actually movements to implement the ideas, norms, and practices of the larger Black Power movement into the professional structures of American social work. As such, they are examples of movement institutionalization in the civil sphere—a part of the process of civil institutionalization, defined as the process of the routine implementation of movement ideas and practices in the institutions of the civil sphere. This development is essential to understanding how movements create, or fail to create, social change in the institutions that shape our lives.

The impact of unequal power relations can be felt throughout society. Certainly, inequality permeates social institutions beyond the state. Workplaces and educational institutions, for example, are sites where social relations happen—sites that simultaneously structure and reflect human relationships. This social fact is especially clear to those who face discrimination in the institutions they interact with in the course of their daily lives. African Americans who entered organizations that were previously either all white or in which black people were marginalized absolutely could not ignore this.

American organizations that existed prior to the civil rights movement were formed in, and often explicitly worked to maintain, racial exclusivity. So during the Black Power era, African Americans often entered organizations that were unprepared to wholly incorporate their bodies or their ideas. Integration more or less followed a predictable pattern, in which African Americans attempted to create change and whites responded by defending the status quo. As a result, it is impossible to think about the institutionalization of these movements into the civil sphere without understanding the struggle to make it happen in the first place. These cases suggest a model for understanding social movement institutionalization that places the actors responsible for demanding institutional change at the forefront rather than at the margins.

In the absence of movement-motivated leadership in an organization, interest group members—movement adherents within the institution—must engage in an intra-organizational social movement (IOSM) to institutionalize movement goals. The activists within these organizations may or may not have direct relationships to the movement they wish to institutionalize. They may be, or may have been, movement participants; participation is not strictly necessary. These movements may also, as discussed earlier, appropriate existing mobilizing structures or construct new ones. In general, there is no singular outcome that can be expected of an IOSM. On the one hand, target organizations may absorb some of the movement's elements, generating movement-motivated changes from within. Another possibility is the creation of what Rojas (2010) calls "counter-centers" within organizations. These counter-centers could take the form of standing committees or caucuses that reflect the original mobilization. On the other hand, activists may create new separate organizations within a field. The numerous black professional associations that were formed in the 1960s and 1970s are a prime example.

To be sure, there are lots of ways in which IOSMs can vary. However, I propose that all IOSMs perform at least three essential tasks in the institutionalization of larger movement goals: translation, tactical development, and issue maintenance (see table 7.2). This process also includes the management of emotional reactions to the prospect of power sharing and other forms of institutional change that may affect relationships and interactions between challengers and power-holders.

First, IOSMs are responsible for framing interests in a way that is relevant to the target institution. As adherents of the goals and ideas of the

TABLE 7.2 Functions of Intra-Organizational Social Movements

Translation	Frames interests of larger movement as relevant for the target organization
Tactical Development	Establishes and or adopts a tactical repertoire in relation to organizational norms and practices of the target organization
Issue Maintenance	Keeps movement issues on the table by maintaining issue visibility and by retaining control over issue framing

movement who are also embedded in the institutional logic of the target, IOSMs do the work of translating the movement into their organization. These movement goals may be translated into the policies of organizations or may be implemented as new norms and values within an institution. In the cases of the NABSW and the TCM, they advocated policies and norms related to new racial practices and increased social activism.

Black social workers met, hashed out, and reworked the appropriate goals and frames for implementation within their organizations. This was largely an exercise in identifying the structures within the profession that could be targeted for change. For example, black social workers made specific demands about curricular change, arguing that "schools of social welfare should move diligently to develop curricula that relate to the urban and rural needs of Black and Brown and minority group students, faculty, and the community, as well as the understanding by the white community of their participatory role in the disfunctioning of all groups of people."[5] This is a direct importation of the Black Power movement's focus on institutional racism into the institutional structures of the profession of social work. Similarly, when black psychologists called for a shift in focus from a "preoccupation with the ghetto as a source of the problems to a consideration of the institutions, practices and forces within the larger white community that contribute so heavily to the maintenance of the status quo," they were asking white researchers to turn to the problem of white racism rather than black pathology in a way that was in line with the Black Power movement's shift in focus from assimilation and integration to a black-centered model of racial justice.

Secondly, IOSMs develop tactical repertoires that are both constrained and enabled by the norms and practices of the target as well as the tactics of the larger movement. In the case of black social workers and other black professionals, the professional convention intersected with the Black Power movement to shape the repertoire such that taking over convention elements became a central tactic in their activism. The use of strategic absences was another important tactic. Strategic absence is a tactic designed to highlight a lack of commitment to movement issues on the part of a target organization by implying that the meeting or event is irrelevant to those absent. It was sometimes used in conjunction with meeting takeovers, like when black social workers' walked out of the 1968 NCSW conference. The Congressional Black Caucus (CBC) also used this tactic with a certain amount of poetry in their boycott of Nixon's 1971 State of the Union address when after being denied the president's audience for more than a year they wrote, "We now refuse to be a part of your audience." To the CBC, Nixon's refusal to hear them or to hear the opinions of black Americans indicated that his opinions on the state of the union in relation to black people could not "possibly be accurate, relative, or germane." Their absence was an obvious statement on Nixon's presidency and the way that he had been dealing with their concerns. The hypervisibility of African Americans in many of the white-dominated organizations of the period made their absence obvious. African Americans used this to their advantage to illustrate to others within their organizations their irrelevance when it came to dealing with African American issues.

Third, IOSMs engage in issue maintenance. Issue maintenance has two components. First, people within organizations interested in incorporating movement goals must take on the responsibility of keeping their issues on the table. Much of what black social workers had to do was to sustain an engagement with issues that were important to them through continuous conversations and correspondence with each other, their white coworkers, board members, and bosses in a way that maintained the visibility of their issues. However, the maintenance of movement concerns within organizations requires more than just reminding people of the movement's grievances, or more than just keeping the issue upfront and visible. Issue maintenance also refers to the practice of retaining control over the framing of these issues. For example, when black social workers within the NFS sought a black associate director, they had to resist the white-dominated leadership's inclination to transform what they thought was meaningful representation by someone who held movement-related ideas into an issue of symbolic or demographic representation. And when the NABSW launched their campaign against licensure, they wrote position papers, published articles, testified before Congress and state legislatures, and more. They had to simultaneously focus on the issue while continuing to rearticulate and reframe the problem as they conceived of it. Whereas proponents of licensing framed licensure as an issue of gaining validity as professionals, the NABSW reframed it as an issue of racial exclusion by placing the interests and experiences of African American clients and social workers at the center of the debate.

These three functions—translating movement issues, developing tactical repertoires, and issue maintenance—are certainly not the only roles that IOSMs can play. Yet these three tasks will likely be central to any intra-organizational movement intent on implementing social change. Based on this examination of black social workers' movement within their profession, I also suggest that analyses of IOSMs pay close attention to emotional processes. The management of emotions and the emotional dynamic between black and white social workers was a central problematic in this movement.

EMOTIONAL LABOR, OR "MAU MAUING"
THE SOCIAL WORKERS

Bringing Black Power into the social work profession required a certain amount of emotional labor.[6] As Wendy Moore (2008) points out in her study of race in elite law schools, students of color "must manage their emotions and the ways in which they choose to express them in order to negotiate the contradictions between their experiences in a racialized space and the institutional norms that equate objectivity with calm, disconnected emotive responses" (143). But black social workers also performed another sort of emotional labor in dealing with the emotional reactions that their white colleagues had to their demands.

In 1966, Stokely Carmichael published an essay on Black Power in the *New York Review of Books*. In it, he makes a poignant statement about white responses to Black Power that is worth quoting at length. He writes, "to most whites, Black Power seems to mean that the Mau Mau[7] are coming to the suburbs at night. The Mau Mau are coming, and whites must stop them." He points out that white Americans discuss "plots to 'get Whitey,'" which aids in the creation of "an atmosphere in which 'law and order' must be maintained." The function of this discourse, Carmichael argues, is to shift the responsibility for action "from the oppressor to the oppressed" (6).

He also addressed white reactions: "Whites chide, 'Don't forget—you're only 10 percent of the population; if you get too smart, we'll wipe you out,'" while white liberals "complain, 'What about me—don't you want my help any more?'" Carmichael slams these responses from white liberals in particular, characterizing them as "people supposedly concerned about black Americans," but who "think first of themselves, of their feelings of rejection." "Or," he notes, "they admonish, 'You can't get anywhere without coalitions,' when there is in fact no group at present with whom to form a coalition in which blacks will not be absorbed and betrayed." He then reproaches how white liberals accuse Black Power advocates "of 'polarizing the races' by [their] calls for black unity, when the true responsibility for polarization lies with whites who will not accept their responsibility as the majority power for making the democratic process work" (6).

After a discussion of what black people can do and what Black Power really means, Carmichael poses a philosophical discussion over whether white people are capable of condemning themselves for white racism—a question he had been exploring in his speeches and writings for some time. He writes,

> As for white America, perhaps it can stop crying out against "black supremacy," "black nationalism," "racism in reverse," and begin facing reality. The reality is that this nation is racist; that racism is not primarily a problem of "human relations" but of an exploitation maintained—either actively or through silence—by the society as a whole. Camus and Sartre have asked, can a man condemn himself? Can whites, particularly liberal whites, condemn themselves? Can they stop blaming us, and blame their own system? Are they capable of the shame which might become a revolutionary emotion?
>
> (8)

Here, Carmichael reflects on and challenges a prominent concept of the civil rights movement, namely Martin Luther King Jr.'s argument that the goal of the movement was "to awaken a sense of shame within the oppressor" (King 1956, as quoted in Garrow 1986). In Carmichael's view, white people were incapable of the shame and self-condemnation that King thought would be so revolutionary as to lead to a beloved community, so the Black Power movement would need to do it for them. Indeed, "revolutionary shame" was not the predominant white emotional reaction to Black Power.

Carmichael's point is especially germane in light of the emotional work that black professionals had to engage in within their professions. Writing in 1966, his words predict how many white social work professionals would respond to the demands of black social workers to incorporate the goals of the Black Power movement into the profession. The Techni-Culture Movement within the National Federation of Settlements is particularly illustrative of this. White social workers spoke of being "under attack" from black social workers and were defensive about the "race work" that they were doing. Carmichael's observation that white liberals would recenter the issue on their own feelings of rejection when confronted with Black Power bore out in the way that some in the NFS referred to the toll such reforms would take on existing white talent and how they reflected on their role as a part of the establishment. Judith Trolander (1987) would portray the rise of black leadership in the movement as an "abrupt takeover" that "was a slap in the face to many whites," which led many white settlement leaders to say, "'to hell' with the blacks" (211). Margaret Berry also confirms that "some white people, who have fought effectively for inclusiveness, now feel hurt or betrayed when they are excluded."

In 1970, Tom Wolfe published *Radical Chic and Mau Mauing the Flak-Catchers*, a literary examination of the relationship between black rage and white guilt that he saw as inherent in black white relations during the Black Power era. It was actually a collection of two essays on the subject: "Radical Chic," which dealt with white liberal fetishization of black radicalism, and "Mau Mauing the Flak Catchers," which made a case that black radicals used self-righteous anger to intimidate white liberals, social service workers in particular. He paints a picture of Black Power advocates aggressively marching down to city halls and the Office of Economic Opportunity in camouflage fatigues and leather jackets with plans to intimidate the poverty workers into funding programs they created and giving them jobs. The latter essay basically argues that African Americans capitalized on white fear by intimidating them for their own economic gain. In doing so, he creates a scene in which black people use the steam of the Black Power movement to harass well-meaning social programs and to scare the white do-gooders who worked in them.

The use of the phrase "Mau-Mauing" is particularly symbolic. While the exact origin of the term "Mau Mau" is debated, it is generally used to refer to the Kikuyu people in Kenya who led an uprising against British imperialism between 1952 and 1960. The Mau Mau were painted by the British as a violent and brutal threat to whites and became an international symbol of black anti-imperialism. This symbolism certainly resonated with segments of the American Black Power movement. For instance, several black soldiers returning from service in the Vietnam War formed a radical organization called De Mau Mau, equating their struggle to the anticolonial struggles throughout Africa (Horne 2009).

The term "Mau-Mauing," however, became widely understood as the strategic use of black anger to induce white reactions, and was popularly used to indicate a belief that black radicals were manipulating white fear as a con or hustle of sorts. In an atmosphere of heightened white fear of African Americans, this snarky term was intended to capture the emotional dynamic between Black Power advocates and white liberals, and served as an implicit indictment of both. However, how one views this dynamic is a matter of perspective.

Certainly, expressions of anger are a common feature of social movements. However, the racial dynamic of these particular sorts of displays complicates our understanding of them. For one, the notion of Mau Mauing, or to blame black activists of Mau Mauing, shifts the focus from white racism (even in its liberal forms) to black anger. This focus on black anger relies on specific racist tropes that paint both black men and women as unreasonably angry, dangerous, and violent while simultaneously depicting the white parties involved as innocent victims of black indignation rather than as active participants in liberal racism. Because these themes are all too common in American racism, discussions of emotion in race-based social movements cannot be race-neutral (see Feagin 2010, and Feagin and Harvey-Wingfield 2010 for a related analysis). Instead, these sorts of interactions have to be viewed in context.

In the context of American race relations, it is essential to recognize that white reactions to black movements are indeed emotional reactions. This is particularly important here because emotionality has tended to be studied only as it relates to groups challenging the status quo. Early theories of social movement development grew out of the distinction between "social organization," or institutionalized social life, and "collective behavior," characterized by crowds, riots, and mass movements (Park 1967). This distinction between rational and irrational social behavior was upheld by psychological and political science theories that attempted to explain social movements through concepts like "relative deprivation," a term which describes the disparity between what a group has and what they feel they should have (Gurr 1970). Gurr (1968) argues that "a psychological variable, relative deprivation, is the basic precondition for civil strife of any kind, and that the more widespread and intense deprivation is among members of a population, the greater is the magnitude of strife in one or another form" (1104). In this way, these early theories tended to treat "popular protest as a form of social pathology" (Aminzade 1984:437). Despite the depiction of social movement participants as deviant and social movements as natural acts of desperation, it is through this early tradition that social movements came to be seen as both agents of social change (Blumer 1951) and the "expression of a wider process of transformation" (Della Porta and Diani 1999:5).

As a reaction to these early characterizations of protestors as irrational and emotional, sociologists spent the 1970s and 1980s attempting to correct these narratives of social movements by rationalizing collective behavior. The most significant reaction to this idea, resource mobilization theory, holds that grievances, which are relatively stable and universal, explain very little about why social movements emerge (McCarthy and Zald 1973, 1977; Zald and Ash 1966; Snyder and Tilly 1972). Because of this, the theory pays close attention to the mechanisms that facilitate action and create the possibility for a social movement, such as the availability of various types of resources, and to the organized, rational nature of social movements. This is done through two points of analysis: (1) a focus on social movement organizations rather than individual actors, which provides a less social-psychological approach, and (2) an investigation into the dynamic accounting for the emergence, development, accomplishments and decline of social movements. Specifically, resource mobilization theory pays particular attention to factors such as the availability of resources to social movement organizations and the position of individuals in social networks, thereby stressing "the rationality of participation in social movements" (Klandermans 1984:583).

Political opportunity models are a response to both collective behavior and, in some cases, resource mobilization theories. Political opportunity theorists (Tilly 1978; McAdam 1999; Tarrow 1983, 1988, 1989; Kriesi 1995; Koopmans 1993) share a focus on the relationship between institutionalized politics and social movements. These models highlight two different relationships between conventional politics and social movements. First, they are concerned with how changes in the institutionalized political arena can create openings for social movement activity. Their second concern is with the difference in social movement dynamics based on the political characteristics of the nation of movement origin (McAdam, McCarthy, and Zald 1996).

Both resource mobilization and political process models rejected the early strict social psychological explanations of social movement participation. However, some scholars argue that the pendulum has swung too far away from social psychology. This same move has also led social movements scholars away from the analysis of grievances. For example, Aminzade and McAdam (2001) argue that as a response to "questionable assumptions about irrationality which devalued the movements in which many of them had actively participated, proponents of a resource mobilization approach were typically unwilling to incorporate emotions into their analysis" (21). In this way, these scholars bought into the problematic notion that equates "rationality with legitimacy and emotion with irrationality" (21). So, in order to show the rational nature of these movements, "they ignored emotions and implicitly accepted the assumptions of rational choice theory" (21).

However, in the last twenty years sociologists have made a return to the study of emotions in social movements. Analysts have focused on how movements manipulate emotions both as a means and an end, in addition to how emotions shape the actions of movements (Jasper 2011). A bona fide subfield of social movements studies has since emerged with a focus on emotion. The study of emotion within social movements has thrown the spotlight on the importance of emotion both as a motivating force for collective action at both the individual and collective levels and as an important dynamic within movements (Aminzade and McAdam 2001).

Researchers have also examined the role of emotion in recruiting activists, gaining confidence from movement advocates, and in developing sympathy from outsiders among many others (see Goodwin and Jasper 2006). Still, movements scholars have failed to turn the analytical lens of "the sociology of emotion" towards movement targets. This has reinforced the notion that to seek power is emotional and to hold on to power is rational or void of emotion. This is a particularly problematic frame in race-based movements because it strengthens the stereotype that people of color are emotional while white people are rational.

The truth is, white members of target organizations clearly responded at times with anger, resentment, shame, or guilt. These emotional reactions were a very real part of the movement-making process for black social workers. Black activists not only had to manage white emotional responses but also their image as emotional actors. From feeling attacked or "hurt and betrayed" when black communities and social workers rejected their help to expressing shock at the development of a black movement in the profession, the emotional responses of white social workers shaped their reaction to their black colleagues. These emotions, in concert with other racialized beliefs about African Americans, shaped both the course and outcome of these movements. Indeed, the very notion of organizational legitimacy is tied to an emotional process. Accusing the NFS of not being racially progressive created a very different reaction among the leadership of that organization than that of the NCSW leadership in the same situation.

While this study is not about these emotional processes per se, it certainly points to the need for students of social movements to address emotional processes among power holders and movement targets. This is an avenue of research that has the potential to further develop theory around emotion in movements and to help activists to better understand and engage emotions among targets. In all, to understand movements within organizations (at least those allied with a larger level movement), analysts should pay attention to how the organizational context both enables and constrains the movement.

IMPLICATIONS AND OUTCOMES

What do these cases help us understand about the conditions under which activists construct or appropriate mobilizing structures when organizing within institutions?

First, that target response to challenges is crucial. If the target institution responds somewhat favorably to the initial demands, challengers may be more likely to appropriate existing structures than those mobilizing within institutions that are hostile or indifferent to their ideas. Much of this is determined by the target institution's organizational identity. The extent to which the identity of the target organization requires ideological receptivity to the proposed ideas will shape both their response to the challengers as well as the perception of receptivity by activists. In other words, whether or not an organization has a culture that is receptive to challenges outside of its normal way of doing things is essential to understanding movement outcomes. Along these same lines, movements that challenge the legitimacy of target organizations in meaningful ways may be more likely to find ways to appropriate existing structures rather than creating separate ones.

The second implication for understanding whether groups will appropriate or create mobilizing structures is legacy and leadership. How likely are different types of challengers to integrate versus separate? Leadership may provide some insights here. In these particular cases, the different ideological and political leanings of the NABSW and TCM leaders explain a great deal. Yet their beliefs were still clearly situated in the larger context of the dominant black movement politics of the era. The Black Power movement—with its encouragement of Black Power, black pride, and the creation of independent black organizations—provided a clear design for black organizing during this period. Here, the Techni-Culture Movement case is an outlier in that the leader was something of a holdout for integration. Though the nature of the historical record favors remembering the organizing efforts that resulted in independent organizations, it does seem that many professions followed the lead of the National Association of Black Social Workers in creating separate organizations.

I have focused here on the differences in these movements within organizations to highlight the theoretical implications for understanding emergent mobilization. However, it is important to understand that these two cases were a part of a much bigger network of actions by black insiders. Social work students and faculty all across the country were organizing on their campuses for curricular changes, increased activism, and fair treatment of black students and professors. Black social workers were publishing and presenting papers on issues that were relevant to the black community and that questioned the profession's racial ideas and practices. Moreover, these challenges were also a part of a larger push to bring the movement home by African Americans in many other professions. So while their differences elucidate how dissimilar organizational types affect movements within organizations, both of these mobilizations need to be understood as parts of a wider effort to implement the Black Power movement that was going on in many arenas: the larger black radical march through the institutions.

Social movement outcomes are always hard to measure because it is difficult to determine the extent to which observed changes occur because of existing social movements as opposed to other social forces. However, in more closed systems like the social work profession, it is a bit easier to attribute changes to organizational actors and observe clear outcomes, like the fact that the NFS went into the 1970s under black leadership or how the discourse on transracial adoption was forever changed by NABSW actions. But there are other outcomes that were at least partially due to black social workers' activism. First, the very creation of the NABSW, black student organizations in schools of social work, and black caucuses in other social welfare fields changed the organizational structure of the profession, creating spaces for black social workers that simply did not exist before. These served and continue to serve as professional support systems and monitors for the field. These structures also transformed the organizational landscape of the profession in a way that attracts more African Americans and other people of color to it. Secondly, the shift in social work education to a focus on diversity beginning late in the 1960s that solidified into a focus on the structural causes of inequality in the 1980s and 1990s is unmistakably connected to black activism in the field. Finally, it was at the insistence of African Americans embedded in the profession that academic work on race and racism within the discipline of social work became increasingly credible and visible.

Overall, black social workers were among a cadre of new Black Power professionals who challenged and reworked existing norms across the various professions to reflect a Black Power ethic. In forging professional places for themselves in a new post-civil rights racial order, they in effect laid the blueprint for what it meant to be "authentically" black in the professional world. They were a part of the generation who developed the standards by which one would be judged as either "really black" or an "Uncle Tom" as African Americans moved into previously white-dominated professional worlds in great numbers. Values like "telling it like it is," calling out racist behavior when one sees it, and maintaining loyalties to the black community rather than to white employers are still a part of the constellation of principles that black professionals must, if not adhere to, then contend with as they negotiate their professional lives. The concept of racial solidarity is obviously not new to black people, nor was it the invention of the Black Power movement, but the organization of black professional associations helped to codify these sorts of standards, first through caucuses, confabs, manifestos, and codes and then through setting norms in daily interaction and in the conferences and publications of their organizations.

8

Conclusion

INSTITUTIONALIZING BLACK POWER

BECAUSE THE BLACK POWER MOVEMENT has been marginalized in the sociological study of social movements, its impacts have been underestimated. While the black cultural transformation it ushered in is critically important, the movement also had significant institutional outcomes. The Black Power movement shaped interracial interactions in established and emerging integrated organizations, and was the dominant organizing frame for African Americans seeking change within them during the late 1960s and early 1970s. The content of the movement gave form to the relationships within the organizations that African Americans found themselves in. While the civil rights movement had made great strides against racial discrimination, it had concerned itself primarily with access to institutions and organizations that had previously been closed to African Americans. But when access was finally gained, the work was not done. Indeed, African Americans mobilized Black Power ideas, norms, strategies, and tactics within a variety of organizations to hold them accountable for new norms of interracial interaction and to craft organizational structures that promoted racial equality. These struggles often resulted in the development of independent black organizations, which was in line with a central call of the Black Power movement. Most of the independent organizations that developed were founded on Black Power principles and sought to support the goals of the movement, which included challenging white racism, affirming a unique black identity, providing safe spaces to develop black agendas, and protecting the interests of African Americans embedded their institutional contexts. These institutional changes and independent organizations, many of which still exist today, are primary outcomes of the Black Power movement that are worthy of further investigation, and suggest the need for reexaminations of this era as a period of racial transformation and the movement itself as an important precursor to contemporary projects for racial equity that have benefited the black middle class.

RACE RELATIONS IN TRANSITION

Tensions and uncertainties surrounded the uneasy transition to the fuller, more complete integration happening in U.S. society during the Black Power movement. Rising numbers of black professionals entering integrated workplaces intersected with the dominance of the Black Power ideology to create some tense interracial interactions. This assessment of black social workers organizing during the movement reveals a complex set of relationships between blacks and whites, often characterized by black desires to hold whites accountable for the changes to racial etiquette and practice required by the Black Power movement along with white responses of resentment, fear, and defensiveness. These relational tensions were played out in struggles over institutional change within the profession.

This study also reflects a much broader transformation in relations between blacks and whites in American society. However, there is a relative dearth of studies that attempt to delve into the relational aspects of race relations during the transition to integration. Elizabeth Lasch-Quinn's *Race Experts* (2001) is one example. In her book, she attempts to analyze "what happened to racial etiquette in the era of integration" (8) through an examination of popular culture sources, developments in black scholarship, and the development of the "diversity industry." She writes a seething critique of the so-called race experts—the diversity counselors, academics, activists, etc.—whom she claims hijacked the colorblind vision of the civil rights movement, turning it on its head to actually reinscribe racial oppression by valuing difference rather than disavowing it. Drawing on both contemporary and historical popular culture sources, ranging from Tom Wolfe's essay "Radical Chic" to the film *Jerry McGuire*, Lasch-Quinn argues that a cultural script of black assertiveness and white submission and guilt became the central mode of "doing the interracial thing" as a result of the Black Power era.

My points of agreement with Lasch-Quinn (and this line of argument in general) are few. I do agree that it is necessary to examine this crucial transition period in race relations, and that there are insights from this period that help us to understand how American society has progressed in the project of racial justice. However, my research does not support her notion that racial etiquette shifted in such a way that black assertiveness was met with white submission. Rather, an analysis of these interactions in the field of social work shows that black demands for respect, representation, and new organizational arrangements to support these shifts were more often met with white resentment and anger rather than submission as Lasch-Quinn would suggest. Whites did not stop using belittling and patronizing language about their black colleagues even in the face of black assertion. From arguing that people of color were "beguiled by their own rhetoric" when they made demands to accusing them of being "guilty of overkill" when they were given concessions, many white reactions primarily served to downplay black concerns. Further, white leadership often found ways to subvert black demands with partial responses and symbolic concessions, continuing to feel that they knew what was best. So contrary to Lasch-Quinn's assertions, this research does not find whites simply cowering in the face of a big black threat. Still, though it is this relationship that she argues resulted in the current state of diversity politics, it is simply not the case that black requirements for racial sensitivity by whites made the bed we now lie in. Lasch-Quinn and other critics of identity politics would have us believe that whites were more than willing to throw out all racial distinctions and that black people, because they insisted on affirming a uniquely black identity and asserting new ways of doing race, are to blame for ongoing racial inequality. But the historical record simply does not support this characterization.

On the contrary, it is elite responses, rooted in a desire to maintain power relations "as is" while doling out token representation and engaging in symbolic celebrations of difference rather than really answering the call to relinquish privilege and control in favor of more egalitarian race relations that resulted in the "multiculturalism" we still see today. It is true that many whites responded to Black Power with fear, which lead them to cling more tightly to the power they had. In the case of social work professional associations, this reaction was framed as a desire to value "establishment" and to not be pressured into giving up old ways of doing things just because "hot-blooded" militant blacks said so. But the central problematic of U.S. race relations is white power, white privilege, and white racism, not some sort of adherence to domination in a general neutral sense. In this way, it is white resistance to Black Power that resulted in us missing the racial equality boat the movement may have launched.

REVISITING BLACK POWER

The important and lasting impact of African American activism in the professions forces us to rethink what Black Power was in a way that expands the boundaries of the movement. To be sure, the Black Power movement is more important than popular accounts let on. While the Black Panther Party and similar organizations were vital parts of the movement, their story is not the whole story. The truth is, African Americans who were both inspired and emboldened by the movement's ideas and figures brought Black Power with them into the institutional context of their lives. Indeed, African American professionals struggled to insert themselves and their interests into civil society through movement-like phenomena within organizations. This Black Power "march through the institutions" should be seen as a part of the movement that, while not the same as more radical manifestations of the movement, had an important impact in society. These efforts to carve out space in existing institutions and build new institutions for the purpose of developing, guarding and promoting black interests shaped and continue to shape the civil sphere in the United States.

In all, black organizing within the professions had at least three important effects. First, the creation of black professional associations—along with the creation of black studies programs, black student associations, and so forth—changed the organizational landscape that all individuals encounter as we make our way through professional training and development. The existence of black professional associations in many of the professions continues the tradition of maintaining the black institutional space that African American professionals built during the Black Power era. Secondly, that black professional associations were so strongly influenced by Black Power created a blueprint for a black professional identity and a commitment to "race politics" as a new professional ethic, an ideology which continues today and works to create a real dividing line around what it means to be authentically black in the world of professional work. Third, the activism of black professionals changed the norms of interaction between blacks and whites, creating frames for understanding workplace racism and how to go about challenging it. In many ways, these norms provide a more effective vehicle for challenging workplace racism than the relatively impotent policies developed around racial harassment. While the law purportedly protects people of color from discrimination in hiring decisions, it does little to protect them from the kinds of interpersonal racism that African Americans embedded in white organizations often face. The development of new professional norms that provide people of color a framework for checking and managing racist behavior from white colleagues is in some cases the only protection that African Americans have in the workplace, particularly against the kinds of racism that create hostile work environments.

Along with these impacts, white responses to black professional organizing laid the roots for a form of corporate and educational "diversity" project that is now nearly completely devoid of its liberatory roots in the Black Power movement. Elite responses, firmly rooted in white emotional reactions to being the targets of dissent in these institutional spaces, created a framework for conciliatory symbolic concessions that were never intended to result in actual power sharing. In other words, white resistance to relinquishing privilege—coupled with Black Power's emphasis on representation and identity—in many ways paved the path to multiculturalism. Indeed, contemporary forms of diversity and multiculturalism are often examples of the tokenism and symbolic representation that Black Power advocates struggled against: acts of recognition, celebration even, that are devoid of any challenge to existing power relations. They are exactly what Carmichael and Hamilton (1966) warned against when they said that, "Black visibility is not Black Power" (48).

Finally, these middle class black professionals, inspired by the Black Power movement, sought a solution to the white subordination of the black community through the racialization of social issues. One way to conceive of this outcome is that, whether intended or not, black social workers' solution to white patronization of the black poor can sometimes be characterized as a changing of the guard from white to black officials rather than a real challenge to the practice of social control. As Adolph Reed (1979) put it, "the movement failed because it succeeded." He argues:

Through federal funding requirements of community representation, reapportionment of electoral jurisdictions, support for voter "education" and growth of the social welfare bureaucracy, the Black elite was provided with broadened occupational opportunities and with official responsibility for administration of the Black population. The rise of Black officialdom in the latter 1970s signals the realization of the reconstructed elite's social program and the consolidation of its hegemony over Black life.

(84)

In other words, by placing black bodies in previously white positions, the movements of the period, combined with new directions in social welfare, did little to overthrow the structure of power relations that maintained domination writ large. Their success in changing professional structures and organizations, however, suggests that Black Power had unexpected benefits for the black middle class.

BLACK PROFESSIONAL ASSOCIATIONS

Citing the economic losses that black families experienced between 1968 and 1988, Audreye Johnson wrote, "NABSW arose out of the climate of times." The founding of the National Association of Black Social Workers and other organizations like it were certainly responses to economic and social crises and to white racism. But they arose out of more than just the quantitative and qualitative condition of African Americans at the time. The NABSW and its counterparts were also products of the dominance of Black Power as a political and social ideology. Many of these organizations, however, are still in existence today, which begs the following questions: do they still reflect a black power ethic? Do they still serve the same functions as they did in the late 1960s and early 1970s?

The Black Power influence is certainly still obvious in the NABSW. Their history of struggle continues to be central to the organization's contemporary identity. In the message from National Conference Co-chairs Zelma Smith and Judith D. Jackson printed in the 2008 commemorative program of the 40th meeting of the NABSW in Los Angeles, they write, "Remember why you are here! Also remember that our ancestors and founders made the supreme sacrifice to establish this significant and meaningful organization. The challenges we face today are no less than those that confronted our forefathers and foremothers. As they accepted their roles in the history of the struggle, so must we accept our roles and struggles." Then-president Gloria Batiste-Roberts also wrote:

> 40 years ago NABSW began with a dream in California that has now grown into a vibrant national organization with international influence. So, in honor of our 40 years of advocacy and activism, we have returned to California to reflect on where we have been and to honor those whose shoulders carry us still. As NABSW moves into its fifth decade, we will use our time together this week to articulate and recommit ourselves—as a group and as individuals—to 40 more years of commitment to our community.[1]

The organization clearly pays homage to their founders and sees their legacy as crucial to their current identity.

Black professional associations, while having moved closer to the professional development side of their concerns, still retain an element of the earlier focus on protest. The NABSW, for example, continues to write position papers on issues they see as important to the black community, such as a 2002 published paper on welfare reform. The organization also maintains a civil liberties and social justice task force.

Black professional associations often take on issues of interest to their profession that may not be conceived of as such by their white counterparts. One case in point is the official statement issued by Association of Black Sociologists (ABS) on the Trayvon Martin case in 2010. In February 2010, Martin, a 17-year-old African American boy, was shot and killed in Florida by George Zimmerman, a neighborhood watchman. His murder resulted in nationwide protests. In releasing such a statement, the Association of Black Sociologists affirmed its commitment to activism and encouraged sociologists to continue to use their research and other resources in the struggle against racism. The statement reads, in part,

> As an organization historically committed to community action and social transformation, the Association of Black Sociologists (ABS) stands in support of these protest efforts. We encourage all ABS members to contact your local, state, and national legislators to continue to challenge the Justice Department and FBI to thoroughly investigate the crime, apprehend Zimmerman, and secure justice not only for Trayvon Martin and his family, but

also for the nation as a whole. Furthermore, continued pressure is required to amend, reevaluate, and in many cases repeal "Stand Your Ground" legislation across this country—laws tantamount to state-sanctioned use of deadly force against innocent individuals. ABS members are encouraged to remain vigilant in the continued struggle to monitor and proactively respond to all forms of inequality experienced by marginalized people.[2]

While the activism of today's black professional associations is certainly different than the kind of activism they engaged in during the Black Power movement, it reflects a continued commitment to social justice. Statements like this suggest that black professional associations still have something unique to offer those black professionals who are interested in creating a more just and equal society.

Members of black professional associations have varied motivations for membership and can have as many different needs from their associations as there are members. Still, there is evidence that many intend to continue serving the dual functions of professional development and advancement on the one hand and addressing issues important to the black community on the other. In her 2012 presidential address, Sandra Barnes, 36th president of the Association of Black Sociologists (ABS), challenged members to

> re-imagine and re-embrace a time and a tradition of Black Sociology that reflects: 1. Our rich inheritance and customs associated with social activism; 2. Community service informed by rigorous research; 3. Dogged determinism to dismantle negative structural forces that undermine the lived experiences of oppressed groups everywhere; and 4. Personal initiative and sacrifice to think of others before ourselves.[3]

Both Dr. Batiste-Roberts and Dr. Barnes issue challenges to their members to recommit to the fight for social justice in black communities. This reflects the fact that while black professional associations today are primarily focused on professional development and coordination, the commitment to activism and racial justice remains. As such, this book identifies the space of possibility for black professional associations moving forward. One of the most important ways that black professional associations can continue to do racial justice work is by identifying the spaces within their field that affect people of color and concentrating their work there. Much like how black psychologists addressed the issue of racism in IQ testing and black social workers addressed racism in the child welfare system, today's black professional associations can focus their work to create meaningful social change within their unique spheres of influence.

Methods

THIS PROJECT IS BASED PRIMARILY on extensive archival research of several different collections of organizational records and personal papers of social work organizations and professionals. I also benefited from the generosity of a few individual social workers who shared papers from their personal collections, and was fortunate to be able to collect oral histories from some key figures in the development of Black Power mobilization within social work. In addition, I conducted participant observation at NABSW conferences to get a sense of how the historical legacy of the organization's founding shapes the contemporary organization and analyzed secondary sources for historical organizations on other professions. I used theory guided process tracing (TGPT) to examine the ways in which movement gains became institutionalized within formal organizations (Aminzade 1993).

TGPT as a method requires that researchers construct "theoretically explicit narratives that carefully trace and compare the sequences of events constituting the process" under examination (Aminzade 1993:108). These narratives "allow us to capture the unfolding of social action over time in a manner sensitive to the order in which events occur. By making the theories that underpin our narratives more explicit, we avoid the danger of burying our explanatory principles in engaging stories." Aminzade (1993) also argues that comparing sequences allows us to explore whether there are similar sequences across cases and to examine the "causes and consequences of different sequence patterns" (108). In this research project, I both traced the process of movement institutionalization and used the strategy of comparing cases to uncover the causal mechanisms that led to different outcomes in the two organizational movements.

The focus on organizational processes is particularly well-suited to historical sociological research. As Skocpol (1987) points out, "social relationships are the key objects of research, as embodied in networks, communities, associations, or large-scale complex organizations." It is through these "concrete, relational units," she continues, "that lived experiences and structural transformations meet." These are the processes that are most amenable to historical sociological methods. This project seeks to explore this development by understanding how the intense transformation brought on by the civil rights and Black Power movements affected relationships and processes within the profession of social work to understand how institutional change occurs—or fails to occur—after a movement wave creates social change.

What I found is that institutional change happens because the struggle continues. All Americans were not willing, enthusiastic participants in the rights revolution and were certainly not interested in anything called "Black Power." Black people embedded in social institutions had to continue to push the contexts of their lives to catch up to the new black identity being forged in the Black Power revolution. Their stories are at least partially told in the documents of organizations, in the meeting takeovers, in the letters between colleagues, in the transcripts of meetings and conferences, and in the newsletters and announcements they produced. These stories are an important part of how real change happens, or at least has the potential to happen, when a powerful social movement grips a society.

In order to trace the process of movement institutionalization in these cases, I carefully analzyed both organization-level and personal papers. Many of the collections I utilized are exceptionally complete and contain many different kinds of documents. I relied most heavily on the minutes or complete transcripts of committee meetings, staff meetings, special meetings, conferences, and training courses. I also studied written correspondence such as letters and memos, news clippings, publications (i.e. organization newsletters and mailings), written statements, and "sense of meeting" documents. I supplemented the official collections of organization and personal papers with the private (published and unpublished) collections of black social workers active during the period under examination.

Starting from a set of theoretical and conceptual ideas, I developed questions about the empirical case. Then, by scouring finding aids and through in-depth conversations with archivists, I made decisions about which boxes and folders to examine. I spent over a year exploring and re-exploring documents, starting with a preliminary scan of the relevant collections and creating a descriptive database system with FileMaker Pro to categorize each relevant document with a summary. I also photocopied hundreds of documents so that I would have my own personal "mini-collection" of sorts related to issues of race, social movements, and organizational change. Lastly, I took great care to engage the iterative relationship between my theoretical conceptions and what I could actually observe in the archives in order to feel confident that the questions I was asking, or what I was looking for, would help me to reach my project's objectives before beginning the data collection in earnest. The database template is the outcome of that process.

Figure Ap.1 is a screenshot of the FileMaker Pro record template that is the result of my preliminary research, which allowed me to refine the descriptive and analytical categories I was interested in. The database allowed me to record the location of the document, check relevant categories, provide a summary, indicate whether I had a copy available, and specify what kind of document it was (e.g. minutes, letter, brochure, etc.). I also had space to provide initial thoughts and interpretations on the document. By the end of my research, I had a searchable database of hundreds of documents with a reference to it archival location and/or its location in my mini-collection.

Once the database and photocopies of relevant documents was complete, I conducted both inductive and deductive coding of the archival sources. The documents were analyzed by organizing them temporally, by organization, and by topic. This process tracing method involved creating timelines of "events" (e.g. meetings, speeches, mailings, letters, etc.) that related to issues of civil rights, Black Power, race in general, and/or dissent by black social workers for each organization to get a handle on what actually happened. Then, I reread the timelines more closely for recurring themes, ideas, and issues related to the topic at hand over time to decide how to organize the narrative and decide whether (and how) my analytic frames—relating to organizational theory, social movements, and race relations—related to the data.

Document Title Document

Date Date

Collection Name Collection

Box Number Box Number

File Number File Number

Topic

- ☐ Racial Discourse
- ☐ Movement Discourse
- ☐ Direct Pressure
- ☐ NABSW
- ☐ Techni-Culture Movement
- ☐ Conference Disturbance
- ☐ Alinsky
- ☐ Riots

- ☐ Gender
- ☐ Black Caucus
- ☐ Poor People's March
- ☐ March on Washington
- ☐ Civil Rights Movement
- ☐ Drake Study
- ☐ Who We Are/What We Do
- ☐ Training Center

- ☐ Militants/Radicals
- ☐ Participating in Social Action
- ☐ Labor
- ☐ Poverty
- ☐ Culture of Poverty Explanations
- ☐ Internal Dissent
- ☐ General Social Work Info
- ☐ Urban, Ghetto, Inner-city

Summary Summary

Copy? Copy

Document Type

- ☐ Board Meeting Minutes
- ☐ Executive Committee Minutes
- ☐ SEA Committee Minutes
- ☐ Other Committee/Minutes/Define in Summary
- ☐ Brochure
- ☐ Training Manual
- ☐ Letter/Define in Summary
- ☐ Mailing
- ☐ Newsletter

- ☐ Newspaper Clipping
- ☐ Financial Records
- ☐ Conference Proceedings
- ☐ General Publication
- ☐ Outside Publication
- ☐ Statements to Congress or House
- ☐ Internal Report or Statement
- ☐ External Report or Summary

Thoughts/ Interpretations Thoughts/Interpretations

FIGURE AP.1 FileMaker Pro record template.

ORAL HISTORIES

While my main data sources were primary documents, I also conducted oral history interviews with prominent activists in the movements under examination. I used these histories to triangulate findings, check facts and interpretations, and to shed light on participant perceptions. The interviews lasted between two and three hours, and covered respondents' recollections of their involvement and the trajectory of their work in the NABSW and the NFS. I followed a simple interview guide to help the respondents recall specific events or issues. For the most part, however, the interviews involved long stretches of storytelling about the events from that period in their life. In all of the interviews, we also engaged in useful dialogue about the project itself and my interpretations of the events that they had been involved in.

Historians and social scientists alike have contested the merits of using oral history as a research method, but I believe that the method is particularly useful in triangulating data from archival sources when participants are available. In this way, oral histories are used less as a record of social fact than as a barometer of the validity of written sources. Though critics have argued that human memory is an imperfect record of the past, as Alessandro Portelli (1991) notes, "oral sources are credible, but with *different* credibility. The importance of oral testimony may lie not in its adherence to fact, but rather in its departure from it, as imagination, symbolism, and desire emerge. Therefore, there are no 'false' oral sources" (68).

Despite the potential pitfalls of oral histories, their use in this project has been extremely valuable. While the recollection of a few activists isn't enough to analyze the development of a movement, it was critical for me to have their memory as a check against what I was seeing in the archives and my own interpretation of their thinking at the time. For example, my sense throughout the analysis of the primary documents was that these movements were very much male-centered and that there was some level of tension between men and women. In asking activists about the relationship between men and women during these campaigns, it became clear that, indeed, this was the case. Dr. Better would personally confirm this by discussing the fact that relations had seemed somewhat egalitarian in her recollection, except that women were never considered for leadership positions. It was important to me to verify if mentions of a demand for male leadership were, in this case, actually indicative of a larger gendered process in the movements. The oral history interviews provided that verification.

Moreover, while human memory provides an imperfect record of human history, when the question at hand is about participant's feelings, perceptions, or reactions during historical events, sometimes memory is all we have. Therefore, there are questions for which there are no other sources but recollection. One case in point was that I had very little record of how TCM activists responded to Walter Smart after he was hired as associate director or once he was promoted to executive director. Only through my conversation with Dr. Karanja, who when asked what they thought of him said that they perceived him to be a "company man," could I confirm what had been little more than an educated assumption on my part. Further, oral histories helped me to get a handle on what social workers at the time saw as important to explain the emergence of their movement. For example, all of the social workers I interviewed singled out the urban rebellions in the late 1960s as central forces in the impetus to organize.

In all, this methodological approach provided important insights into organizational dynamics during the period under examination. As organizational actors were navigating the tumult of uncertainty presented by both external and internal movement dynamics, they were constantly reviewing, reflecting, adjusting, and readjusting. Documents and the imperfect human memory cannot tell all, but it is possible to catch a glimpse of these processes through them. Organizational records do provide a story (though certainly not the only story) about organizational change. Through careful process tracing and strategic narrative construction analysts can piece together a picture of conflict in organizations. It has been my intention to do this as accurately as possible for the cases at hand.

ARCHIVAL SOURCES

Garland Jaggers Document Collection, published as an appendix to Jaggers 2003.

Lexis-Nexis Black Power Microfilm Series, accessed at the Schomburg Center for Research in Black Culture.

Margaret Berry Personal Papers, Social Welfare History Archives, University of Minnesota.

National Association of Social Workers and Predecessor Organizations, Social Welfare History Archives, University of Minnesota.

National Federation of Settlements and Neighborhood Centers Records, Social Welfare History Archives, University of Minnesota.

Shirley Better Personal Papers, Private Collection.

Verne Weed Collection for Progressive Social Work, Social Welfare History Archives, University of Minnesota.

ORAL HISTORY RESPONDENTS

Shirley Better

Jay Chunn

Douglas Glasgow

Garland Jaggers

Sokoni Karanja (formerly Lathan Johnson)

ORAL HISTORY GUIDING QUESTIONS

Tell me a little bit about how you got into social work.

What was it like being a social worker during the civil rights era?

How do you think the Black Power movement affected social workers?

How did you get involved with the NABSW/TCM?

Why did you become president of the organization? (if applicable)

What were the major issues of concern during your presidency? (if applicable)

What is your take on why the NABSW/TCM was started?

What were the conflicts with mainstream social work that lead to the founding?

What were the conflicts between black social workers themselves about these issues?

Were the disagreements about issues or tactics?

Would you say there were disagreements between men and women?

Did most black social workers see themselves as activists during this period?

Was the profession in general leaning towards more social action or not?

In addition to forming new organizations, what other ways did black social workers challenge the profession?

In retrospect, how do you think the activism of black social workers within the profession changed social work as a whole, or did it?

Would you be open to follow up questions if they arise?

Anything else you want to tell me about this time in your life?

Founding Dates of Black Professional Associations

1966	Black Stuntmen's Association
1967	National Black Law Students Association
	Negro Airmen International
1968	Association of Black Psychologists
	Association of Black Sociologists
	National Association of Black Social Workers
	National Black Catholic Clergy Caucus
	National Black Sisters' Conference
	National Conference of Black Lawyers
1969	Congressional Black Caucus
	National Association of Black Accountants
	Caucus of Black Economists (later the National Economic Association)
	African American Women's Clergy Association
1970	Association of Black Anthropologists
	Black Awareness in Television
	Black Caucus of the American Library Association
	Black Retail Action Group
	International Association of Black Professional Fire Fighters
	National Alliance of Black School Educators
	National Black Caucus of Local Elected Officials
	National Black Child Development Institute
	National Black MBA Association
1971	Conference of Minority Public Administrators
	Conference of Minority Transportation Officials

National Black Nurses Association

National Organization of Black Architects (later renamed the National
Organization of Minority Architects)

National Podiatric Medical Association

1972   Coalition of Black Trade Unionists

National Black McDonald's Operators Association

National Black Police Association

National Organization for the Professional Advancement of Black
Chemists and Chemical Engineers

National Association for the Study and Performance of
African-American Music

National Association of Minority Women in Business

National Minority Supplier Development Council

1974   Association of Black Cardiologists

Black Flight Attendants of America

International Black Writers and Artists

National Association of Blacks in Criminal Justice

National Conference of Black Mayors

1975   Black Data Processing Associates

National Association of Black County Officials

National Association of Black Journalists

National Society of Black Engineers

1976   Association of Black Women Attorneys

National Association of Black Owned Broadcasters

National Black Coalition of Federal Aviation Employees

National Organization of Black Law Enforcement Executives

Organization of Black Airline Pilots

1977   National Society of Black Physicists

1978   Black Filmmakers Foundation

National Black Association for Speech-Language and Hearing

1979   Association of Black Women in Higher Education

Black Entertainment and Sports Lawyers Association

In keeping with disciplinary standards, I have used *Chicago Manual of Style* author/ date style citations in the notes. However, for ease of reading, I have followed humanities style when documenting primary sources, manuscript collections, interviews, and other firsthand accounts.

FOREWORD

1 Not her real name.
2 The black freedom movement describes the ideologically diverse organized struggle against racial oppression unfolding among African Americans from the mid-1950s through the early 1970s, although its roots extend decades earlier.

1. INTRODUCTION: RACE, RESISTANCE AND THE CIVIL SPHERE

1 I use the terms "black" and "African American" interchangeably. In keeping with convention, I do not capitalize the word "black" when referring to African Americans. However, it was a common practice of Black Power advocates to capitalize the word. I retain the original capitalization in quotes.
2 Shirley Better, oral history interview by Joyce Bell, May 28, 2006, audio recording, in author's possession. See also Jaggers 2003; Johnson 1988; Vasey 1968.
3 Better, interview.
4 Ibid.

5   "Position Statement of the National Association of Black Social Workers," May
    29, 1968, appendix to Jaggers 2003.

6   Ibid.

7   Ibid.

8   Glide Memorial Church has a long history of providing space for counter-
    conventions in San Francisco. During the 1960s Glide Memorial church pro-
    vided safe spaces for several radical organizations including the American In-
    dian Movement and the Black Panthers ("Our Story," accessed June 19, 2013,
    http://66.211.107.100/page.aspx?pid=412). The Society for Women in Sociol-
    ogy also held a counter-convention there in 1969.

9   Larry Dum, "400 Black Social Aides Walk Out of Meet Here," *San Francisco
    Examiner*, May 28, 1968; Better, interview; Jay Chunn, oral history interview
    by Joyce Bell, May 22, 2006, audio recording, in author's possession. See also
    Jaggers 2003.

10 Better, interview.

11 Ibid.

12 Mary Fainsod Katzenstein (1998) provides an excellent account of how the
    women's movement was brought into the military and church. Her study de-
    tails the changes made in these powerful yet (at least in the case of the church)
    non-governmental sites.

13 There is considerable debate over the definition and usage of the term "civil
    society." I adopt a simple definition that refers to associational life without en-
    gaging in debates over the relationship between civil society, the state, and the
    market. For excellent treatments of the debate over the concept, see Alexander
    2006; Bryant 1993; Edwards 2004; and Kumar 1993.

14 McAdam and Scott (2005) argue that the institutionalization of the rights
    revolution, and the black movement in particular, happened in two processes:
    the creation of regulatory fields and the broad effect of the rights revolution on
    other established fields during the latter (post-1970) period of the black move-
    ment. Several excellent studies detail the first process. Stryker and Pedriana
    (2004), for example, focus on how protest increases the capacity of the state
    to enforce the rules ushered in or otherwise reinforced by movements. Simi-
    larly, Walton's (1988) study of civil rights regulatory agencies describes the ways
    in which the civil rights movement was institutionalized within the state as
    an enforcement tool. Kenneth Andrews's (2004) research has focused on how
    the civil rights movement affected electoral politics in the American South.

John Skrentny (2002) has also explored the creation of civil rights regulatory agencies and the rise of affirmative action policy as a result of the civil rights movement.

15   I use the term "intra-organizational social movements" to distinguish from the state-level social movements I reference throughout, such as the civil rights, Black Power, and welfare rights movements.

16   Zald and Berger (1978) introduced the idea that movement-like processes often occur within organizations. They argue that these phenomena are important to understand because "they affect the major priorities of organizations, the control of organizational resources, organizational survival, and growth" (824). They further argue that these internal movements "reflect the larger trends and politics of society" in that "social movements in organizations are often the situs for the working out of political issues . . ." (825).

2. RE-ENVISIONING BLACK POWER

1   For an excellent review of the Black Power studies subfield, see Joseph 2008. See also Goldberg and Griffey 2010, on Black Power in the construction industry; Tibbs 2012, on the role of the movement on prisoner unions; and the essays in Warren-Hill and Rabig 2012 on Black Power, community development, and business.

2   "Massive resistance" was the name given to the practice of resisting school integration after the *Brown* decision. White politicians as well as ordinary citizens fiercely protected segregation. This resistance served as the impetus for the direct action phase of the civil rights movement (see Webb 2005 for a full analysis).

3   There are several books detailing the history of the Black Panther Party. See Jones 1998 and Foner 1995.

4   The Black Power movement experienced extreme state repression. Ranging from the direct execution of movement leaders and the imprisonment of activists to the infiltration and destruction of movement organizations, this repression of the Black Power movement was central to its decline in the 1970s.

5   COINTELPRO is the acronym for the U.S. government's Counter Intelligence Program, which monitored, infiltrated, and disrupted various movement groups. Their records, which became available under the Freedom of Information Act, have been important in the study of radical movements.

6   The National Conference on Black Power, resolutions, July 23, 1967, in *The Black Power Movement, Part 1: Amiri Baraka from Black Arts to Black Radicalism*, reel 1. Black Studies Research Sources: 2001.

7   Ibid.

8   Ibid.

3. BLACK POWER PROFESSIONALS

1   The Voting Rights Act of 1965 was a follow-up piece of legislation that outlawed literacy tests and other discriminatory voting practices and allowed for federal oversight of the voting process.

2   Many important black political figures drew this connection, including Malcolm X and Stokely Carmichael. There are also important writings by black scholars on the subject. See also Cruse 1962 and Allen 1969.

3   U.S. Congress, Senate Congressional Record, 92nd Cong., 1st sess., March 30, 1971, speech by Charles C. Diggs Jr., as cited in Barnett 1975.

4. "A NICE SOCIAL TEA PARTY": THE ROCKY RELATIONSHIP BETWEEN SOCIAL WORK AND BLACK LIBERATION

1   Larry Dum, "400 Black Social Aides Walk Out of Meet Here," *San Francisco Examiner*, May 28, 1968.

2   Memorandum, "Social Action Methods in the Practice of the National Federation of Settlements and Neighborhood Centers," February 18, 1960, box 23, folder 5, National Federation of Settlements and Neighborhood Centers (NFSNC) Records, Social Welfare History Archives, University of Minnesota. Hereafter cited as NFSNCR.

3   Ibid.

4   Executive Committee Meeting Minutes, 1963, box 1, folder 4, NFSNCR.

5   Ibid.

6   Gertrude Keefe to Gladys Duppstadt, 1963, box 33, folder 11, NFSNCR.

7   National Federation of Settlements (hereafter cited as NFS), report, *Settlement Participation in the March on Washington*, October 1963, box 33, folder 14, NSFNCR.

8   Ibid.

9   Ibid.

10 Letter to Margaret Berry, "Re: Role of Settlements in Civil Rights," n.d., box 33, folder 11, NFSNCR.

11 Ibid.

12 NFS, *Settlement Participation in the March on Washington.*

13 NFS, report, *General Purpose of Sub-Committee on Civil Rights,* 1964, box 23, folder 1, NFSNCR.

14 Arthur Hilman, "Notes and Comments on the Alinsky Approach," n.d., box 19, folder 2, NFSNCR.

15 NFS, *Report on Civil Rights Questionnaire,* April 1964, box 23, folder 2, NFSNCR.

16 Ibid.

17 Margaret Berry (1915–2002) was an internationally recognized leader in social work, and was the executive director of the National Federation of Settlements from 1959 to 1971. Her presidency would be marked by profound challenges, especially regarding race within social work. Berry, a white woman, would eventually find herself at the center of the struggles by black social workers to gain leadership within the profession.

18 NFS, *Executive Report to the Board,* January 1965, box 1, folder 5, NFSNCR.

19 National Urban League, press release, May 22, 1964, box 33, folder 14, NFSNCR.

20 Ibid.

21 DeLeslie Allen, "The Role of the Settlement in Civil Rights," speech given at the Annual Meeting of the Delaware Valley Settlement Alliance, October 11, 1965, box 169, folder 1, NFSNCR.

22 Ibid.

23 Ibid.

24 Ibid.

25 Ibid.

26 St. Clair Drake, report, *Race Relations in a Time of Rapid Social Change,* 1966, box 149, folder 5, NFSNCR.

27 *National Federation of Settlements Roundtable,* newsletter, December 1966, box 185, folder 16, NFSNCR.

28 Ibid.

29 Herbert Brunson, "Final Report on Freedom Community Centers," box 1, folder 7, NFSNCR.

30 Margaret Berry to Social Welfare History Archives staff during archive collection process, n.d., box 150, folder 1, NFSNCR.

31 Reports, Al Rhodes and Coleman Miller to Margaret Berry, 1966–1969, box 150, folder 1, NFSNCR.

32 Ibid.

33 Ibid.

34 Ibid.

35 The Mississippi Sovereignty Commission was a domestic spy operation (similar to COINTELPRO) that was actively monitoring Mississippi civil rights movement activities between 1956 and 1977. Their records were released by a court order as a result of a lawsuit brought forward by a group led by the ACLU.

36 Margaret Berry to Social Welfare History Archives staff during archive collection process, n.d., box 150, folder 1, NFSNCR.

37 Herbert Brunson, *Final Report on Freedom Community Centers*, box 1, folder 7, NFSNCR.

5. "WE STAND BEFORE YOU, NOT AS A SEPARATIST BODY": THE TECHNI-CULTURE MOVEMENT TO GAIN VOICE IN THE NATIONAL FEDERATION OF SETTLEMENTS

1 Quoted in *National Federation of Settlements (NFS) News and Round Table*, "Hammering out the American Dream," July 1968, box 158, folder 8, NFSNCR.

2 Resolutions of the Black Caucus of the Inner City Violence Conference, Chicago, Ill., October 7, 1968, box 158, folder 8, NFSNCR.

3 Ibid.

4 Ibid.

5 *The Black Caucus Position Paper on New Directions for Settlements*, 1968, box 158, folder 8, NFSNCR.

6 Ibid.

7 Black Caucus to NFS Leadership, memorandum, "Rationale for Conference," box 45, folder 3, NFSNCR.

8 The Detroit Revolutionary Union Movement organization was a militant black union of autoworkers that was organized to respond to racism in their workplace and within the autoworkers' unions. See Geschwender 1977; Georgakas and Surkin 1998.

9 Response to survey on support for Black Conference, n.d., box 3, folder 7, NFSNCR.

10 Margaret Berry to John Austin, January 8, 1970, box 3, folder 7, NFSNCR.

11 Black Caucus of the NFS to NFS leadership and executive board, memo-
    randum, "Why and How a Techni-Culture Conference," box 158, folder 8,
    NFSNCR.

12 "Technicolor" is the name of the process of creating color film. The term was
    popular in the mid to late 1960s and coincides with the popularization of color
    television.

13 Black Caucus to NFS Leadership, memorandum, "Rationale for Conference,"
    box 45, folder 3, NFSNCR.

14 Ibid.

15 John Austin to Margaret Berry, February 6, 1970, box 3, folder 7, NFSNCR.

16 Margaret Berry to John Austin, March 4, 1970, box 3, folder 7, NFSNCR.

17 "Techni-Culture Conference Statement," report presented to the NFS Board
    of Directors, Chicago, Ill., February 28, 1970, box 45, folder 3, NFSNCR.

18 Clipping, *The Cincinnati Post and Times Star,* May 30, 1970, box 158, folder 8,
    NFSNCR.

19 NFS, transcript, annual business meeting, May 30, 1970, box 43, folder 6,
    NFSNCR.

20 Ibid.

21 Margaret Berry to executives and board presidents of Member Houses, July 8,
    1970, box 116, folder 1, NFSNCR.

22 Ibid.

23 NFS, minutes of the executive committee meeting, October 2, 1970, box 2,
    folder 4, NFSNCR.

24 Margaret Berry to John Austin, January 8, 1970, box 3, folder 7, NFSNCR.

25 Margaret Berry to John Austin, March 4, 1970, box 3, folder 7, NFSNCR.

26 "Techni-Culture Conference Statement."

27 Lindsay Miller, clipping, "Daily Closeup," *New York Post*, February 11, 1972,
    box 132, folder 5, NFSNCR.

28 Walter Smart, testimony before Subcommittee of the Committee on Resolu-
    tions and Platform, 1972 Republican National Convention, box 23, folder 6,
    NFSNCR.

29 NFS, full-page promotion advertisement, n.d., box 129, folder 19, NFSNCR.

30 For a full treatment of this conflict, see Trolander 1982.

31 NFS, packet of materials about Alinsky and his organizations distributed to
    member agencies, February 1967, box 19, folder 2, NFSNCR.

32 Margaret Berry to member organizations, September 9, 1966, box 23, folder 5,
    NFSNCR.

33 Houston Community Center, report, "Story of Black Power Dialogue with a Community Center," box 169, folder 1, NFSNCR.

34 Ibid.

35 Eleanor Hardy, report, *Rendering Settlement Services in a Predominately Black Community*, 1967, box 169, folder 1, NFSNCR.

36 DeLeslie Allen, memorandum to board presidents, October 1967, box 169, folder 1, NFSNCR.

37 Ibid.

38 NFS, minutes of the Board Training Institute, October 19, 1968, box 133, folder 11, NFSNCR.

39 National Federation of Settlements and Neighborhood Centers, *News and Round Table*, January 1969, box 158, folder 8, NFSNCR.

40 Margaret Berry, address delivered to the General Assembly of the NFS Conference, Houston, Tex., May 23, 1968, box 133, folder 11, NFSNCR.

41 Meeting minutes, New Directions Committee meeting with Connecticut and Rhode Island regional agencies, October 18, 1968, box 133, folder 11, NFSNCR.

42 Ibid.

43 Ibid.

44 NFS, minutes, executive committee meeting, April 19, 1968, box 2, folder 2, NFSNCR.

45 NFS, minutes, New Directions Committee meeting, May 22, 1968, box 133, folder 11, NFSNCR.

46 Margaret Berry, "All Points of View." *NFSNC News and Round Table*, January 1969, box 158, folder 8, NFSNCR.

47 See Aminzade and McAdam 2001; Hercus 1999; and Jasper 1998 for an introduction to the literature on social movements and emotions.

48 Aminzade and McAdam 2001 (pp. 49–50) discuss the methodological difficulties of examining historical documents for emotional tone.

49 John Austin to Margaret Berry, June 4, 1970, box 3, folder 7, NFSNCR.

50 Mrs. Anderson Page to Margaret Berry, June 22, 1970, box 3, folder 7, NFSNCR.

51 Gordon Herstlet to John Austin, 1970, box 117, folder 1, NFSNCR.

52 Margaret Berry, address delivered to the General Assembly of the NFS Conference, Houston, Tex., May 23, 1968, box 133, folder 11, NFSNCR.

53 James Adams, "Strange Welcome: Convention Finds Policy Under Fire From Hosts," *Cincinnati Enquirer*, May 30, 1970, box 23, folder 6, NFSNCR.

54 John Austin to Margaret Berry, July 1, 1968, box 3, folder 6, NFSNCR.

55 Margaret Berry to John Austin, July 11, 1968, box 3, folder 6, NFSNCR.

56 Margaret Berry to John Austin, March 8, 1970, box 3, folder 6, NFSNCR.

57 James Adams, "Strange Welcome: Convention Finds Policy Under Fire From Hosts."

58 NFS, bulletin, Techni-Culture Conference, n.d., box 158, folder 8, NFSNCR.

59 Ibid.

6. "WE'LL BUILD OUR OWN THING": THE EXIT STRATEGY OF THE NATIONAL ASSOCIATION OF BLACK SOCIAL WORKERS

1 For other accounts of the NABSW movement, see Bell 2007 and Reid-Meritt 2010.

2 National Association of Social Workers (NASW), Proceedings of NASW's National Social Action Workshop on the Urban Crisis, April 25–27, 1968, box 3, folder 34, Verne Weed Collection for Progressive Social Work Records, Social Welfare History Archives, University of Minnesota. Hereafter cited as Verne Weed Collection.

3 Charles V. Hamilton is a political scientist and coauthor of *Black Power: The Politics of Liberation in America* with Stokely Carmichael. Carmichael and Hamilton were the first authors to develop and systematically apply the concept of institutional racism. Alvin Poussaint is a renowned expert on African American psychiatry. His work focuses on the role of racism in African American mental health. In 1965 he served as the southern field director of the Medical Committee, which provided health care to southern activists and worked towards desegregating southern hospitals. He is also a founding member of Jesse Jackson's Operation PUSH (People United to Serve Humanity). Richard Cloward was a sociologist and activist who was the cofounder of the National Welfare Rights Organization. During the late 1960s, he and his wife Frances Fox Piven were publishing on the issue of welfare rights and were advocates of radical changes in social welfare.

4 NASW, Proceedings of NASW's National Social Action Workshop on the Urban Crisis, 1968, box 3, folder 34, Verne Weed Collection.

5 Ibid.

6 Ibid.

7 Ibid.

8 Ibid.

9 Audreye Johnson, "A Week of History: NABSW May 26–30, 1968," paper delivered at NABSW conference, 1978, Shirley Better personal collection.

10 Douglas Glasgow, oral history interview by Joyce Bell, April 4, 2008, audio recording, in author's possession.

11 Ibid.

12 Garland Jaggers, oral history interview by Joyce Bell, April 3, 2008, audio recording, in author's possession; Glasgow, interview.

13 See discussion below on Confab in Black conference.

14 John C. Kidneigh, "The New York Conference Story," in National Conference on Social Welfare, *Official Proceedings of the Annual Meeting: 1969* (Ann Arbor: University of Michigan Library, 2005), 178–84.

15 Margaret Berry, essay, "Partial View of 96th NCSW, May 25–29, 1969," box 3, folder 7, Margaret Berry Papers, Social Welfare History Archives, University of Minnesota. Hereafter cited as MBP.

16 John C. Kidneigh, "The New York Conference Story."

17 Berry, "Partial View of 96th NCSW, May 25–29, 1969."

18 Ibid.; Francis X. Cline, clipping, "Militants Renew Protest at Welfare Conference." *New York Times*, May 27, 1969, box 3, folder 7, MBP.

19 Eve Edstrom, clipping, "Radicals' Demands Stun and Polarize Welfare Leaders," *The Washington Post*, June 1, 1969, box 3, folder 7, MBP.

20 Jay Chunn, oral history interview by Joyce Bell, May 22, 2006, audio recording, in author's possession; Berry, "Partial View of 96th NCSW, May 25–29, 1969."

21 Berry, "Partial View of 96th NCSW, May 25–29, 1969."

22 Ibid.

23 Ibid.

24 Cline, "Militants Renew Protest at Welfare Conference."

25 Berry, "Partial View of 96th NCSW, May 25–29, 1969."

26 Ibid.; Francis X. Cline, "Group Will Seek Militants' Fund," *New York Times*, May 27, 1969.

27 Sumati N. Dubey, John B. Turner, and Magdalena Miranda, "Black Unity & Self Determination: Social Welfare Implications," in National Conference on Social Welfare, *Official Proceedings of the Annual Meeting: 1969* (Ann Arbor: University of Michigan Library, 2005), 118–130.

28 Howard Prunty, "The New York Story—A Participants Viewpoint," in National Conference on Social Welfare, *Official Proceedings of the Annual Meeting: 1969* (Ann Arbor: University of Michigan Library, 2005), 185–193.

29 Edstrom, "Radicals' Demands Stun and Polarize Welfare Leaders."; Berry, "Partial View of 96th NCSW, May 25–29, 1969."

30 Chunn, interview.

31 National Association of Black Social Workers (NABSW), "Position Statement of the National Association of Black Social Workers," May 26, 1969, Garland Jaggers Document Center, included as an appendix to Jaggers 2003. Hereafter cited as GJDC.

32 Better, interview.

33 Chunn, interview.

34 Association of Black Catalysts (ABC), conference summary, "Chicago Catalysts Declare War on White Racism," n.d., GJDC.

35 Ibid.; Johnson 1975.

36 ABC, "Chicago Catalysts Declare War on White Racism."

37 ABC, "Invitation to Participate in a Confab in Black," n.d., Shirley Better personal collection.

38 ABC, "Chicago Catalysts Declare War on White Racism."

39 Ibid.

40 Ibid.

41 Ibid.

42 Ibid.

43 ABC, *This is Our Bag: Code of Ethics for Black People*, appendix to Johnson 1975.

44 Ibid.

45 Ibid.

46 Ibid.

47 Ibid.

48 Ibid.

49 Ibid.

50 William T. Greene, "Editorial," *NABSW News*, January 1973, box 1, folder 14, Verne Weed Collection.

51 Shirley Better, Founders Forum speech, 2005. Shirley Better personal collection.

52 Ibid.

53 Jaggers, interview.

54 Glasgow, interview.

55 Chunn, interview; NABSW, "Position Paper on Welfare Reform," 1977, box 3, folder 41, Verne Weed Collection.

56 Leora Neal, "Black Adoption Program," *ABSW New York Chapter News*, January 1975, box 3, folder 41, Verne Weed Collection.

57 Sokoni Karanja (formerly Lathan Johnson), oral history interview by Joyce Bell, May 30, 2006, audio recording, in author's possession.

58 Jaggers, interview.

59 ABC, "Chicago Catalysts Declare War on White Racism."

60 Greene, "Editorial."

61 Better, interview.

62 NABSW, "Position Statement of the National Association of Black Social Workers Concerning Neutralizing Racism in Schools of Social Welfare in General and Berkeley School of Social Welfare in Particular," n.d., box 3, folder 7, MBP.

63 Berry, "Partial View of 96th NCSW, May 25–29, 1969."

64 NABSW, "Position Statement of the National Association of Black Social Workers Concerning Neutralizing Racism in Schools of Social Welfare."

65 Ibid.

66 Glasgow, interview.

67 Ibid.

68 NABSW, memorandum, "Statement of Understanding," May 28, 1969, box 3, folder 10, MBP.

69 Ibid.

70 Ibid.

71 Ibid.

72 NABSW, "Position Statement of the National Association of Black Social Workers."

73 NABSW, "National Association of Black Social Workers Position Paper on NASW Proposed Certification Legislation," November 13, 1972, box 1, folder 14, Verne Weed Collection.

74 The distinction between the different types of representation is essential here. Hanna Pitkin (1967) offers a useful approach to conceptualizing representation. She describes four views of representation: formalistic, descriptive, symbolic, and substantive. Formalistic representation refers to the process by which representation comes to be. It has two elements, authorization (the right to act on behalf of the represented) and accountability (the responsibility to act on behalf of the represented). Descriptive representation refers to the extent to which representatives look like the represented. This could just as easily be called demographic representation, or representation based on shared characteristics. Symbolic representation refers to the extent to which a representative stands for the represented. In other words, the kind of representation that

means something important to the represented. Substantive representation is the kind of representation in which a representative acts in the best interest of the represented. This depends on the ability of the representative to assess and act on the interests of those they represent. See also Dovi 2011 on Pitkin's framework.

75 NABSW, "Statement to the State Legislative Higher Education Committee on Licensing," November 10, 1975, box 1, folder 14, Verne Weed Collection.

76 Ibid.

77 Ibid.

78 The RASSW was a Marxist-oriented group of activist social workers, most of whom were white.

79 RASSW, "Position Paper on Licensing Proposal," n.d., box1, folder 14, Verne Weed Collection.

80 NABSW, "Statement to the State Legislative Higher Education Committee on Licensing," November 10, 1975, box 1, folder 14, Verne Weed Collection; Chunn, interview.

81 Leonard E. Tate, "The Absurdity of Licensure," *NABSW News*, 1974, box 1, folder 14, Verne Weed Collection.

82 See Dyeson 2004 for a history of social work licensure.

83 Jay Chunn, essay, n.d., Jay Chunn personal collection.

84 Dum, "400 Black Social Aides Walk Out of Meet Here."

85 Chunn, interview.

86 Better, interview.

87 NABSW, "Position Statement of the National Association of Black Social Workers."

88 Ibid.

89 NABSW, "Trans-Racial Adoption Statement," *NABSW News*, 1974, box 1, folder 14, Verne Weed Collection.

90 Ibid.

91 Ibid.

92 Leora Neal, "Black Adoption Program."; Chunn, interview; Better, interview.

93 Leora Neal, "Black Adoption Program."

94 Ibid.

95 Ibid.

96 Ibid.

97 ABC, *This is Our Bag: Code of Ethics for Black People.*

98 NABSW, "Code of Ethics," 1971, GJDC.

99 Ibid.

100 NASW, Proceedings of NASW's National Social Action Workshop on the Urban Crisis, 1968, box 3, folder 34, Verne Weed Collection.

101 Karanja, interview.

102 See Hull et al. 1982; Brown 1992; Williams 2008

103 Will Connolly, clipping, "Welfare's New Thrust," *San Francisco Monitor*, June 6, 1968, box 3, folder 14, MBP.

104 ABC, "Chicago Catalysts Declare War on White Racism."

105 Ibid.

106 Chunn, interview.

107 Glasgow, interview.

108 Jaggers, interview.

109 Better, interview; Chunn, interview.

7. EXIT AND VOICE IN INTRA-ORGANIZATIONAL SOCIAL MOVEMENTS

1 Audreye Johnson to Howard Prunty, June 8, 1969, GJDC; Dewey Lawrence, memorandum, Report on New York NCSW to Detroit Association of Black Social Workers general membership meeting, June 26, 1969, GJDC.

2 NABSW, "Position Statement of the National Association of Black Social Workers," May 29, 1968, GJDC.

3 Karanja, interview.

4 James Adams, "Strange Welcome: Convention Finds Policy Under Fire From Hosts." *Cincinnati Enquirer*, May 30, 1970, box 23, folder 6, NFSNCR.

5 Ibid.

6 The concept of emotional labor comes from Arlie Hochshild (1983), who suggested that people who work in service occupations sell particular kinds of emotional displays. For example, waitresses are expected to maintain a cheerful emotional display whether or not it corresponds to their actual feelings. This emotional display is a part of what sells the restaurant experience. It has since been extended to include the kinds of work that people within other sorts of organizations undertake to maintain appropriate emotional displays. Moore's (2008) conception is one of these.

7 While the origin of the term "Mau Mau" is debated, it is generally used to refer to the Kikuyu people, who led an uprising against British imperialism in Kenya in between 1952 and 1960. The Mau Mau were painted by the British as a violent and brutal threat to whites and became an international symbol of black

anti-imperialism. The Mau Mau symbolism resonated with segments of the U.S. Black Power movement.

8. CONCLUSION: INSTITUTIONALIZING BLACK POWER

1   National Association of Black Social Workers, conference booklet, *Ma'at, Sankofa, & Harambee: 40 Years Strong: 40th Annual Conference Souvenir Journal*, April 1–5, 2008, in author's possession.

2   Association of Black Sociologists, e-mail sent to members, "Statement in Support of Trayvon Martin Protests," March 27, 2012, in author's possession.

3   Sandra Barnes, "Presidential Address," August 12, 2012, Annual Meetings of the Association of Black Sociologists, Denver, Colo.

REFERENCES

Abbott, Andrew. 1988. *The System of Professions: An Essay on the Division of Expert Labor.* Chicago: University of Chicago Press.

Albert, Stuart, and David A. Whetten. 1985. "Organizational Identity." In *Research in Organizational Behavior*, vol. 7, edited by L. L. Cummings and Barry Staw, 263–95. Greenwich, Conn.: JAI Press.

Alexander, Jeffrey C. 2006. *The Civil Sphere.* New York: Oxford University Press.

Alinsky, Saul D. 1971. *Rules for Radicals: A Practical Primer for Realistic Radicals.* New York: Random House.

Allen, Robert L. 1969. *Black Awakening in Capitalist America.* Garden City, N.Y.: Doubleday.

Aminzade, Ronald. 1984. "Reinterpreting Capitalist Industrialization: A Study of Nineteenth Century France." *Social History* 9(3): 329–351.

———. 1993. *Ballots and Barricades: Class Formation and Republican Politics in France, 1830–1871.* Princeton, N.J.: Princeton University Press.

Aminzade, Ronald, and Doug McAdam. 2001. "Emotions and Contentious Politics." In *Silence and Voice in the Study of Contentious Politics*, edited by Ronald Aminzade, Jack A. Goldstone, Doug McAdam, Elizabeth J. Perry, William H. Sewell Jr., Sidney Tarrow, and Charles Tilly, 14–50. New York: Cambridge University Press.

Andrews, Kenneth T. 2004. *Freedom Is a Constant Struggle: The Mississippi Civil Rights Movement and Its Legacy.* Chicago: University of Chicago Press.

Baraka, Imamu Amiri. 1972. "Toward the Creation of Political Institutions for All African Peoples: Gary and Miami." *The Black Collegian.* Nov./Dec. issue.

Barnett, Marguerite Ross. 1975. "The Congressional Black Caucus," *Proceedings of the Academy of Political Science* 32:36.

Beck, Bertram M. 1976. "Settlements in the United States—Past and Future." *Social Work* 21(4):268–272.

Bell, Joyce M. 2007. *Bringing the Movement Home: Black Social Workers' Struggle for Power in the Profession, 1966–1976*. Ph.D. diss., University of Minnesota. ProQuest (3273112).

Benson, J. Kenneth. 1971. "Militant Ideologies and Organizational Contexts: The War on Poverty and the Ideology of 'Black Power.'" *The Sociological Quarterly* 12:328–339.

Berry, Margaret. 1965. "Points and Viewpoints: Mr. Gans is Challenged." *Social Work* 10:1.

Biles, Roger. 1992. "Black Mayors: A Historical Assessment." *The Journal of Negro History* 77(3):109–125.

Biondi, Martha. 2012. *The Black Revolution on Campus*. Berkeley: University of California Press.

Blackwell, James E. 1974. "Role Behavior in a Corporate Structure: Black Sociologists in ASA." In *Black Sociologists: Historical and Contemporary Perspectives*, edited by James E. Blackwell and Morris Janowitz, 341–367. Chicago: University of Chicago Press.

Blumer, Herbert. 1951. "Collective Behavior." In *New Outline of the Principles of Sociology*, edited by Alfred McClung Lee, 166–222. New York: Barnes and Noble.

Bonilla-Silva, Eduardo. 2003. *Racism Without Racists: Colorblind Racism and the Persistence of Racial Inequality in the United States*. New York: Rowan and Littlefield.

———. 2001. *White Supremacy and Racism in the Post-Civil Rights Era*. Boulder, Colo.: Lynne Rienner Publishers, Inc.

Bradley, Stefan M. 2009. *Harlem vs. Columbia University: Black Student Power in the Late 1960s*. Urbana: University of Illinois Press.

Brown, Elaine. 1992. *A Taste of Power: A Black Woman's Story*. New York: Doubleday.

Brown, H. Rap. 1967. *Die Nigger Die!: A Political Autobiography of Jamil Abdullah Al-Amin*. Chicago: Chicago Review Press.

Brown, Michael K., Martin Carnoy, Elliott Currie, Troy Duster, David B. Oppenheimer, Marjorie M. Schultz, and David Wellman. 2003. *Whitewashing Race: The Myth of a Color-Blind Society*. Berkeley: University of California Press.

Bryant, Christopher. 1993 "Social Self-Organization, Civility and Sociology: A Comment on Kumar's 'Civil Society.'" *British Journal of Sociology* 44(3):397–401.

Burns, Andrea A. 2013. *From Storefront to Monument: Tracing the Public History of the Black Museum Movement*. Amherst: University of Massachusetts Press.

Carlton-LaNey, Iris. 1999. "African American Social Work Pioneers' Response to Need." *Social Work* 44(4):311–321.

Carlton-LaNey, Iris, and Sandra Carlton Alexander. (2001). "Early African American Social Welfare Pioneer Women: Working to Empower the Race and the Community." *Journal of Ethnic and Multicultural Diversity in Social Work* 10(2):67–84.

Carmichael, Stokely. 1966. "What We Want." *New York Review of Books* 7(4):5–6, 8.

Carmichael, Stokely, and Charles V. Hamilton. 1992 [1967]. *Black Power: The Politics of Liberation*. New York: Vintage Books.

Carr, Leslie G. 1997. *"Color-blind" Racism*. Thousand Oaks, Calif.: Sage.

Carson, Clayborne. 1995. *In Struggle: SNCC and the Black Awakening of the 1960s*. Cambridge, Mass.: Harvard University Press.

Cazenave, Noel A. 2007. *Impossible Democracy: The Unlikely Success of the War on Poverty Community Action Programs*. Albany: State University of New York Press.

Clarke, Cheryl. 2005. *The Days of Good Looks: The Prose and Poetry of Cheryl Clarke, 1989–2005*. New York: Carroll and Graff.

Conyers, James E. 1992. "The Association of Black Sociologists: A Descriptive Account from an 'Insider.'" *The American Sociologist* 23(1):49–55.

Council on Social Work Education. 1971. *Educational Policy and Accreditation Standards*. Rev. ed. Alexandria, Va.: Author.

———. 1973. *Educational Policy and Accreditation Standards*. Rev. ed. Alexandria, Va.: Author.

Coontz, Stephanie. 1992. *The Way We Never Were: American Families and the Nostalgia Trap*. New York: Basic Books.

Crenshaw, Kimberlé Williams. 1988. "Race, Reform, and Retrenchment: Transformation and Legitimation in Antidiscrimination Law." *Harvard Law Review* 101(7):1331–1387.

———. 1997. "Colorblind Dreams and Racial Nightmares: Reconfiguring Racism in the Post-Civil Rights Era." In *Birth of a Nation'hood: Gaze, Script, and Spectacle in the O. J. Simpson Case*, edited by Toni Morrison and C. Lacour, 97–168. New York: Pantheon Books.

Cruse, Harold W. 1962. "Revolutionary Nationalism and the Afro-American." *Studies on the Left* 2(3):12–25.

Della Porta, Donatella, and Mario Diani. 1999. *Social Movements: An Introduction*. Malden, Mass.: Blackwell.

Doane, Ashley W., and Eduardo Bonilla-Silva. 2003. *White Out: The Continuing Significance of Racism*. New York: Routledge.

Dovi, Suzanne. "Political Representation." In *Stanford Encyclopedia of Philosophy*, Winter 2011 edition. Stanford University, 1997–. Article published January 2, 2006; revised October 17, 2011. http://plato.stanford.edu/archives/win2011/entries/political-representation.

Drake, St. Clair, and Horace R. Clayton. 1993 [1945]. *Black Metropolis: A Study of Negro Life in a Northern City*. Chicago: University of Chicago Press.

Dutschke, Rudi. 1969. "On Authoritarianism." In *The New Left Reader*, edited by Carl Oglesby, 243–253. New York: Grove Press.

Dyeson, Timothy. 2004. "Social Work Licensure: A Brief History and Description." *Home Health Care Management and Practice* 16(5):408–411.

Edwards, Michael. 2004. *Civil Society*. Cambridge: Polity Press.

Ehrenreich, John H. 1985. *The Altruistic Imagination: A History of Social Work and Social Policy in the United States*. Ithaca, N.Y.: Cornell University Press.

Feagin, Joseph. 2001. *Racist America: Roots, Current Realities, and Future Reparations*. New York: Routledge.

———. 2010. *The White Racial Frame: Centuries of Racial Framing and Counter-Framing*. New York: Routledge.

Fisher, Jacob. 1980. "Social Work Today, 1934–1942, and the Dissenting Left for Which it Spoke." *Catalyst* 3(1):3–22.

Flanagan, Richard M. "Lyndon Johnson, Community Action, and Management of the Administrative State." *Presidential Studies Quarterly* 31(4):585–608.

Foner, Phillip S., ed. 1995. *The Black Panthers Speak*. Boston, Mass.: Da Capo.

Foucault, Michel. 1980. "Two Lectures." In *Power/Knowledge: Selected Interviews and Other Writings, 1972–1977*, edited by Colin Gordon, 78–108. New York: Pantheon.

Gaines, Kevin. 1996. *Uplifting the Race: Black Leadership, Politics, and Culture in the Twentieth Century*. Chapel Hill: University of North Carolina Press.

Gallagher, Charles A. 2003. "Color-blind Privilege: The Social and Political Functions of Erasing the Color Line in Post Race America." *Race, Gender, and Class* 10(4):22–37.

Gans, Herbert J. 1964. "Redefining the Settlement's Function for the War on Poverty." *Social Work* 9(4):5–7.

Garcia, Alejandro. 1990. "An Examination of the Social Work Profession's Efforts to Achieve Legal Regulation." *Journal of Counseling and Development* 68(5):491–497.

Garrow, David. 1986. *Bearing the Cross: Martin Luther King, Jr., and the Southern Christian Leadership Conference.* New York: William Morrow.

Georgakas, Dan, and Marvin Surkin. 1998. *Detroit: I Do Mind Dying; A Study in Urban Revolution.* Updated edition. Cambridge, Mass.: South End Press.

Geschwender, James A. 1977. *Class, Race, and Worker Insurgency: The League of Revolutionary Black Workers.* New York: Cambridge University Press.

Gilkes, Cheryl Townsend. 1982. "Successful Rebellious Professionals: The Black Woman's Professional Identity and Community Commitment." *Psychology of Women Quarterly* 6(3):289–311.

Gioia, Dennis A., Majken Schultz, and Kevin Corley. 2000. "Organizational Identity, Image, and Adaptive Instability. *Academy of Management Review* 25(1):63–81.

Goldberg, David, and Trevor Griffey. 2010. *Black Power at Work: Community Control, Affirmative Action, and the Construction Industry.* Ithaca, N.Y.: Cornell University Press.

Goodwin, Jeff, and James M. Jasper. 2006. "Emotions and Social Movements." In *Handbook of Sociology of Emotions,* edited by Jan E. Stets and Jonathan H. Turner, 611–635. New York: Springer.

Gordon, Linda. 1994. *Pitied But Not Entitled: Single Mothers and the History of Welfare, 1890–1935.* New York: The Free Press.

Gramsci, Antonio. 2005 [1971]. *Selections from the Prison Notebooks.* Translated and edited by Quintin Hoare and Geoffrey Nowell Smith. New York: International Publishers.

Gurr, Ted. 1968. "Psychological Factors in Civil Violence." *World Politics* 20(2):245–278.

———. 1970. *Why Men Rebel.* Princeton, N.J.: Princeton University Press.

Haines, Herbert. 1997. "Black Radicalization and the Funding of Civil Rights: 1957–1970." In *Social Movements: Readings on Their Emergence, Mobilization, and Dynamics,* edited by Doug McAdam and David Snow, 440–442. Los Angeles: Roxbury.

Hall, Stuart. 1996. "Gramsci's Relevance for the Study of Race and Ethnicity." In *Stuart Hall: Critical Dialogues in Cultural Studies,* edited by David Morley and Kuan-Hsing Chen, 411–444. New York: Routledge.

Harrison, Ira E. 1987. "The Association of Black Anthropologists: A Brief History." *Anthropology Today* 3(1):17–21.

Harrison, Michael I., and John K. Maniha. 1978. "Dynamics of Dissenting Movements Within Established Organizations: Two Cases and a Theoretical Interpretation." *Journal for the Scientific Study of Religion* 17(3):207–224.

Hartmann, Douglas, and Joyce M. Bell. 2011. "Race-Based Critical Theory and the 'Happy Talk' of Diversity in America." In *Illuminating Social Life: Classical and Contemporary Theory Revisited*, 6th edition, edited by Peter Kivisto, 259–277. Thousand Oaks, Calif.: Sage.

Hayden, Tom. 1967. *Rebellion in Newark: Official Violence and Ghetto Response.* New York: Random House.

Hercus, Cheryl. 1999. "Identity, Emotion, and Feminist Collective Action." *Gender and Society* 13(1):34–55.

Higginbotham, Evelyn Brooks. 1993. *Righteous Discontent: The Women's Movement in the Black Baptist Church, 1880–1920.* Cambridge, Mass.: Harvard University Press.

Hill-Collins. 1986. "Learning from the Outsider Within: The Sociological Significance of Black Feminist Thought." *Social Problems* 33(6):S14-S32.

Hine, Darlene Clark. 2003. "Black Professionals and Race Consciousness: Origins of the Civil Rights Movement, 1890–1950." *Journal of American History* 89(4):1279–1294.

Hirschman, Albert O. 1970. *Exit, Voice, and Loyalty: Responses to Decline in Firms, Organizations, and States.* Cambridge, Mass.: Harvard University Press.

Hochschild, Arlie Russell. 1983. *The Managed Heart: Commercialization of Human Feeling.* Los Angeles: University of California Press.

Horne, Gerald. 2009. *Mau Mau in Harlem?: The U.S. and the Liberation of Kenya.* New York: Macmillan.

Hull, Gloria T., Patricia Bell Scott, and Barbara Smith. 1982. *All the Women Are White, All the Men Are Black, But Some of Us Are Brave.* New York: The Feminist Press at City University of New York.

Jacoby, Russell. 1987. *The Last Intellectuals: American Culture in the Age of Academe.* New York: Noonday Press.

Jaggers, Garland. 2003. *That Rare Moment in History.* Detroit: Author.

Jani, Jayshree S., Dean Pierce, Larry Ortiz, and Lynda Sowbel. 2011. "Access to Intersectionality, Content to Competence: Deconstructing Social Work Education Diversity Standards." *Journal of Social Work Education* 47(2): 283–301.

Jasper, James M. 2011. "Emotions and Social Movements: Twenty Years of Theory and Research." *Annual Review of Sociology* 37: 285–303.

———. 1998. "The Emotions of Protest: Affective and Reactive Emotions In and Around Social Movements." *Sociological Forum* 13(3):397–424.

Jasper, James M., and Jane Poulsen. 1993. "Fighting Back: Vulnerabilities, Blunders, and Countermobilization by the Targets in Three Animal Rights Campaigns." *Sociological Forum* 8(4):639–657.

Jeffries, Judson L., ed. 2006. *Black Power in the Belly of the Beast.* Urbana: University of Illinois Press.

Jewell, K. Sue. 2003. *Survival of the African American Family: The Institutional Impact of U.S. Social Policy.* Westport, Conn.: Praeger.

Johnson, Audreye E. 1988. *The National Association of Black Social Workers, Inc.: A History for the Future.* New York: The National Association of Black Social Workers, Inc.

———. 1976. "The National Association of Black Social Workers, Inc.: A View of the Beginning." *Black Caucus Journal of NABSW* 7(1):13–17.

———. 1975. *The National Association of Black Social Workers: Structural and Functional Assessment by Leaders and Members.* Unpublished Ph.D. diss., University of Denver.

Jones, Charles E. 1998. *The Black Panther Party Reconsidered.* Baltimore: Black Classic Press.

Joseph, Peniel. 2006. *The Black Power Movement: Rethinking the Civil Rights-Black Power Era.* New York: Routledge.

———. 2007. *Waiting 'Til the Midnight Hour: A Narrative History of Black Power in America.* New York: Macmillan.

———. 2008. "Historians and the Black Power Movement." *Organization of American Historians Magazine of History* 22(3):8–15.

———. 2010. *Dark Days, Bright Nights: From Black Power to Barack Obama.* New York: Basic Civitas Books.

Josey, E. J. 2000. "Black Caucus of the American Library Association: The Early Years." In *Handbook of Black Librarianship,* 2nd editon, edited by E. J. Josey and Marva DeLoach, 83–99. Lanham, Md.: Scarecrow Press.

Karstedt-Henke, Sabine 1980. "Theories for the Explanation of Terrorist Movements." In *The Politics of Internal Security* edited by E. Blankenberg, 198–234. Frankfurt: Suhrkamp.

Katzenstein, Mary Fainsod. 1998. *Faithful and Fearless: Feminist Protest Inside the Church and Military.* Princeton, N.J.: Princeton University Press.

Kelley, Robin D. G. 1997. *Yo' Mama's Disfunktional!: Fighting the Culture Wars in Urban America.* Boston: Beacon.

————. 2003. *Freedom Dreams: The Black Radical Imagination*. Boston: Beacon.

Killian, Lewis. 1981. "Black Power and White Reactions: The Revitalization of Race-Thinking in the United States." *Annals of the American Academy of Political and Social Science* 454:42–54.

Klandermans, Bert. 1984. "Mobilization and Participation: Social- Psychological Expansions of Resource Mobilization Theory." *American Sociological Review* 49(5):583–600.

Koopmans, Ruud. 1993. "The Dynamics of Protest Waves: West Germany, 1965–1989." *American Sociological Review* 58(5):637–658.

Kotlowski, Dean. 1998. "Black Power—Nixon Style: The Nixon Administration and Minority Business Enterprise." *Business History Review* 72(3):409–445.

Kriesi, Hanspeter. 1995. "The Political Opportunity Structure of New Social Movements: Its Impact on Their Mobilization." In *The Politics of Social Protest: Comparative Perspectives on States and Social Movements*, edited by J. Craig Jenkins and Bert Klandermans, 167–199. Minneapolis: University of Minnesota Press.

Kumar, K. 1993. "Civil Society: An Inquiry into the Usefulness of a Historical Term." *The British Journal of Sociology* 44(3):375–395.

Ladner, Joyce, 1973. *The Death of White Sociology*. New York: Random House.

Landry, Bart. 1988. *The New Black Middle Class*. Berkeley: University of California Press.

Lasch-Quinn, Elisabeth. 1993. *Black Neighbors: Race and the Limits of Reform in the American Settlement House Movement, 1890–1945*. Chapel Hill: University of North Carolina Press.

————. 2001. *Race Experts: How Racial Etiquette, Sensitivity Training, and New Age Therapy Hijacked the Civil Rights Revolution*. New York: W. W. Norton.

Lounsbury, Michael, Marc J. Ventresca and Paul M. Hirsch. 2003. "Social Movements, Field Frames and Industry Emergence: A Cultural-Political Perspective on US Recycling." *SocioEconomic Review* 1:71-104.

Mahoney, James. 2000. "Path Dependence in Historical Sociology." *Theory and Society* 29(4):507–48.

Marable, Manning. 1984. *Race, Reform, and Rebellion: The Second Reconstruction in Black America, 1945–1982*. Jackson: University Press of Mississippi.

Mayes, Keith A. 2009. *Kwanzaa: Black Power and the Making of the African-American Holiday Tradition*. New York: Routledge.

McAdam, Doug. 1999. *Political Process and the Development of Black Insurgency, 1930–1970*. Revised edition. Chicago: University of Chicago Press.

McAdam, Doug, John McCarthy, and Mayer N. Zald. 1996. "Opportunities, Mobilizing Structures, and Framing Processes: Toward a Synthetic, Comparative Perspective on Social Movements." In *Comparative Perspectives on Social Movements: Political Opportunities, Mobilizing Structures, and Cultural Framings,* edited by Doug McAdam, John McCarthy, and Mayer N. Zald, 1–20. New York: Cambridge University Press.

McAdam, Doug, and W. Richard Scott. 2002. "Organizations and Movements." Paper presented at the annual meeting of the American Sociological Association, Chicago, Ill.

——. 2005. "Organizations and Movements." In *Social Movements and Organization Theory,* edited by Gerald F. Davis, Doug McAdam, W. Richard Scott, and Mayer N. Zald, 4–40. New York: Cambridge University Press.

McCarthy, John D., and Mayer N. Zald. 1977. "Resource Mobilization and Social Movements: A Partial Theory." *American Journal of Sociology* 82(6):1212–41.

——. 1973. *The Trend of Social Movements in America: Professionalization and Resource Mobilization.* Morristown, N.J.: General Learning Press.

Morris, Aldon. 1984. *The Origins of the Civil Rights Movement: Black Communities Organizing for Change.* New York: The Free Press.

Morris, Aldon, and Suzanne Staggenborg. 2004. "Leadership in Social Movements." In *The Blackwell Companion to Social Movements,* edited by David A. Snow, Sarah A. Soule, and Hanspeter Kriesi, 171–196. Malden, Mass.: Blackwell.

Moore, Sharo E., and Surjit Singh Dhooper. 2000. *Instructor's Manual for Social Work Practice with Culturally Diverse People.* Thousand Oaks, Calif.: Sage.

Moore, Wendy Leo. 2008. *Reproducing Racism: White Space, Elite Law Schools, and Racial Inequality.* Lanham, Md.: Rowman & Littlefield.

National Advisory Commission on Civil Disorders. 1968. *Report of the National Advisory Commission on Civil Disorders.* New York: Bantam Books.

National Association of Social Workers. 1973. *Legal Regulation of Social Work Practice.* Washington, D.C.: Author.

Nelson, Alondra. 2011. *Body and Soul: The Black Panther Party and the Fight Against Medical Discrimination.* Minneapolis: University of Minnesota Press.

Nelson, Bryce. 1969. "Psychologists: Searching for Social Relevance at APA Meeting." *Science* 165(3898):1101–1104.

Office of History and Preservation, Office of the Clerk of the U.S. House of Representatives. 2008. *Black Americans in Congress, 1870–2007.* Washington, D.C: U.S. Government Printing Office. Accessed August 13, 2012. http://baic.house.gov/historical-essays/essay.html?intSectionID=41.

Office of Policy Planning and Research, United States Department of Labor. 1965. *The Negro Family: The Case for National Action.* Accessed December 2012. http://www.dol.gov/oasam/programs/history/webid-meynihan.htm#.UModq9PjlR1.

Ogbar, Jeffrey. 2004. *Black Power, Radical Politics, and African American Identity.* Baltimore: Johns Hopkins University Press.

Omi, Michael, and Howard Winant. 1994. *Racial Formation in the United States: From the 1960s to the 1990s.* New York: Routledge.

Orfield, Gary. 2001. *Schools More Separate: Consequences of a Decade of Resegregation.* Cambridge, Mass.: Harvard University Press.

Park, Robert E. 1967. *On Social Control and Collective Behavior.* Edited by Ralph Turner. Chicago: University of Chicago Press.

Pinderhughes, Diane. 1990. "NCOBPS: Observations on the State of the Organization." *National Political Science Review* 2:213–21.

Pins, Arnulf M. "Changes is Social Work Education and Their Implications for Practice." *Social Work* 16(2):5–15

Pitkin, Hanna F. 1967. *The Concept of Representation.* Berkeley: University of California Press.

Popple, Philip, and P. Nelson Reid. 1999. "A Profession for the Poor? A History of Social Work in the United States." In *The Professionalization of Poverty, Social Work and the Poor in the Twentieth Century,* edited by Gary R. Lowe and P. Nelson Reid, 9–29. New York: Aldine Transaction.

Portelli, Alessandro. 1991. *The Death of Luigi Trastulli and Other Stories: Form and Meaning in Oral History.* Albany: State University of New York Press.

Potocky, Miriam. 1997. "Multicultural Social Work in the United States." *International Social Work* 40:315–326.

Raeburn, Nicole C. 2004. *Changing Corporate America from Inside Out: Lesbian and Gay Workplace Rights.* Minneapolis: University of Minnesota Press.

Reed, Adolph. 1979. "Black Particularity Reconsidered." *Telos* 1979(39): 71–93.

Reid-Merritt, Patricia. 2010. *Righteous Self-Determination: The Black Social Work Movement in America.* Baltimore: Imprint Editions.

Reisch, Michael, and Janice Andrews. 2001. *The Road Not Taken: A History of Radical Social Work in the United States.* Philadelphia: Brunner Routledge.

Robinson, Cedric. 1997. *Black Movements in America.* New York: Routledge.

Rogers, Ibram. 2012. *The Black Campus Movement: Black Students and the Racial Reconstitution of Higher Education, 1965–1972.* New York: Palgrave Macmillan.

Rojas, Fabio. 2010. *From Black Power to Black Studies: How a Radical Social Movement Became an Academic Discipline.* Baltimore: Johns Hopkins University Press.

Rustin, Bayard. 1965. "From Protest to Politics: The Future of the Civil Rights Movement." *Commentary*, February: 25–31. Accessed December 2012. http://www.commentarymagazine.com/article/from-protest-to-politics-the-future-of-the-civil-rights-movement/

Ryan, William. 1971. *Blaming the Victim*. New York: Pantheon.

Sanders, Charles. 1970. "Editorial." *Black Caucus* 3(1): 2–4.

Sauber, S. Richard, and Harold J. Vetter. 1983. *The Human Services Delivery System*. New York: Columbia University Press.

Schindler, Ruben, and Edward Allan Brawley. 1987. *Social Care at the Front Line: A Worldwide Study of Paraprofessionals*. New York: Tavistock Publications.

Schurman, Rachel. 2004. "Fighting 'Frankenfoods': Industry Opportunity Structures and the Efficacy of the Anti-Biotech Movement in Western Europe." *Social Problems* 51:243–268.

Scott, BarBara. 2006. *Presidential Address*. Annual Meeting of the Association of Black Sociologists. Montreal, Canada.

Selznick, Philip. 1948. "Foundations of the Theory of Organization." *American Sociological Review* 13:25–35.

Silverman, Arnold R. 1993. "Outcomes of Transracial Adoption." *Adoption* 3(1): 104–118.

Singh, Robert. 1998. *The Congressional Black Caucus: Racial Politics in the U.S. Congress*. Thousand Oaks, Calif.: Sage.

Skocpol, Theda. 1987. "Social History and Historical Sociology." *Social Science History* 11:17–30.

Skrentny, John D. 2002. *The Minority Rights Revolution*. Cambridge, Mass.: Harvard University Press.

Smith, Robert C. 1981. "Black Power and the Transformation from Protest to Policies." *Political Science Quarterly* 96(3):431–443.

———. 1992. "'Politics' Is Not Enough: On The Institutionalization of the Afro-American Freedom Movement" In *From Exclusion to Inclusion: The Long Struggle for African American Political Power*, edited by Ralph Gomes and Linda Williams, 97–126. New York: Greenwood Press.

———. 1978. "The Changing Shape of Urban Politics: 1960–1970." *The Annals of the American Academy of Political and Social Science* 439:6–28.

Snow, David A., E. Burke Rochford Jr., Steven K. Worden, and Robert D. Benford. 1986. "Frame Alignment Processes, Micromobilization, and Movement Participation." *American Sociological Review* 51(4):464–481.

Snyder, David, and Charles Tilly. 1972. "Hardship and Collective Violence in France: 1830 to 1960." Working paper. Ann Arbor: University of Michigan Center for Research on Social Organization.

Stack, Carol. 1974. *All Our Kin: Strategies for Survival in a Black Community*. New York: Harper and Row.

Stryker, Robin, and Nicholas Pedriana. 2004. "The Strength of a Weak Agency: Enforcement of Title VII of the 1964 Civil Rights Act and the Expansion of State Capacity, 1965–1971." *American Journal of Sociology* 110:709–760.

Suchman, Mark C. 1995. "Managing Legitimacy: Strategic and Institutional Approaches." *Academy of Management Journal* 20(3):571–610.

Swartout, Kristy A., ed. 2006. *Encyclopedia of Associations*. 44th Edition. Farmington Hills, Mich.: Gale Group.

Tarrow, Sidney. 1983. "Struggling to Reform: Social Movements and Policy Change During Cycles of Protest." Western Societies Program Occasional Paper, No. 15. Ithaca, N.Y.: New York Center for International Studies, Cornell University.

———. 1988. "National Politics and Collective Action: Recent Theory and Research in Western Europe and the United States." *Annual Review of Sociology* 14:421–40.

———. 1989. "Struggle, Politics, and Reform: Collective Action, Social Movements, and Cycles of Protest." Western Societies Program Occasional Paper, No. 21. Ithaca, N.Y.: New York Center for International Studies, Cornell University.

Tibbs, Donald F. 2012. *From Black Power to Prison Power: The Making of Jones v. North Carolina Prisoners' Labor Union*. New York: Palgrave Macmillan.

Tilly, Charles. 1978. *From Mobilization to Revolution*. Reading, Mass.: Addison-Wesley.

Trolander, Judith Ann. 1975. *Settlement Houses and the Great Depression*. Detroit: Wayne State University Press.

———. 1982. "Social Change: Settlement Houses and Saul Alinsky, 1939–1965." *Social Service Review* 56(3):346–367.

———. 1987. *Professionalism and Social Change: From the Settlement House Movement to Neighborhood Centers, 1886 to the Present*. New York: Columbia University Press.

———. 1997. "Fighting Racism and Sexism: The Council on Social Work Education." *Social Service Review* 71(1):110–134.

Tropman, John E., and Rebecca L. Stotzer. 2005. "National Conference on Social Welfare." In *The Encyclopedia of Social Welfare History in North America*, edited by John M. Herrick and Paul H. Stuart, 253–255. Thousand Oaks, Calif.: Sage.

Turner, Ralph, and Lewis Killian. 1972. *Collective Behavior.* 2nd edition. Englewood Cliffs, N.J.: Prentice Hall.

United States National Advisory Commission on Civil Disorders. 1968. *Report of the National Advisory Commission on Civil Disorders.* New York: Bantam.

United Way of America. "History." Accessed June 19, 2013. http://national.united-way.org/about/history/.

Van DeBurg, William L. 1992. *New Day in Babylon: The Black Power Movement and American Culture, 1965–1975.* Chicago: University of Chicago Press.

Vasey, Wayne. 1968. "The San Francisco Story." In the *Official Proceedings of the Annual Meeting: 1968,* by National Conference on Social Welfare, 156–163. Ann Arbor: University of Michigan Library.

Wacquant, Loïc. 2001. "Deadly Symbiosis: When Ghetto and Prison Meet and Mesh." *Punishment and Society* 3(1):95–134.

Walker, Edward. 2005. *Polity Membership, Movement Cultures, and Iron Laws: Three Types of Institutionalization in Social Movement Theory.* Unpublished ms.

Walkowitz, Daniel J. 1999. *Working With Class: Social Workers and the Politics of Middle-Class Identity.* Chapel Hill: University of North Carolina Press.

Walters, Ronald W. and Robert C. Smith. 1999. *African American Leadership.* Albany: State University of New York Press.

Walton, Hanes. 1988. *When The Marching Stopped: The Politics of Civil Rights Regulatory Agencies.* Albany: State University of New York Press.

Warren Hill, Laura, and Julia Rabig. 2012. *The Business of Black Power: Community Development, Capitalism, and Corporate Responsibility in Postwar America.* Rochester, N.Y.: University of Rochester Press.

Webb, Clive, ed. 2005. *Massive Resistance: Southern Opposition to the Second Reconstruction.* New York: Oxford University Press.

Wencour, Stanley, and Michael Reisch. 1989. *From Charity to Enterprise: The Development of American Social Work in a Market Economy.* Urbana: University of Illinois Press.

West, Michael O. 2012. "Whose Black Power?" In *The Business of Black Power: Community Development, Capitalism, and Corporate Responsibility in Postwar America,* edited by Laura Warren Hill and Julia Rabig, 274–304. Rochester, N.Y.: University of Rochester Press.

Williams, Cenie. 1969. "Message From the President." *Black Caucus Journal* 2(1):8-10.

Williams, Rhonda Y. 2008. "Black Women and Black Power." *Organization of American Historians Magazine of History* 22(3):22–26.

————. 2011. "'To Challenge the Status Quo by Any Means': Community Action and Representational Politics in 1960s Baltimore." In *The War on Poverty: A New Grassroots History, 1964–1980*, edited by Annelise Orleck and Lisa Gayle Hazirjian, 63–86. Athens: University of Georgia Press.

Williams, Robert L. 2008. "A 40-Year History of the Association of Black Psychologists." *Journal of Black Psychology* 34(3):249–260.

Williams, Robert L., William Dotson, Patricia Don, and Willie S. Williams. 1980. "The War Against Testing: A Current Status Report." *Journal of Negro Education* 49(3):263–273.

Wilson, William Julius. 1980 [1978]. *The Declining Significance of Race: Blacks and Changing American Institutions*. Chicago: University of Chicago Press.

Wingfield, Adia Harvey. 2010. "Are Some Emotions Marked 'Whites Only'? Racialized Feeling Rules in Professional Workplaces." *Social Problems* 57(2):251–268.

Withorn, Ann. 1984. *Serving the People: Social Services and Social Change*. New York: Columbia University Press.

Woodard, K. Komozi. 1999. *A Nation Within a Nation: Amiri Baraka (LeRoi Jones) and Black Power Politics*. Chapel Hill: University of North Carolina Press.

Wolfe, Tom. 2009 [1970]. *Radical Chic and Mau Mauing the Flak Catchers*. New York: Picador.

Zald, Mayer N., and Michael A. Berger. 1978. "Social Movements in Organizations: Coup d'Etat, Insurgency, and Mass Movements." *American Journal of Sociology* 83(4):823–861.

Zald, Meyer N., and Roberta Ash. 1966. "Social Movement Organizations: Growth, Decay and Change." *Social Forces* 44:327–340.